The Great Contest

WELLINGTON IN THE FIELD.

After a Portrait by Sir Thomas Lawrence.

This was Wellington's favourite campaigning costume. The frock-coat was dark blue, the cloak grey lined with white. The telescope he carried all through Spain and Belgium and afterwards gave to Lord Stanhope.

The Great Contest

Britain, Wellington & the War with Napoleonic France, 1800–1815

ILLUSTRATED WITH 92 PICTURES & MAPS

Charles Oman

Edited by John H Lewis

LEONAUR

The Great Contest
Britain, Wellington & the War with Napoleonic France, 1800-1815
by Charles Oman
Edited by John H Lewis

ILLUSTRATED WITH 92 PICTURES & MAPS

FIRST EDITION

Leonaur is an imprint of Oakpast Ltd

Copyright in this form © 2018 Oakpast Ltd

ISBN: 978-1-78282-786-3 (hardcover)
ISBN: 978-1-78282-787-0 (softcover)

http://www.leonaur.com

Publisher's Notes

Contents

Introduction by the Editor

Readers familiar with the scholarship and published works of the historian, Sir Charles William Chadwick Oman (1860-1946) may possibly be confused by the publication of this book since its title will certainly be unfamiliar. The reason for that circumstance, should it arise, is simple to explain for this is a book that Oman never wrote. However, the reader should not be alarmed by this revelation since the content of 'The Great Contest' is assuredly comprised of the excellent academic research, insightful analysis and conclusions of Charles Oman delivered with the readability and the economy of phrase which has made him perennially essential as an historian.

Readers will be aware that Oman wrote extensively on many subjects and periods of history and, most relevantly for those interested in the period of time covered by this book, on the subject of the history of the Peninsular War in Spain, Portugal and the South of France within a multi-volume work which has received the highest praise from students of the Napoleonic Wars since its publication. Indeed, Oman's history of the Peninsular War, first published in 1902, has been highly regarded as a history of the total conflict to the degree that Oman was considered by many in consequence to be the foremost authority on the subject following the publication of Sir William Napier's *magnum opus,* the first volume of which appeared in 1828.

The great historian of the British Army, Sir John Fortescue, (1859-1933), collaborated with Oman for those passages of his own multi-volume, 'History of the British Army' which concerned the war in the Iberian Peninsula. Although Fortescue was not always in accord with Oman's conclusions there is little doubt that his own work benefited substantially from the research Oman had already undertaken and published on the subject.

7

Although Fortescue's writings were extensive on the subject of the war against Napoleonic France he did not publish a work solely dedicated to the Peninsular War. I believe Fortescue's writings on that subject were not available in isolation until they were gathered together and edited by me and published by Leonaur in 2016. Fortescue's writings on the Waterloo Campaign have also been extracted from his history of the British Army and published separately. Together, Oman and Fortescue were without parallel as historians in their field and there can be little doubt that subsequent authors on the subject have leant upon their scholarship, though for some reason both historians are now sometimes by some people considered to be dated. How much original source material has emerged in the last century concerning the British wars against Napoleonic France which may have substantially influenced the published material of later military historians is difficult to estimate or imagine.

Though it is a subjective point view having read both Fortescue and Oman to some degree, I believe Oman was Fortescue's master in terms of academic clarity and quality of prose. Simply put, he wrote a more enjoyable book to read which carries his reader almost effortlessly through his subject and that is a rare talent.

Despite his fine work on the Peninsular War which concluded in 1814, Oman as has been admitted, never wrote a comprehensive single-volume work intended for publication which embraced the entire struggle between Britain and Napoleonic France including the Waterloo Campaign against Napoleon in 1815 which terminated in the defeat of the emperor on the muddy slopes beyond Waterloo, thus embracing all the events and consequences of that 'great contest'. This book is an attempt in measure to rectify that unfortunate shortcoming.

Though this period of history is universally known as the 'Napoleonic Age' it is fair to note this term does not fairly describe it from the British historical perspective, for though the British nation was in continual conflict with France, Napoleon himself was notably absent from the battles and fields of conflict where British sailors and soldiers fought. From the British perspective this period was surely, 'The Age of Wellington', for as a military commander Arthur Wellesley dominated the stage with his successes from the moment he entered the fight until, in the role of nemesis, he defeated Napoleon utterly and finally in his only battle against him.

However, whilst this book is dominated by battles, there are other aspects to warfare. Most histories of the events of 1815 conclude immediately following the Battle of Waterloo itself without considering the subsequent effects upon Britain and Europe in the post-war period as though the closing of the curtain upon Napoleon would bring an immediate end to the collateral effects of the Napoleonic era, though it had disrupted the political and economic affairs of the entire continent and beyond for decades.

This book has been created by the joining together in chronological order of four outstanding smaller works of history written by Oman concerning this period. The text which opens and concludes the book is taken from Oman's, 'England in the Nineteenth Century' published in 1899. Within this text at the appropriate point has been inserted Oman's independently published, superb concise history of the Peninsular War and his analysis of 'The Hundred Days Campaign, 1815'.

Included in the Waterloo Campaign section of the text readers will discover Oman's outstanding research into the casualties sustained by the French Army during the 1815 conflicts which was originally published in two separate articles and provides essential detail of losses of officers and men. This information illuminates the degree of engagement in which each unit was involved by the extent to which it suffered as a result of action. Readers familiar with the Battle of Waterloo may have concluded that there would inevitably be high losses among the cavalry of the French *cuirassier* regiments for example, but given the familiar legends surrounding the actions of the Grenadiers of the Imperial Guard during the closing stages of the battle, most readers will be surprised to learn that it actually suffered comparatively light casualties.

These smaller works, though superb, would be unlikely to be published in modern times separately, whereas combined they have created, by virtue of their common author, a work of almost seamless chronology.

The book concludes by returning to Oman's nineteenth century history which explains the effects of the war and embraces Wellington's short and inauspicious political career. Thus, this history gives context to this riveting period delivered by the pen of a master. Given the concise nature of the book it occurred to the publisher that this text would provide an ideal overview for those who were new to the subject as well as those who were more familiar with it but who would value a hitherto unpublished text in this form by Oman. To illuminate the text this edition has been substantially enhanced with maps and illustrations which, of course, did not appear in any of the originally published versions of any of the constituent parts.

John H. Lewis, 2018

CHAPTER 1

The Peace of Amiens

When the nineteenth century opened, on New Year's Day 1801, England was still engaged in the weary war with revolutionary France. The struggle had already raged for eight years and seemed as far from an end as ever. It made little difference to its character that the government with which the contest had to be fought out was no longer the corrupt Directory of Barras. The military despotism of the new First Consul, Napoleon Bonaparte, was quite as hostile to England, and infinitely more formidable. Till he had tried his strength against her and learnt the limitations of his power, Bonaparte was not likely to come to terms.

Moreover, Britain had just ascertained that it should have to fight him single-handed. The last of its powerful continental allies was now about to withdraw from the struggle. Austria had already opened negotiations for peace with the First Consul: since the defeat Hohenlinden (December 3, 1800) her position seemed untenable, and she was glad to be permitted to retire from the war, still retaining her ill-gotten gains in Italy, the lands of the unfortunate republic of Venice.

Bonaparte had resolved to let her off easily: not only did he wish to have his hands free for the duel with Great Britain and the internal reorganisation of France, but he was jealous lest Moreau, the victor of Hohenlinden, might dictate peace at the gates of Vienna, and so cast into the shade his own achievements at Marengo in the previous summer. Hence came the peace of Lunéville (February 9, 1801), which took Austria out of the struggle against Bonaparte for more than four years.

Russia, the other ally of England in the war of 1798-9, had already made her peace with France: the eccentric Czar Paul had not only thrown over the British alliance, but had ranged himself on the side of Britain's enemies. Inspired by a perverse and wrong-headed admiration for the person of the First Consul, he had set himself to aid him by every means in his power. In December, 1800, he had formed a

League of the Baltic Powers: Sweden, Denmark, and Prussia declared an "Armed Neutrality" during the remainder of the struggle between England and France.

Though not nominally directed against the former power, the "Armed Neutrality" was practically a declaration of hostility against her, for the confederates undertook to oppose—if necessary, by force of arms—the English doctrine that a neutral flag did not cover the goods of a belligerent on the high seas. The theory that neutral ships might be searched for contraband merchandise, whenever and wherever they were met, was strongly held by British statesmen, and had already caused much friction with Denmark and other powers. The hot-headed *Czar* had followed up his declaration of Armed Neutrality by seizing the English ships ice-bound in Russian ports and throwing their crews into prison—proceedings which left no doubt as to his future policy.

In 1801, therefore, England had to face not only her old enemy across the Channel, but the new league of the Baltic states. The prospect was not cheering, for the internal condition of the United Kingdom was anything but satisfactory. The last throes of an Irish rebellion had died down, and in 1800 Castlereagh had bribed and cajoled the Parliament on St. Stephen's Green to vote away its own legislative independence and consent to the Union with Great Britain. But if the position in Ireland was less desperate than it had been three years before, the general aspect of domestic affairs was gloomy. Dearth had prevailed all through 1800, and the rise in the price of bread had been followed by its usual consequences of discontent and riot.

The National Debt was piling itself up at the most fearful rate—the revenue had been in 1800 only £39,000,000, while the expenditure had been £63,000,000; the immense difference between the two had to be made up by borrowing. The military enterprises of Great Britain had been uniformly unsuccessful, save indeed in India. The last of them, the invasion of Holland in 1799, had been perhaps the worst managed of the whole series. It was true that British forces had been as regularly victorious at sea as they had been unfortunate on land, but even the greatest triumphs—Camperdown, St. Vincent, and the Nile—had been defensive rather than offensive successes. Britain had prevented France and her allies from insulting its own shores, or from gaining a mastery in the waters of the Mediterranean.

But Jervis, Duncan, and Nelson had been powerless to check the establishment of a French domination on the mainland of Western

Europe. The Royal Navy had swept the mercantile marine of France, Spain, and Holland from the seas, and the nation had appropriated their carrying trade. Yet, since the great enemy had never been mainly dependent on its seaborne commerce, and since the woes of Dutch or Spanish merchants were not likely to touch Bonaparte's heart, the British could bring comparatively little pressure to bear upon France. It was not till he tried his worst against Great Britain and found that he could not hope to deal her any serious blow, that the First Consul evinced any real desire for peace. Meanwhile he hoped to retain his new conquest of Egypt, and to bring to the aid of the shattered navies of France and Spain the fresh naval resources of the Baltic powers.

It was not under the guidance of William Pitt, whose unswerving hand had hitherto directed the foreign policy of Great Britain, that the last year of the Revolutionary war was destined to be fought out. Early in 1801 he resigned his office, on a question which, important enough in itself, was yet but a side issue in this time of stress and peril. While negotiating the details of the Union with Ireland, he had pledged his word to the Irish Catholics to introduce in the new United Parliament legislation for the relief of their many political disabilities. This he was preparing to do, when he found that the old king was determined to put his veto on any such action. Of the many deep-rooted prejudices of George III. none was more violent than his dislike for Romanists, and he had contrived to persuade himself that to give his assent to such a bill as Pitt was drafting would involve him in a breach of his Coronation Oath, "to defend the Protestant Church as by law established." When informed of the king's resolve, Pitt resigned (February, 1801): his exaggerated sense of loyalty to his old master prevented him from forcing matters to the point of actual conflict between king and ministry. He has been much censured, both for leaving the helm of state when the foreign danger was still so great, and for refusing to bring stronger pressure on the king, who, in spite of his obstinacy, might have yielded at the actual moment of friction.

With Pitt some of his personal friends retired from office. but the Tories still retained their hold on the government and Continued to carry out Pitt's policy in every detail. The new prime minister was Henry Addington, Speaker of the House of Commons, a man of narrow views and limited ability, chiefly notable for his subservience to the crown and his utter want of originality. Addington, and not Pitt, was the man destined to bring the great Revolutionary war to its end, though to his predecessor must be given the credit of devising the

13

A Plan of the Operations of the British Forces in Egypt from the Landing in Aboukir Bay on the 8th March to the BATTLE of ALEXANDRIA 21st March, 21 inclusive.

MEDITERRANEAN SEA

Aboukir Bay

Lake Aboukir

Lake Mareotis

Scale of Miles

ORDER of BATTLE of the BRITISH ARMY.

ORDER of BATTLE of the FRENCH ARMY,
Menou, Commander in Chief.

REFERENCE.

Published by W. Faden, Geographer to His Majesty & to His Royal Highness the Prince of Wales, Charing Cross, May 18th 1801.

measures which finally brought it to a successful conclusion.

Before leaving office, Pitt had made arrangements for the carrying out of two great expeditions, both of which were destined to win complete success. The first was aimed against the new French colony in Egypt. An English Army, concentrated in the Mediterranean, was to land in the Delta and assail the French from the sea, cross the desert, and strike into the valley of the Nile south of Cairo. As it chanced, the Indian Army arrived too late to take any part in the fighting, the larger expedition having done all the work.

The French general Menou, who had to face the attack, chanced to be wholly incompetent. He was an eccentric and histrionic personage, who had embraced Mohametanism to please Bonaparte, and thought more of his poses and of his proclamations than of strategy. He divided his troops up into two bodies, so that the 20,000 English who landed at Aboukir, under Sir Ralph Abercromby, were superior to each fraction, though far inferior in number to the whole army of Egypt. Two fights in front of Alexandria broke the main force of the French, though the gallant Abercromby fell in the moment of victory. After short sieges the two halves of Menou's army, shut up the one in Cairo and the other in Alexandria, laid down their arms, and all Egypt was in British hands (March-July, 1801). Bonaparte's dream of an Eastern empire had come to a disastrous end. This was inevitable from the first; without command of the sea such an outlying possession could not possibly be maintained.

Not less complete was the success of the English in the Baltic against the signatories of the declaration of Armed Neutrality. The bitter northern winter, which seals up the Russian and Swedish ports, prevented the early concentration of the allied fleets. Before the ice had broken up, an English squadron had been sent off, with orders to throw itself between the scattered divisions of the enemy, and to destroy them in detail.

Such a plan was absolutely necessary, for if the confederate navies could have massed themselves they might have taken the sea with more than fifty ships of the line, and the British squadron numbered no more than eighteen. Nelson sailed with them, but only as second-in-command: by some inexplicable stupidity of those in charge at the Admiralty, he had been placed under the orders of Sir Hyde Parker, a respectable veteran destitute of all initiative and dash. The squadron reached the Sound on March 30, and three days later attacked Copenhagen, while the Russians and Swedes were still wholly ignorant

ALEXANDRIA. LANDING OF THE BRITISH ARMY IN ABOUKIR BAY.

of their approach.

The Danes had protected their capital and arsenal by a line of floating batteries interspersed with ships of war. Parker thought their front almost too formidable to be attacked, but finally gave Nelson permission to go in with twelve ships and do his best. The approach lay up a narrow channel between sandbanks, on which more than one of the English ships went aground. But Nelson forced his way up to the enemy and engaged with them in the most furious cannonade of the whole Revolutionary war. No other of England's enemies fought their ships with such splendid obstinacy as the Danes: for some time, Nelson seemed to be making so little progress that his cautious superior hung out signals desiring him to draw off and retire. But Nelson turned his blind eye to the signals and persisted in the fight till the Danish floating batteries were burnt or sunk.

Although the shore forts still held out, the Prince Regent of Denmark then yielded to Nelson's summons and consented to suspend his adherence to the Armed Neutrality. The British fleet was then directed against Cronstadt, but its presence in Russian waters turned out to be unnecessary. Ten days before the Battle of Copenhagen the Czar Paul had fallen, the victim of a palace conspiracy. His constant petty tyranny and his mad caprices had driven his nobles to desperation, and on the night of March 23, 1801, he was strangled in his bedroom by a band of his own courtiers. His son and successor, Alexander, at once reversed his policy, released the English prisoners, and declared that the Baltic league was at an end.

Thus, the new and formidable weapon which Bonaparte had intended to turn against Great Britain was shattered, a few months before the last French garrison in Egypt was driven to surrender. Foiled in both quarters, the First Consul at last began to make genuine overtures for peace: his earlier offers had no reality in them. Addington and his cabinet were far from realising the bitter hatred of England which Bonaparte nourished in his heart and believed that a permanent pacification with him presented no insuperable difficulties. The negotiations, which commenced in the summer of 1801, dragged on for many months, and the definitive Treaty of Amiens was only signed on March 27, 1802.

By it England acknowledged the government of the First Consul, and accepted accomplished facts, by recognising the new boundaries of France and of her vassals, the Batavian, Helvetic, and Cisalpine Republics—new names which cloaked the identity of the Seven United

17

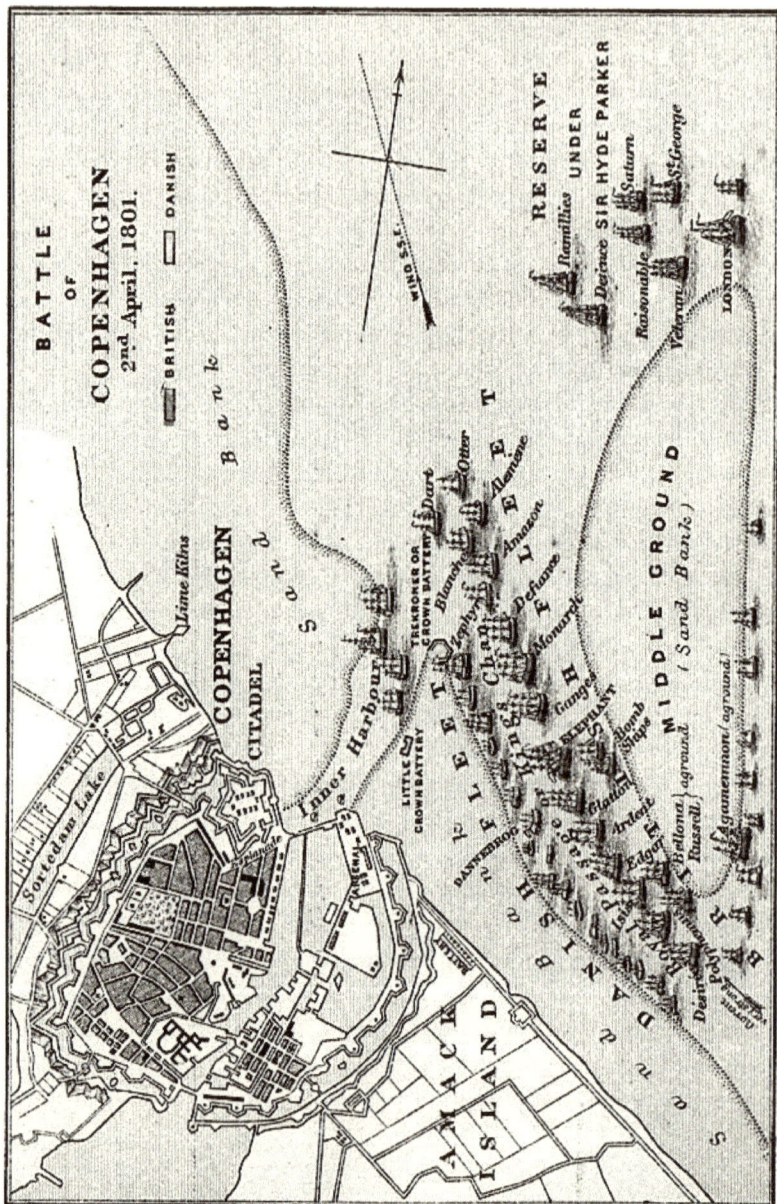

BATTLE
OF
COPENHAGEN
2nd April. 1801.

BRITISH   DANISH

Provinces, of the Swiss Confederates, and of Lombardy. Great Britain restored to France all her lost colonies in the West and East Indies; but Bonaparte—always liberal with the property of his unfortunate allies—allowed the conqueror to retain the Spanish island of Trinidad in the West, and in the East the important Dutch settlement of Ceylon. Charles IV. of Spain and the Batavian Republic, however, received back the rest of the possessions of which they had been stripped, the former recovering the island of Minorca, the latter the Cape of Good Hope, both points of high strategical importance which English statesmen surrendered with deep regret.

One more among the numerous clauses of the treaty requires mention—England had just captured Malta, which Bonaparte, in 1798, had lawlessly seized from the Knights of St. John without any declaration of war. The treaty provided that this important island, the key of the central Mediterranean, should be evacuated by the British forces and restored to its original owners, when the Order should have been reconstituted and remodelled. Herein lay the germs of much future trouble.

By the Treaty of Amiens England, perhaps, gave up more than was absolutely necessary. Her position was a very strong one after the French failures in Egypt and the Baltic; and it was only a genuine wish for peace, and a misplaced confidence in the good intentions of Bonaparte, which led the Addington ministry to give up so many valuable conquests. England, in spite of all her financial burdens, had still plenty of strength left in her. The expense of the war, monstrous as it had been, was almost made up to her by the extraordinary growth of English commerce since 1793. The destruction of the mercantile marine of France, Spain, and Holland had led to an unparalleled expansion in British trade.

In 1793 the export of British manufactures had been to the value of £14,700,000; in 1801 it had risen to £24,400,000. Similarly, at the earlier date Britain had re-exported £5,400,000 of foreign and colonial goods; in 1801 the figures had tripled and were recorded as £17,100,000. The number of British ships at sea had risen from 16,000 to 18,000, in spite of all French privateering. If Britain had failed to prevent the establishment of the French domination on the continent of Western Europe, France had failed quite as signally in her attempts to demolish British commercial and maritime supremacy. During the heat of the war Britain had grasped the control of Southern India, by putting down Bonaparte's ally, Tippoo Sultan of Mysore

19

(1799); the "Great Proconsul" Wellesley was, at the very moment of the Treaty of Amiens, watching his opportunity to lay the foundations of British power in the central and northern regions of Hindostan by interfering in the affairs of the Mahratta states, a project which he was to take in hand before the year 1802 had expired.

Yet, even when all these facts are taken into consideration, there can be no doubt that Addington and his cabinet were fully justified in concluding peace with France. War is such a fearful burden, and its chances are so incalculable, that no government which is offered an honourable and not unprofitable peace should hesitate to accept it, merely because there is some prospect of obtaining yet better terms at some future date. The one mistake made was in thinking that Bonaparte was sincerely anxious for an equitable pacification and wished to dwell beside us as a quiet neighbour. But the statesmen of 1801 could not know his character as we know it after a study of his whole career; they were quite excusable if they were deceived by his plausible verbiage and allowed him some credit for the magnificent and praiseworthy sentiments which he professed.

CHAPTER 2

The Struggle with Bonaparte

The peace from which so much had been hoped was to endure for no more than thirteen months. But in March, 1802, well-nigh all men on the island side of the Channel believed that the struggle with France had reached its end, and thought that a period of rest, economy, and retrenchment had set in. Britain was to turn to account the complete sovereignty of the seas and the new Indian empire which she had gained, and, by a careful development of trade and manufactures, was to free herself from the burden of her vast national debt.

The army and navy were reduced with a haste that was to produce much trouble ere the year was out. So great were the expectations that were entertained of the prosperity that was to result from the peace, that when the French ambassador arrived in London, his carriage was actually drawn through the streets by the populace, and a general illumination testified to the national joy. Great numbers of English at once embarked on continental travel—a pleasure which had been denied them for more than eight years, and for which many of them were to pay dearly in 1803.

Bonaparte's objects in coming to terms with England had been twofold. He wished for an interval of quiet in which to prepare for that assumption of regal power which he had already determined to carry out. But he also wished to recover the lost French colonies, and to gain time to rebuild the shattered French Navy, which in 1802 had been reduced to less than forty ships of the line. In a few years he intended to create a new fleet, which should be able to dispute with that of Britain the mastery of the seas. Moreover, observing the enthusiasm with which peace was greeted in England, he fancied that British Government would wink at several new aggressions which he was contemplating on the continent. Rather than renew the war, he imagined that the weak Addington would submit to many humiliations. In this respect he wholly misconceived the situation; he underrated the wariness and national pride of his opponents to an absurd degree.

Only a few months had elapsed after the Treaty of Amiens had been signed, when the First Consul began to take in hand some measures which were certain to irritate England. In September he annexed to France Piedmont and the rest of the continental territories of the King of Sardinia, though that unfortunate monarch had given him no provocation whatever. Parma was at the same time appropriated, though compensation was in this case given to the dispossessed Bourbon duke. Soon after Bonaparte sent 30,000 men into Switzerland and overturned there a government which was not sufficiently subservient to his interests. When England protested against this high-handed action, he merely replied that she had no concern with continental affairs, since there was no mention of Piedmont or the Helvetic Republic in the Treaty of Amiens. On his part he began to declaim against the British Government because Malta had not yet been evacuated: Britain had agreed to restore the island to the Order of the Knights of St. John, but since they had not yet been reorganised, British troops were still in possession. However, actual preparations for their departure had begun when the First Consul's action caused them to be suspended.

Even before these matters of foreign policy had come to a head, Bonaparte had created much ill feeling in England by making some extraordinary demands from the British Government. He proposed that Britain should expel from British shores the princes of the old royal family of France and certain other refugees, a request for the violation of English hospitality which was naturally refused. He also made an astonishing demand for the suppression of certain English newspapers and pamphlets, wherein his conduct and policy were being discussed with the usual freedom of political papers. When Lord Hawkesbury made the natural reply that in England the press was free, and that it was not British wont to expel foreign exiles who had done nothing against British laws, the First Consul pretended to regard himself as outrageously insulted (August 17, 1802).

His ill-will was notably manifest in the regulations against English trade which he maintained. He utterly refused to sign any commercial treaty, and caused crushing duties to be laid on English goods, not only in France, but throughout the territories of her vassal republics. He also sent agents and spies all over Great Britain and the British empire, to discover British exact military and commercial resources. The final outbreak of wrath against him on the British side of the Channel was largely caused by the publication of the papers of one of his agents, General Sebastiani, which were filled with elaborate plans for putting the French again in possession of Egypt, and for undermining English trade in the Levant.

It was no wonder that in the winter of 1802-3 the English ministers made up their minds that another war was probably in sight. They resolved to retain a firm hold on Malta, and to delay the surrender of the Cape of Good Hope, Pondicherry, and such other French possessions as had not yet been given back. When Parliament met in March, the prime minister announced that the army and navy, instead of being further reduced, would require certain additions. It was the news of these measures which led Bonaparte to show his hand: he summoned the English ambassador, Lord Whitworth, to the Tuileries, and, in the presence of a large assembly, delivered an angry harangue at him. He accused the English cabinet of violating the Treaty of Amiens with deliberate treachery, cried that they should have war if they wanted it, "but if they are the first to draw the sword, I shall be the last to put it back into the scabbard. Woe to those who violate treaties; they shall answer for the consequences to all Europe" (March 13, 1803).

After such a scene the Addington cabinet felt that war was inevitable; they began hurriedly to refit the British dismantled fleet, and to re-embody British disbanded battalions. Bonaparte, on the other hand, began to move troops from inland France towards the shores of the Channel, and set naval preparations afoot in all his ports, especially in the new arsenal of Antwerp. Some negotiations, half-hearted on both sides, dragged on for nearly two months more; but when the First Consul insisted that Britain should not only recognise the legality of his doings in Italy and Switzerland, but also at once evacuate

Malta, it was obvious that there could be no yielding. On the 12th of May, 1803, the British ambassador left Paris, and the declaration of war followed.

It is probable that at first Bonaparte had merely intended to bully and hector the British Government into condoning his annexations in Italy and had assumed his aggressive airs in the full confidence that Addington and his cabinet would give way. When they refused to yield an inch, and met his menaces with a declaration of war, he showed all the irritation of a man deceived in his expectations. His first act was a sign of blind wrath, an act unparalleled in previous generations, though unfortunately it was to have a complete reproduction in 1914. He seized all the English tourists and travellers who were passing through France for pleasure or business, and put them in confinement, as if they had been prisoners of war. They were about 10,000 in number, and Bonaparte actually had the cruelty to keep them confined during the whole of the war.

Even more unlucky than the interned of Rühleben, they were ten years in bonds. Another sign of his wrath was that he persistently continued to accuse the British Government of hiring assassins to attempt his life—ascribing all conspiracies against him whether the work of royalist fanatics or discontented republicans, to English gold.

Thus, began the second half of the great French war—the struggle with Bonaparte as opposed to the struggle against the principles of the Revolution. The two episodes are one in so far as they are regarded as constituting the great test-struggle between England and France, the last serious effort made by a foreign power to destroy British commercial and maritime supremacy by force of arms. Napoleon in this respect only continued the work of the Jacobins, and the short Peace of Amiens was a break so insignificant that we need hardly regard it at all. Up to 1802 the game had been a drawn one, and the adversaries had only paused for a moment to draw breath before resuming their duel.

But the character of the struggle was profoundly modified by the fact that from 1803 onwards the British were no longer fighting against the principles of the Revolution, but against a military despot of unparalleled genius, who had fought his way up from the obscure position of a lieutenant of artillery to that of the arbitrator of Europe, and had showed his ability to direct the anarchic energy of revolutionary France to his own ends. France under Bonaparte only resembled France under Robespierre in the unscrupulous vigour of her assaults on her neighbours. After having long posed as the prophetess of licentious liberty, she now became the apostle of despotism; and England, therefore, was able to appear once more as the protectress of the liberties of Europe against a tyrant, abandoning her previous position as the defender of order against anarchy, which she had occupied since 1792.

The Republicans had talked of freeing the masses in England from the government of a corrupt oligarchy: Bonaparte made no pretence of any such philanthropic aim, and merely spoke of destroying the power and wealth of Great Britain because she stood in his way. All through his career it is most notable how a hatred for this country pervades and explains all his widespread schemes. From the day when, as a young artillery officer, he drove the British garrison out of Toulon, to the day when he saw the broken columns of his Old Guard rolling down the slope of Waterloo, it was always England that stood before him as the enemy of his schemes and the final object at which his blows were levelled. His invasion of Egypt in 1798 had been aimed against the British Indian empire, and Britain had foiled him.

His policy after the rupture of the Peace of Amiens had always before it as its ultimate end the maritime and commercial ruin of England. He strove to accomplish it first by open invasion and maritime war, later by the more circuitous method of compelling all Europe to unite in the league of the "Continental System" and join him in his boycotting of English trade. All his wars with Austria, Prussia, and Russia were to a great extent indirect blows at the insular enemy whom he could not attack on her own soil, for all the confederacies against him were fomented and consolidated by the application of English gold. To win the fight of Friedland or Wagram meant to him that he could force another state into adopting a commercial policy hostile to England, not merely that he could seize territory or impose vassalage on the defeated foe. The final end of all his plans was to crush Great Britain, and the other episodes of the war were but means to that end, only necessary because England's continental allies must be subdued before England herself could be touched.

Bonaparte had many points in his favour while conducting the war against Great Britain. He had all the advantages that come from unity of purpose and despotic power. The ministers of a constitutional state are clogged with the responsibility to Parliament and the nation for all their actions. They have to face the criticism of the opposition and the comments of the press. Moreover, the policy of a cabinet of ten or a dozen men must necessarily be less coherent and self-consistent than that of a single autocrat. When each side had formed a scheme, the ruler of France could provide for its speedy and silent accomplishment; while the English expeditions were too often canvassed in parliament and divulged by the press before they had even left British shores.

Bonaparte was his own finance-minister and his own commander-in-chief; while in England the views of the economist and the soldier were too often clashing in the cabinet, with the result that the one spent more than he intended, though the other was always being checked by insufficient supplies. Several times, as we shall see, Wellington was nearly starved out in Spain, while the ministry were positive that they were spending too much rather than too little on his army. Nothing of the sort could happen in France, where the same hand held the sword and the purse-strings. Bonaparte, too, in his dealings with his allies, could press his demands as a master; England had great difficulty in getting even part of her requirements carried out by confederates who knew that they were serving her as well as themselves, and could therefore get what terms they liked out of her.

CHAPTER 3

The Sea & Invasion

The great war of 1803-1814 falls into two main parts. During the first, Bonaparte aimed at fighting England on the seas, and his fundamental project was the actual invasion of British shores. This period lasted for somewhat over two years, and ended in 1805, when the British Government stirred up against him enemies who kept his army occupied in Central Europe and the Royal Navy destroyed his fleet at Trafalgar. During the second and longer section of the struggle, Bonaparte abandoned his invasion scheme, frankly ceased to dispute the mastery of the seas, and strove to wear down England by cutting off the sources of her commercial prosperity by his "Continental System," a scheme hopeless from the first, and entailing on him in the end the desperate hatred, not only of the governments, but of the peoples of every European state. He finally fell because he had taught every patriot in every land to look upon him as a bitter and irreconcilable personal enemy.

At the first outbreak of the new war in 1803, it would be hard to say which of the two belligerents displayed the greater energy. Bonaparte marched 120,000 veteran troops to the coast of the Channel and set every dockyard in France and Holland to work, in order to build men-of-war to equal the English fleet in numbers. He also constructed vast numbers of large flat-bottomed boats, in which he intended to convey his army across the straits under cover of his war fleet. His own headquarters were placed at Boulogne; to right and left his regiments lay at every port between Ostend and St. Valery. He was thoroughly set upon trying that invasion of the British Isles which the Directory had abandoned as impracticable after the defeats of Camperdown and St. Vincent. A fog, he thought, might cover his crossing, or a gale might drive away the British squadron which observed him, or a lucky concentration of his own ships might for a moment give him the command of the Channel. But in some way or another he was determined that the attempt should be made. His troops were trained to get on board their flat-bottomed boats with extraordinary speed and order, and he boasted that the whole army could embark in France and disembark in England within forty-eight hours—a feat wholly impossible at that time.

On the British side of the Channel the outbreak of war had roused wild anger against Bonaparte for cheating the nation out of the long-desired peace from which so much had been expected. With anger was mixed a strong feeling of apprehension when the magnitude of the preparations at Boulogne became known. The excitement was far greater than that which had been felt during the critical year 1798. While the ministers were planning how best the military forces of the United Kingdom could be drawn out to meet the projected attack, the nation itself came to their aid by forming many hundreds of volunteer corps. In a few months 347,000 volunteers were under arms, besides 120,000 regulars and 78,000 militia. The new levies were very raw, and insufficiently supplied with cavalry and artillery. But their numbers were so great and their enthusiasm so genuine, that, with the regulars to stiffen their resistance, it cannot be doubted that they would have given a good account of Bonaparte, if ever he had succeeded in throwing the whole of his 150,000 men ashore in Kent and Sussex.

The spirit of the nation was displayed with equal clearness by the demand made for the return of Pitt to the helm of the state. Addington, whose efforts to organise the national defence were considered too slow and ineffective, retired from office in the spring of 1804, and Pitt's advent to power was signalised by an outburst of redoubled energy and an unsparing expenditure of public money. Every month that Bonaparte waited before dealing his threatened blow made the project of invasion more chimerical.

The longer the First Consul studied the problem of transporting

Camp at Boulogne

his host across the straits on his light craft, the more difficult it began to appear. Finally, after many months spent in weighing the chances for and against the possibility of invading England before he had secured control of the Channel, Bonaparte seems to have come to the very wise and prudent conclusion that it was too hazardous an undertaking. Instead of placing his army on board of his transports and flat-bottomed boats and launching them on to the narrow seas, he resolved to bring up his war fleet to convey them across. But to collect his line-of-battle ships from the scattered ports where they were being blockaded by the English squadrons was in itself a very hazardous and difficult task. He deferred the operation till 1804, and meanwhile took in hand a piece of domestic policy whose conclusion the rupture of the Treaty of Amiens had interrupted.

He thought the time was ripe for the open restoration of monarchy in France. A royalist conspiracy against his life being detected, he took the opportunity which it gave him to demand a higher and firmer position in the state than that of First Consul. Acting on his secret orders, the French senate requested him to assume the title of emperor—the monarch of so large a realm and the controller of so many vassal states was too great (he thought) to be a mere king. Bonaparte at once accepted the offer, which seemed to fall in with the aspirations of the whole nation.

Jacobinism was wholly dead, and there was a real and widespread enthusiasm for the ruler who had not merely smitten the foreign enemies of France, but had restored order within her boundaries, reorganised her finances, and brought back to the ruined country a considerable measure of internal prosperity (May 18, 1804). Bonaparte compelled the Pope to come to Paris to assist in his coronation: it was a grand if somewhat garish pageant, which went to the hearts of the few surviving members of the old republican party and marked the complete ascendency of despotism in France. At its culminating point, Bonaparte, taking the crown out of the hands of Pius VII., who had been intending to place it on his head, crowned himself instead, and then placed another diadem on the brow of his wife, Josephine Beauharnais. For the future law ran in France in the name of the "Emperor Napoleon," though the state was officially spoken of as a republic for two or three years more, in spite of its new monarchical form (December 2, 1804).

In the autumn of 1804, Napoleon began to take in hand his new scheme for concentrating a naval force in the Channel to cover the passage of his army. He hoped to unite at Boulogne all the scattered French squadrons, and to join to them the navies of Holland and Spain. The latter power had just been forced by him, much against her will, to join the coalition. Charles IV., being summoned to supply the emperor with either ships or money, undertook to pay France an enormous subsidy, trusting thereby to escape an open breach with England. But the Addington cabinet got early news of the treaty, and promptly seized the frigates which were bringing the treasure from America (October 5), whereupon Spain a few months later declared war on England (December 12), and openly joined Napoleon.

This event immensely enlarged the area of naval war: English fleets had now to watch every port of Western Europe, from the Texel in the North Sea to Genoa in the Mediterranean, lest some detachment of the enemy might escape, and, by relieving other blockaded squadrons, concentrate for the moment a force which should outnumber British ships on the all-important belt of sea between Boulogne and the Kentish coast. Everything then depended on the untiring vigilance of British admirals, who had to keep up an endless watch on the hostile ports, and whose weather-beaten ships could never retire for a moment from the wearisome blockade.

Napoleon at last thought out an elaborate and ingenious scheme for drawing together his scattered naval strength. The initiative was to lie with Villeneuve, the admiral commanding at Toulon, whose squadron was being watched by a somewhat smaller English fleet under the ever-watchful Nelson. He was to slip out of his port at the first opportunity, and, evading Nelson, to make for the Straits of Gibraltar. Picking up the Spanish ships at Cartagena and Cadiz, where the English blockading vessels were very few, he was then to strike out westward into the Atlantic, as if intending to deal a blow at the English West Indies. Nelson, the emperor rightly thought, would follow them in that direction.

But after reaching the Caribbean Sea, the Franco-Spaniards were to turn suddenly back and make a dash for Brest, where lay a large French squadron, watched by Admiral Cornwallis and the English Channel fleet. If all went well, Villeneuve could raise the blockade of Brest, for, counting the ships in that port, he would have some sixty vessels to Cornwallis's thirty-five. Nelson meanwhile would be vainly searching the West Indian waters for the enemy who had reached the Channel. Cornwallis must retire or be crushed, and the command of the narrow seas must pass for some weeks into French hands. The invasion could then be accomplished.

Much of this scheme of the emperors was actually carried out. On March 29, 1805, Villeneuve ran out of Toulon in a heavy gale, which had blown Nelson far to the south. He made for the Straits of Gibraltar, while the English admiral was vainly looking for him off Sicily, under the impression that he had sailed for Egypt. Fortunately for the Royal Navy, the Spanish fleet was in such a disgraceful state of disrepair and disorder, that no ships from Cartagena and only six from Cadiz joined the enemy, and Villeneuve had to start on his dash across the Atlantic with only eighteen vessels instead of the thirty on which he had counted (April 9, 1805). On the 13th of May they reached Martinique. After staying some weeks in the West Indies, that the knowledge of his arrival there might get abroad and mislead Nelson, the French admiral started homeward on the 4th of June. His great opponent meanwhile had only received full information as to the route taken by the French as late as May 9 and started for the West just a month later than the French, and with only eleven line-of-battle ships. He reached Barbados on the very day that Villeneuve turned back towards Europe, vainly sought him among the islands for a few days, and then, acting on his own unerring inspiration, turned backward and made sail for Europe. He was now only nine days behind the French, though he had started with a full month to the bad.

Meanwhile all Napoleon's elaborate plans for bringing Villeneuve to Brest, long ere his departure from the West transpired, were wrecked by the chances of war and the activity of the English Admiralty. A fast-sailing English brig sighted the allied fleet moving eastward soon after it left the West Indies. Making an extraordinarily swift passage, this little vessel brought the news to Portsmouth on the 7th of July. Realising its tremendous importance, Lord Barham, the First Lord of the Admiralty, gave prompt orders that a squadron should be sent out into the Atlantic to intercept Villeneuve. This was done with such splendid speed that on July 23 fifteen vessels under Sir Robert Calder met the approaching enemy just as he arrived in sight of Europe, off the Spanish cape Finisterre. After an indecisive action, in which they lost two ships, the allies ran into Ferrol instead of sailing for Brest: Calder's appearance had checkmated them.

Nelson, too, was now back in European waters; on July 20, three days before Calder's action, he reached Gibraltar. All the British squadrons being now within touch of each other, Bonaparte's scheme had practically failed. But Villeneuve made its failure more disastrous than

BATTLE
OF
TRAFALGAR
21st October, 1805.

BRITISH ☐ FRENCH ☐ SPANISH

COMBINED FRENCH & SPANISH FLEET

Cornélie
Neptuno
Scipion
Intrepide
Formidable
Duguay Trouin
San Francisco de Asis
Rayo
Mont Blanc
San Augustin
Fure
Heros
Santisima Trinidad
BUCENTAURE
Neptune
Redoutable
San Leandro
San Justo
Indomptable
Sta Anna
Monarca
Algesiras
Bahama
Swiftsure
Montañes
Themis
Hermione
Argonauta
Prince des Asturias
Argus
San Ildefonso
San Juan Nepomuceno
Achille
Argonaute
Aigle
Pluton
Berwick
Fougueux

Africa

BRITISH FLEET

Euryalus
Britannia
Sirius
Mars
Belleisle
Royal Sovereign
Tonnant
Bellerophon
Colossus
Achilles
Polyphemus
Revenge
Swiftsure
Thunderer
Defiance
Defence
Dreadnought
Prince
Entreprenante
Pickle
Minotaur
Orion
Ajax
Naiad
Agamemnon
Spartiate
Leviathan
Conqueror
Neptune
Temeraire
VICTORY

DIVISION OF VICE ADMIRAL COLLINGWOOD

WIND. S.N.W.

Plan shewing
THE SITE OF
BATTLE

SPAIN

Cadiz
L. Pta Real
Medina-Sidonia
Scene of Action
C. Trafalgar
Tarifa
Algesiras
Gibraltar
Strait of Gibraltar
Tangier
Ceuta
AFRICA

it need have been. Having procured reinforcements at Ferrol, he then moved to Cadiz to pick up the remainder of the Spanish fleet. After joining them, he had thirty-three ships of the line; but outside Cadiz lay Nelson with his own and Calder's squadrons, twenty-seven vessels in all. Villeneuve refused to put out, rightly thinking that his superiority in numbers did not compensate for the inferior quality of his crews. But nevertheless, he had to fight. His master the emperor had heard with disgust and wild anger that the fleet which was to give him the command of the Channel had appeared at Ferrol instead of at Brest and had allowed itself to be turned from its goal by Calder's less numerous squadron. In his vexation Napoleon sent his admiral a letter taunting him with cowardice and bad seamanship and informing him that a successor had been sent to supersede him.

To vindicate his courage, the unfortunate Villeneuve determined to offer battle to Nelson before he was displaced from command. The fleets met off Cape Trafalgar, on October 21, 1805, with the result that might have been expected. Nelson's vessels in two columns burst into the midst of the ill-formed Franco-Spanish line, and silenced or captured ship after ship by their splendid gunnery. The allied rear and centre were annihilated before their van could tack and come into action. Nineteen of Villeneuve's ships, including his own, were taken, and one blew up; only a remnant escaped into Cadiz. But Nelson was mortally wounded by a musket-ball in the thick of the fight. He lived long enough to hear that the victory was complete but expired ere night. His work was done, for Napoleon never again dared to send a large fleet to sea or to risk a general engagement. Had Nelson's indomitable soul sustained his frail body for a few more years, there would have been little but weary blockading work for him to do. He had effectually put an end to all Napoleon's invasion schemes, by destroying more than half the French and Spanish ships which were to have swept the Channel and laid open the shores of Kent.

The turning-point of the great naval campaign of 1805 had been Calder's indecisive action off Cape Finisterre. The moment it had been fought and Villeneuve had turned southward. Napoleon had mentally given up his idea of crossing the Dover Straits and turned his attention to Continental affairs. It was high time, for Pitt had been stirring up against him a formidable coalition. The old monarchies of Europe had been greatly displeased by Napoleon's annexations in Italy and elsewhere. Francis II. of Austria bitterly resented his constant intrigues with the minor German states, and as emperor had a special grievance against him. For in 1804 Bonaparte had violated the territory of the empire in the most outrageous way. He had sent a regiment of horse across the Rhine and kidnapped at night a Bourbon prince, the Duke of Enghien, whom he then tried and shot on a false accusation of being concerned in an assassination plot.

Such a violation of international law and common morality had provoked open protest from Austria and Russia. These two powers were already negotiating for an alliance against France, when Pitt stepped in to offer them enormous subsidies and the active aid of the English fleet. It was hoped that Prussia too would join the coalition; but the ministers of Frederick William III. pursued a mean and double-faced policy, haggling with France and Austria at once, and offering themselves to the highest bidder. They finally helped neither side, but pounced on the electorate of Hanover, with Napoleon's consent, and preserved an ambiguous neutrality.

CHAPTER 4

Europe Ablaze

The French autocrat was not unaware of the Austro-Russian alliance. When he heard of Villeneuve's failure, he dropped for ever his cherished invasion scheme, and, suddenly turning his back on the sea, declared war on his Continental enemies before they were ready for him. The troops from the camp of Boulogne were hurried across France by forced marches, and hurled into Germany, long before the Russians were anywhere near the field of operations. The Austrians alone had to bear the first brunt of the war; their imbecile commander, Mack, allowed them to be surprised before they were concentrated, and was himself captured at Ulm with nearly 40,000 men before the war was many days old (October 20). This disaster left the Austrians so weak that they could not even save Vienna from the invader; the wrecks of their army had to fall back and join the Russians, who were only now coming on the scene.

A month later (December 2, 1805) the French and the allies met in a decisive battle at Austerlitz, a Moravian village, eighty miles north of Vienna. Here the unskilful generalship of the allies exposed them to a bloody defeat, which cost them more than 30,000 men. The Austrians now cried aloud for peace, which Napoleon only granted on very hard terms. He took away Venice and the other Austrian lands south of the Alps, and united them to Lombardy, so forming a "Kingdom of Italy," of which he wore the crown. The Tyrol was given to Bavaria, whose ruler had sided with Napoleon.

Moreover, Francis II. was forced to give up the time-honoured title of "Holy Roman Emperor" which his ancestors had held since 1438, and with it his place as nominal *suzerain* of the other German states. Most of the minor princes between the Rhine and the Elbe were forced to replace their nominal dependence on the Habsburg emperor by a very real servitude to Bonaparte. He formed them into the "Confederation of the Rhine" under his own presidency, and compelled them to place their armies and treasures at his disposal (July to December, 1806).

The news of the defeat of Austerlitz is often said to have been the death-blow of Pitt. This statement is only true in a general way, and the theatrical last words which are put into his mouth, "Roll up the map of Europe; we shall not want it again for twenty years," are not authentic. But there is no doubt that he was bitterly disappointed at the failure of the great coalition which he had raised against Napoleon. His death was really due to the long strain of anxiety during the projected invasion of England, and to his carelessness about his health, of which he was as reckless as he was about his private fortune. He died, a broken man, though aged no more than forty-six, on January 23, 1806. But his policy lived after him, and his successors were to carry it out to a successful end, though only after eight more years of desperate war.

With the battles of Trafalgar and Austerlitz, followed by the death of Pitt, the first stage in the great struggle with the French emperor came to an end. There was no further talk of the invasion of England, nor did Bonaparte attempt any more to dispute the dominion of the seas. But his mind was none the less set on the humiliation of England, though his methods of assailing her became more indirect. He had now in his eye the establishment of a domination over the whole of Europe.

The first step towards the systematic reduction of his neighbours to subjection was the establishment of the "Confederation of the Rhine," whose members were from the first his slaves. The second was the planting out of his relatives as rulers of the smaller states of Europe. In 1806 his brother Joseph was made King of Naples, from which the imbecile Bourbon house were driven out, because they had dared to league themselves with Austria during the war of 1805. A few months later came the crowning of his brother Louis as King of Holland—the Batavian republic being ruthlessly swept away, without any option being given to the Dutch of declaring their wishes as to the government of their land. Bonaparte began to talk of himself as the "successor of Charlemagne," an ominous saying for Germans and Spaniards, since the great Frankish emperor's dominions had extended as far as the Elbe and the Ebro.

Meanwhile Pitt had found no competent successor in England. No statesman commanded sufficient authority with the people or the Parliament to take his place. The result that followed was a coalition ministry. The Whig party, excluded from office for more than twenty years, were invited to take their share in the governance of the realm. Charles James Fox and Sheridan took office, allied to Lord Grenville, long a faithful supporter of Pitt, and to many other Tories, among whom Addington was numbered.

Even the way in which Bonaparte had broken the peace of Amiens had not wholly cured Fox of his idea that peace with France was possible. The invasion scheme being foiled, he thought that the emperor might be willing to come to terms. Accordingly, the Grenville-Fox cabinet entered into negotiations with the enemy in 1806. Napoleon at first used smooth words, but the conditions on which he offered peace were humiliating, considering that England had hitherto not only held her own, but had swept the French fleet from the seas and occupied a great number of French colonies.

To his great regret. Fox was compelled to acknowledge that an honourable and reasonable peace was not procurable. Soon after he died (September, 1806), surviving his great rival Pitt by less than a year. The coalition ministry survived him a few months but resigned in March, 1807. The two elements in it were at variance, and the Whigs made the refusal of George III. to allow them to introduce Catholic Emancipation their excuse for leaving office. A cabinet of pure Tories succeeded them, in which the leading spirit was Spencer Perceval, though the premiership was nominally held by the aged Duke of Portland.

Not many months after the Austrians had yielded to their conqueror, and the Russians had retired sullenly towards the east, the third great Continental power was destined to feel the weight of Napoleon's sword. The weak and selfish ministers of Prussia had stood out from the coalition of 1805 and had sold themselves to Napoleon for the price of the annexation of Hanover—the patrimony of the old King of England. But no sooner was Austerlitz won and the allies crushed, than Napoleon began a series of systematic slights and insults to Prussia. He considered that, by making her bargain with him, she had sold herself to be as much his vassal as were Holland or Bavaria.

The numerous insults which he inflicted on his ally Frederick William III. culminated in an extraordinary piece of bad faith. He had covenanted in 1805 that Prussia should keep Hanover: but, negotiating with England in 1806, he calmly proposed to the English ministers to take back that electorate and restore it to George III. as one of the terms of peace. This came to the ears of the Prussian court and led to such an explosion of wrath that with great haste and hurry Frederick William declared war on France, without giving himself time to prepare his army or to purvey himself allies. He hastily tried to conciliate England, whose king he had robbed of Hanover, and to patch up an alliance with Alexander of Russia, who was still eager to fight, to reverse the verdict of Austerlitz. Both England and Russia came to terms with the Prussians, but not in time to give her practical assistance during the opening days of the war.

Advancing beyond the Elbe in order to overrun the lands of the princes of the "Confederacy of the Rhine," the Prussians found themselves suddenly assailed on the flank by the French Army, which Bonaparte had secretly concentrated under cover of the Thuringian Forest. The Prussian troops had hitherto enjoyed a very high reputation, won in the splendid victories of Frederick the Great. But the accurate drill and stern discipline which they inherited from him, and their undoubted courage in the field, did not save them from a fearful disaster. Guided by aged and incompetent generals, who had not studied Bonaparte's methods of attack, they were caught before they could concentrate, and defeated piecemeal at the battles of Jena and Auerstadt (October 14, 1806).

When Napoleon had once got them on the run, he pursued them so fiercely that division after division was outmarched, surrounded, and compelled to lay down its arms. The king escaped with only 12,000 men, the wreck of a host of 150,000 veterans, to join his Russian ally. Of all the disasters which befell the powers of the Continent when they measured themselves on the field of battle against Bonaparte, this was the most sudden and humiliating. Only a few weeks after the declaration of war the Prussian monarchy was ruined.

After entering Berlin in triumph, the victor pressed on to the east to meet the Russians. His campaign against them was far more difficult and sharply contested. In the first pitched battle, fought at Eylau in a blinding February snowstorm, amid frozen lakes and pine woods, the emperor, though not beaten, failed to drive the enemy from the field. He retired for a space into winter quarters; but when the spring of 1807 came round he pushed forward again, and, after much sharp fighting, crushed the Russians at Friedland (June 14). The *czar* then asked for peace; meeting him on a raft on the river Niemen, the boundary of Russia and Prussia, Napoleon concluded with him the Treaty of Tilsit (July 7, 1807).

The terms of this peace were far harder on Prussia, who had been friendly with France since 1795, than on Russia, who had thrice during the last ten years struck hard at her. Frederick William was stripped of half his dominions, partly to help in making a new kingdom called "Westphalia" for Napoleon's brother Jerome, partly to erect in Poland a vassal state called the "Grand Duchy of Warsaw," destined to act as a French outpost to the east. A crushing fine was laid on the dismembered monarchy, and French garrisons were permanently established in its chief strongholds. Russia, on the other hand, was left intact, and only compelled to sign an agreement to follow Napoleon's policy of attacking England by striking at her trade.

Since Villeneuve's incapacity and Nelson's vigilance had ruined Bonaparte's invasion scheme, another set of designs against Britain had been maturing in the emperor's mind, for her ruin was still the final end of all his policy, and the wars with Continental powers were no more than episodes in the struggle. There was a way in which victories like Austerlitz and Friedland could be turned to account. If all English trade with the states of the Continent could be prohibited, England—Napoleon thought—must grow poor and perish. The enforcement of this policy begins with the "Berlin Decrees," issued soon after Jena, in the autumn of 1806, and was continued by the Milan Decrees of 1807. These ordinances were among the most ingenious devices of the emperor's fertile brain; but, unlike most of the others, were decidedly impracticable from the first.

Everyone was familiar with the idea of a naval blockade, wherein the power supreme at sea places ships before the harbours of its foe and prohibits the ingress or egress of his merchandise. But Bonaparte's idea was the reverse of this: he would institute a land blockade—soldiers and custom-house officers should be planted all round the coasts of France and France's vassals and allies, to exclude British vessels, and so to prevent British manufactures and colonial goods reaching the Continent. The Berlin Decrees declared the British Isles to be in a state of blockade—we are reminded of another decree from Berlin, issued in 1915 by another and a not less bitter enemy. No subject of France or of France's vassal states was to purchase or possess any British merchandise. No vessel of a neutral power—for example, the United States of America—which had touched at a British port or a port of the British colonies, was to be admitted into a Continental haven.

All goods of British manufacture were to be seized, whenever and in whosesoever hands they were found, and confiscated to the crown. These rules were at once imposed on Holland, Italy, Spain, and Germany, and after Tilsit Russia also was cajoled into accepting them. In all Europe, only Turkey, Portugal, Sweden, and the small island kingdoms of Sicily and Sardinia were not included in their effect.

The new Tory government in England promptly took up the challenge. By the "Orders in Council" of 1807 the whole of the coasts of France and France's allies were declared to be in a state of strict blockade, and all vessels—even those under neutral flags—which left or entered them were declared good prizes of war, *unless* they could prove that since leaving home they had touched at a British port. This was a sort of ironical parody of Bonaparte's Berlin Decrees: obviously if both parties carried out their threats, there could be no foreign trade at all in continental Europe.

The main difference between the two sets of Decrees was that from the first England had the power to put her edict in force, while Bonaparte's was a dead letter not worth the paper on which it was written. He could not force his subjects and allies to give up the countless articles of luxury and necessity which they had been accustomed to draw from Britain or Britain's colonies. From the first the proscribed goods contrived to penetrate into Europe despite his orders. They came up the Danube from Turkey, they crept into Spain from Portugal. Smuggling became scientific and was practised on a gigantic scale. From Malta, Sicily, Gibraltar, and the Channel Islands vessels laden with contraband goods sailed every night to throw ashore their wares in Italy and France.

Napoleon never succeeded in excluding British goods, but he succeeded in making the price of them to his unfortunate subjects or allies three or four times the natural amount, for the smuggler's risk of capture had to be highly remunerated. Every time that a German or Spaniard had to pay two shillings a pound for his sugar, or to substitute chicory for his accustomed coffee, he was reminded that the Continental System was the cause of his privations and asked himself what benefit his country was drawing from the French alliance to compensate him for his personal inconvenience.

As the years passed by, and Napoleon's demands grew more exorbitant, the nations chafed more and more against his tyranny, till there followed the great final explosion of wrath in 1813. But in 1807 this was as yet far off, and the full weight of Bonaparte's exactions was unrealised. Meanwhile the suffering brought on England was comparatively insignificant: Britain had still the undisturbed control of the Indian, Chinese, African, and North American trade to draw on, even though British commerce with Europe was restricted. British ports and warehouses were full, and though could not readily use some old markets, yet the stagnation of which Napoleon had dreamed was far from setting in. Such were the effects of the long-pondered scheme which the emperor had devised, a scheme which he carried out with a ruthless disregard for the interests of his subjects and allies, and which was to draw him first into the costly Spanish war of 1808, and then into the disastrous Russian war of 1812.

One of the secret articles of the Treaty of Tilsit had formulated a plan of the emperor's for combining the Russian and Danish fleets, in order to dispute the command of the Baltic with England—a device which Czar Paul had tried once before in 1801. This was easily foiled by the second English attack on Copenhagen (October, 1807). This was technically an assault on a neutral, an act which could not be justified. But the whole Danish fleet was carried off to England. This naval success, however, hardly compensated for the failure of two other expeditions, from which much had been expected.

One was an attempt to seize the Spanish colony of Buenos Ayres in South America, which ended in the ignominious departure of the incompetent General Whitelock under a convention, after half of his small army had been taken prisoners. The other was a mismanaged expedition to Egypt, which led to nothing, and was finally abandoned with some discredit.

The British Army was indeed at this moment at the lowest point or its reputation. Unlike the navy, it had failed in most of the tasks on which it had been sent: only in India had it been uniformly successful. It was not till British men got leaders worthy of their merits in Wellesley and Moore that they were able to show their real value and prove that they were more than equal to the boasted veterans of Napoleon. Their chance was now close at hand.

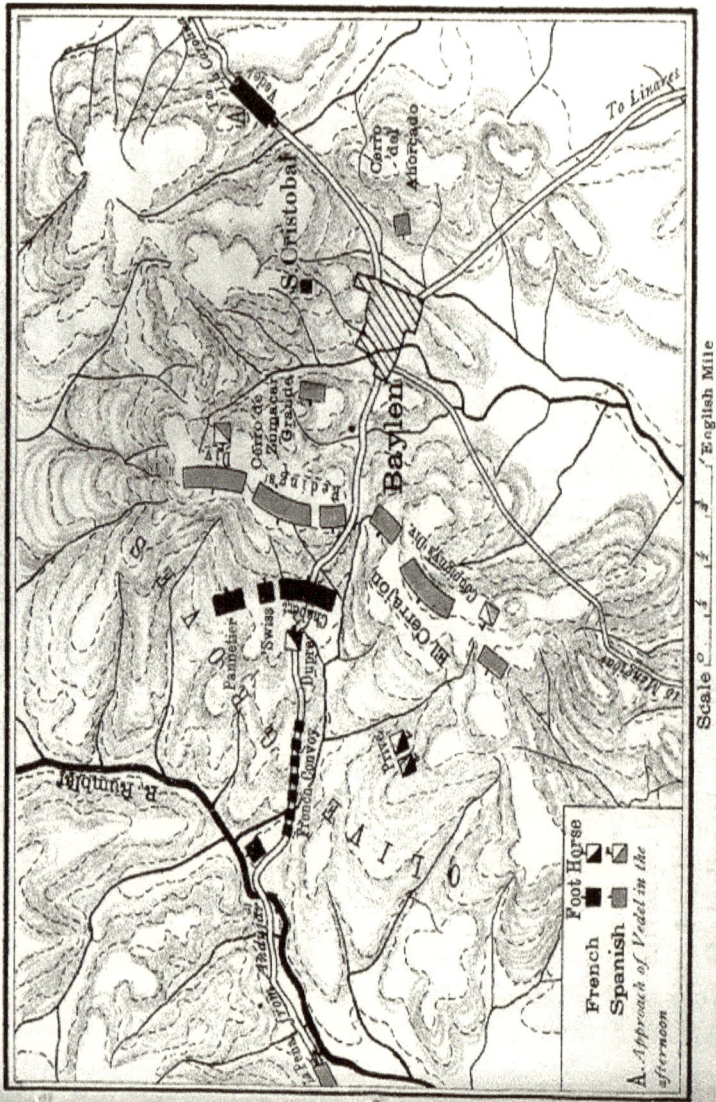

Battle of BAYLEN July 19, 1808. at the moment of DUPONT'S third attack.

French
Spanish

Foot Horse

A. Approach of Vedel in the afternoon

Scale — English Mile

CHAPTER 5

Spain & Portugal

In 1808 Bonaparte conceived the iniquitous idea of seizing the crown of Spain and substituting for its wretched King Charles IV. a monarch of his own choosing. Charles was an obedient ally, but he was so thoroughly incompetent that his assistance did not count for much: the emperor imagined that a nominee of his own would prove a more profitable helper. But the way in which he set about the conquest of Spain was characteristically treacherous and tortuous. He drafted a large army into the Peninsula under the excuse that he was about to attack Portugal, almost the last state in Europe which had not yet accepted the Continental System. Declaring that "the House of Braganza had ceased to reign," he poured his forces into Portugal, whose prince-regent fled overseas to Brazil without attempting to offer resistance. But while one French Army under General Junot had marched on Lisbon, large detachments followed behind, and occupied, under the guise of friends, the Spanish capital Madrid, and the fortresses of Barcelona, Pampeluna, and San Sebastian.

The Spaniards suspected no harm till Napoleon showed his hand by a disgraceful piece of kidnapping. King Charles IV. and his son, Prince Ferdinand, a worthless and useless pair, had been engaged in a bitter quarrel with each other. Bonaparte summoned them both to visit him at Bayonne, just across the French frontier, in order that he might arbitrate between them and heal their quarrel. They were foolish enough to obey this insolent mandate: when they arrived, however, he put them both in confinement, bullied them into signing an abdication, and sent them prisoners into France. He then took the astounding step of appointing his own brother Joseph Bonaparte as the successor of Charles IV., and the numerous French troops scattered through Spain everywhere proclaimed the usurper. The populace of Madrid rose, but was put down with ruthless severity, and Joseph made his appearance in the capital at the head of a strong guard.

Bonaparte had believed that centuries of misgovernment and disorganisation had so broken the spirit of the Spanish nation that his impudent and treacherous scheme could be carried to a successful end. He was soon undeceived: the Spaniards, in spite of the decay of their ancient power and wealth, and the incompetence of their rulers, still possessed a healthy sense of national pride: they were, moreover, the most obstinate, fanatical, and revengeful race in Europe.

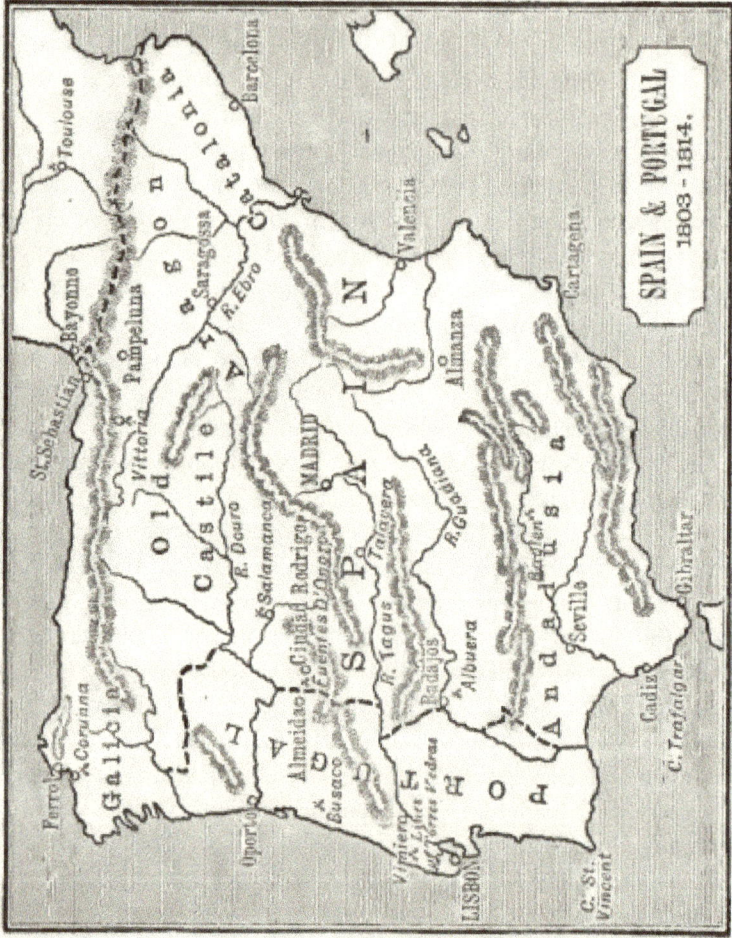

SPAIN & PORTUGAL
1803 - 1814.

Toulouse

Catalonia

Barcelona

Bayonne

Aragon

St. Sebastian

Pampeluna

Saragossa

R. Ebro

Vittoria

Valencia

Cartagena

Castile Old

N

Madrid

Almanza

R. Douro

Salamanca

Ciudad Rodrigo

Fuentes d'Onoro

R. Guadiana

R. Tagus

Talavera

S P A I

Albuera

Seville

Badajos

Granada

Andalusia

Gibraltar

Cadiz

C. Trafalgar

Ferrol

Corunna

Galicia

Oporto

Almeida

Busaco

Torres Vedras

Vimiera

T A L

P O R T U G A L

LISBON

C. St. Vincent

Though deprived of their princes, and confronted with French garrisons treacherously installed in their fortresses, they sprang to arms in every province. In most quarters their raw levies were easily beaten by the French veterans, but a series of fortunate chances enabled the insurgents of the South to surround and capture at Baylen an army under General Dupont, which had forced its way into Andalusia (July 20, 1808). This was the first serious check which the French arms had sustained since Napoleon had been proclaimed emperor, and it had important results. Joseph Bonaparte and his troops had to abandon Madrid, to retire beyond the Ebro, and to ask aid from France.

Meanwhile a second disaster followed hard on the heels of the battle of Baylen. The English Government had sent a small army to Portugal, under Sir Arthur Wellesley, an officer well known for his gallant services in India. This force routed at Vimiero (August 21, 1808) the French troops under Junot, which had occupied Lisbon. The defeat was so crushing that the enemy might have been pursued and driven into the sea without much further trouble. But Wellesley was superseded by a senior officer, Sir Hew Dalrymple, who arrived from England on the night of the battle. This cautious general admitted the French to terms, and by his Convention of Cintra (August 30, 1808), Junot's troops were allowed to quit Portugal with bag and baggage, and to return to France by sea.

Two such checks to the French arms called Bonaparte himself into the field. He hurried over the Pyrenees more than 200,000 of the veterans who had conquered at Austerlitz and Jena and hurled himself upon the Spaniards. The latter were as inferior in numbers as in discipline and military spirit: their ill-organised bands were scattered in all directions, and Napoleon entered Madrid in triumph, and replaced his brother on the throne (December 4, 1808). He hoped to complete the conquest of the Peninsula by crushing the English Army from Portugal, which was now advancing towards him under Sir John Moore—Dalrymple and Wellesley had been recalled to answer before a court-martial for the Convention of Cintra. The emperor moved in his troops from all sides to surround the 25,000 English, but Moore executed an admirably timed retreat, and drew the bulk of the French army after him into the inhospitable mountains of Galicia.

While vainly pursuing the English, Bonaparte suddenly received news which changed all his plans: a new war was imminent in his rear. Austria had now had three years in which to recover from the humiliation of Austerlitz and had completely reorganised her army. She was

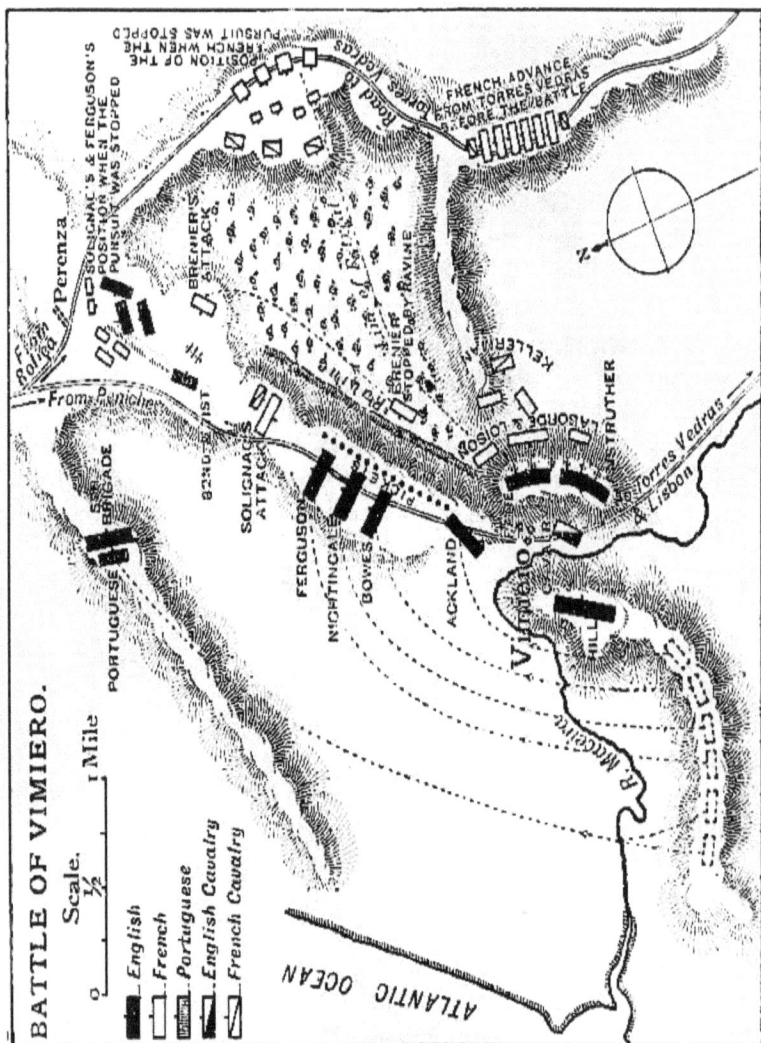

BATTLE OF VIMIERO.

Scale, ½   1 Mile

■ English
□ French
▦ Portuguese
◣ English Cavalry
◿ French Cavalry

From Lourinha / Perenza

SOLIGNAC'S & FERGUSON'S POSITION WHEN THE PURSUIT WAS STOPPED

POSITION OF THE FRENCH WHEN THE PURSUIT WAS STOPPED

FRENCH ADVANCE FROM TORRES VEDRAS BEFORE THE BATTLE

BRENIER'S ATTACK

BRENIER STOPPED BY RAVINE

KELLERMANN

LABORDE & LOISON

STRUTHER

From Peniche

PORTUGUESE BRIGADE

SOLIGNAC'S ATTACK

FERGUSON

NIGHTINGALE

BOWES

ACKLAND

VIMIERO

HILL

To Torres Vedras & Lisbon

R. MACEIRA

ATLANTIC OCEAN

chafing bitterly against Napoleon's dictatorial ways and the restraints of the "Continental System." Seeing the French busy in the Spanish war, she gladly listened to the persuasions of the Perceval cabinet, who offered English aid for a fresh attack on the old enemy. It was the news of this danger in the rear which forced Bonaparte to quit Spain, taking with him his imperial guards, but leaving the rest of his troops behind him. Marshal Soult, to whom the pursuit of Moore was handed over, followed the English to the sea: at Corunna the retreating army, suddenly turned to bay, inflicted a sharp defeat on Soult, and embarked in safety for England (January 16, 1809). Moore fell in the moment of victory, after having taught his followers that the French could be outmanoeuvred, outmarched, and beaten in the open field. His troops had suffered much from their own indiscipline and the bitter weather, but little from the overwhelming force of pursuers.

The Austrian war of 1809 was the most formidable struggle in which Bonaparte had yet engaged. The enemy fought better and were far better managed than in 1800 or 1805: they had also the advantage of the fact that 200,000 of the best troops of France were locked up in the Peninsula. The Archduke Charles, Austria's great general, long held Napoleon in check, and even forced him to recross the Danube after the Battle of Essling. It was not until after many months of bitter fighting that the invaders at last gained a decisive battle at Wagram (July 6, 1809). The fortune of war might perhaps have been turned against the French by the help of England; but the Perceval cabinet most unwisely wasted a fine army by sending it into the swamps of Holland to besiege Flushing and make a vain demonstration on Antwerp. Forty thousand men, who might have overrun North Germany, or recovered Madrid, captured Flushing, but suffered so severely from marsh-fever in the pestilential isle of Walcheren that they had at last to be withdrawn, without having aided the Austrians in the least.

Francis II., meanwhile, was forced after Wagram to sign the peace of Schönbrunn, by which he gave up to Napoleon his whole seacoast in Dalmatia and Illyria, part of Poland, and—bitterest of humiliations—the hand of his daughter Maria Louisa (October 14, 1809). To make this marriage possible, the French emperor callously divorced Josephine Beauharnais, the amiable if frivolous spouse who had shared his fortunes for fourteen years. If he hoped to bind Austria firmly to him by the match, Bonaparte was woefully deceived.

While the Austrian war was being fought out, the French made little progress in Spain. They were now being opposed not only by the

The Battle of Vimiero

Spanish levies, but by a new English Army headed by Wellesley, who had been sent back to the Peninsula when it was recognised that he had been in no wise responsible for the Convention of Cintra. The year 1809 was very glorious to the English arms: Wellesley first drove Marshal Soult out of Portugal, surprising him at Oporto, and forcing him to flee northward with the loss of all his guns and baggage. Then marching into Spain, he joined a Spanish Army under General Cuesta, and defeated at Talavera (July 28, 1809) the French force which covered Madrid. He might even have won back the capital but for the mulish obstinacy of his colleague, and the military incompetence of the Spanish troops, who could not be trusted except behind entrenchments. Talavera was won entirely by the 23,000 English, their allies refusing to advance even when the battle was won. After this heart-breaking experience Wellesley resolved never to cooperate with a Spanish army again, and to trust entirely to his own troops.

Meanwhile the news of Talavera caused the French troops from all parts of the Peninsula to concentrate against the little English Army, which had to beat a cautious retreat to the Portuguese frontier. No result had been gained from the incursion into Spain, save that the troops had learnt to look with confidence on their leader, who received as his reward for his two victories the title of Wellington, under which he was to be so well known.

After the peace of Schönbrunn had been signed, Bonaparte commenced to pour reinforcements into Spain, and even spoke of going there himself "to drive the British leopard into the sea." Ultimately, however, he sent instead his ablest lieutenant. Marshal Masséna, with 100,000 fresh troops. The arrival of these new legions gave fresh vigour to the invaders: they overran most of Southern and Eastern Spain, and only failed when they were confronted in Portugal by the indomitable; army of Wellington. The year 1810 was for the English commander the most trying period of the whole war. Masséna marched against him in overpowering strength, and all that was in his power was to play a slow and obstinate game of retreat, turning back on occasion, as at the very skilfully fought Battle of Bussaco (September 27), to check the heads of the French columns.

In this way he led the enemy on to the gates of Lisbon, in front of which he had erected a very elaborate system of fortifications, the celebrated "Lines of Torres Vedras," extending in a triple range all across the peninsula on which the Portuguese capital stands. Masséna knew nothing of the lines till his army was brought up by running into the

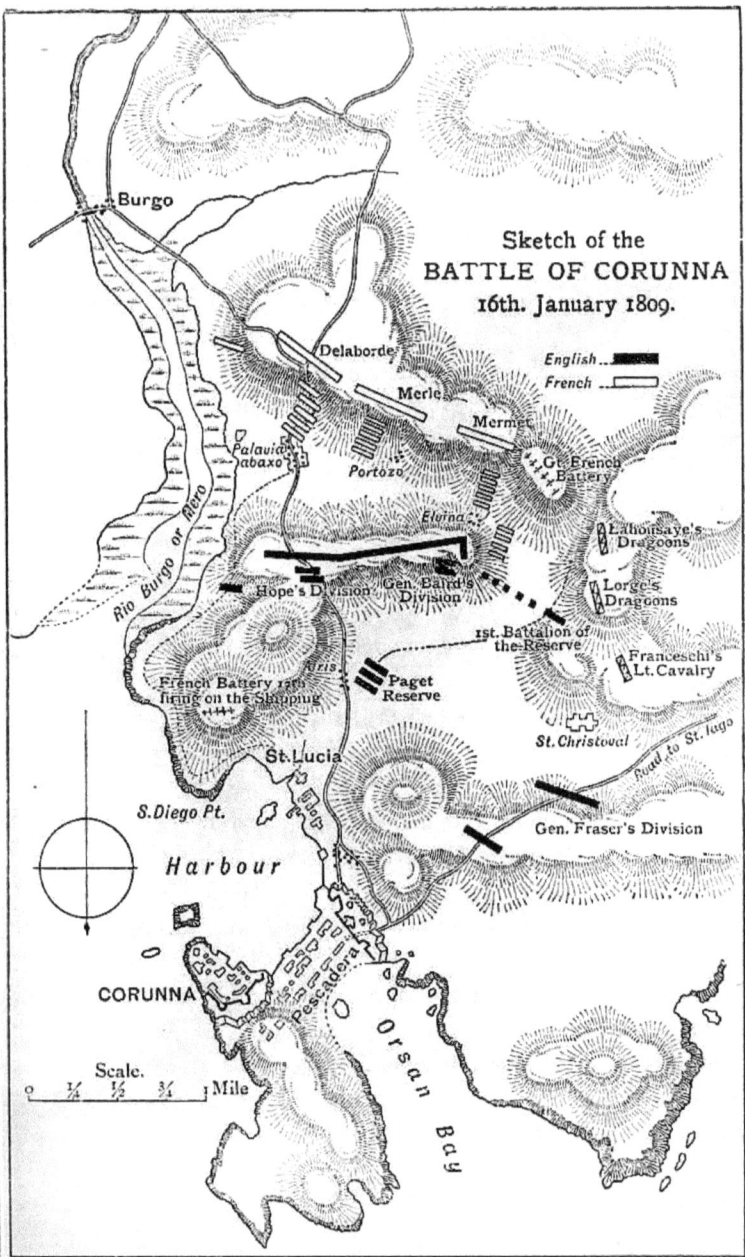

Sketch of the
BATTLE OF CORUNNA
16th. January 1809.

English..
French ..

Burgo

Delaborde

Merle

Mermet

Gt. French
Battery

Palavia
abaxo

Portozo

Elvina

Lahoussaye's
Dragoons

Hope's Division

Gen. Baird's
Division

Lorge's
Dragoons

Rio Burgo or Mero

1st. Battalion of
the Reserve

French Battery 12th
firing on the Shipping

Paget
Reserve

Franceschi's
Lt. Cavalry

St. Christoval

Road to St. Iago

St. Lucia

S. Diego Pt.

Gen. Fraser's Division

Harbour

CORUNNA

Pescadera

Orsan Bay

Scale.
0   ¼   ½   ¾   Mile

first of them (October, 1810). He found them so strong that he dared not risk an attack on them and halted irresolute in their front. Wellington had expected this and had prepared for the contingency by sweeping the whole countryside bare of provisions and causing the peasantry to retire into Lisbon. Masséna's host starved in front of the lines for five months, vainly hoping for aid from Spain. But Wellington had cut their line of communication with Madrid by throwing numerous bands of Portuguese militia across the mountain roads, and no food and very few fresh troops came to help the invaders. When his army was almost perishing from famine, Masséna was constrained to take it back to Spain, suffering so dreadfully by the way that he only brought back two-thirds of the men whom he had led into Portugal (March, 1811).

The retreat of the French from before the lines of Torres Vedras was the turning-point of the Peninsular War, and in some degree the turning-point of Napoleon's whole career, for Masséna's march to the gates of Lisbon marked the last and furthest point of his advance towards the conquest of Western Europe. After this the French were always to lose ground. The emperor kept an enormous army in the Peninsula, but he could never wholly master it. No single region of Spain would remain quiet unless it was heavily garrisoned; the moment that troops were withdrawn it blazed up again into insurrection. The Spanish levies were very bad troops in the open field, and were beaten with the utmost regularity, even if they had two men to one against the French.

But they never lost heart, in spite of their defeats; as was remarked at the time, "A Spanish Army was easy to beat, but very hard to destroy." It dispersed after a lost battle, but the survivors came together again in a few days, as self-confident and obstinate as ever. The regular troops gave the French far less trouble than the "Guerillas"—half armed peasantry, half robbers, who lurked in the mountains, refrained from attacking large bodies of men, but were always pouncing down to capture convoys, cut off small isolated detachments, and harass the flanks and rear of troops on the march. They so pervaded the country that the transmission of news from one French Army to another was a matter of serious difficulty; a message was never certain to get safely to its destination unless its bearer was protected by a guard of five hundred men.

The French habitually shot every *guerillero* whom they caught, and in return the insurgents murdered every straggler that fell into their

THE 42ND RETAKING ELVIZA

THE 23RD LIGHT DRAGOONS AT TALAVERA

hands. The drain on the strength of the army of occupation caused by this lingering and bloody war of retaliation was appalling. It was not for nothing that Bonaparte called the Peninsular War "the running sore" that sapped his strength.

Editor's Note

The events which occurred upon the Iberian Peninsula during this period had special significance for the British from a military perspective. It was in Spain and Portugal that British armies were principally engaged and it was in this theatre that the Duke of Wellington would earn the abiding fame which would place him in the pantheon of his nation's highest regarded military commanders.

So within the framework of the broader history of the Napoleonic Age the Peninsular War will continue to feature in this work in synopsis. However, a more expansive description of the Iberian campaign by Oman also appears in its relevant place in the text.

CHAPTER 6

Napoleon's Zenith & Fall

Meanwhile the emperor was apparently at the very zenith of his power during the years 1809-11. His annexations grew more reckless and iniquitous than ever. He appropriated Holland, expelling his own brother Louis Bonaparte, because he showed some regard for Dutch as opposed to French interests, and had ventured to plead against the "Continental System." Soon after, he annexed the whole German coast-line on the North Sea, and even the south-west corner of the Baltic shore. This again was done in the interest of the Continental System; the Hanseatic towns had not shown sufficient enthusiasm in carrying it out, so he absorbed them and cut short several neighbouring principalities. By this last expansion the "French Empire" stretched from Lubeck to Rome, for the pope had already been evicted from the "Eternal City" in 1809.

In addition, Bonaparte personally ruled the kingdom of Italy, and the Illyrian provinces on the Adriatic. The Rhine Confederation, Switzerland, the Grand Duchy of Warsaw, the French Kings of Spain and Naples were his vassals. Prussia was occupied by his garrisons since 1806. Austria, Russia, Denmark, and Sweden were his more or less willing allies. The English had no friends save in the weak kingdoms of Sicily, Sardinia, and Portugal, and among the still weaker Spanish insurgents.

Meanwhile, even in this dark time, England continued to carry

51

Sierra de Montalban

TALAVERA
DE LA REYNA.

RIVER TAGES

BATTLE
OF
TALAVERA
DE LA REYNA.
27th & 28th July 1809.

SCALES

To Madrid

From Oropesa

English   Spanish   French

Cavalry   Infantry   Artillery

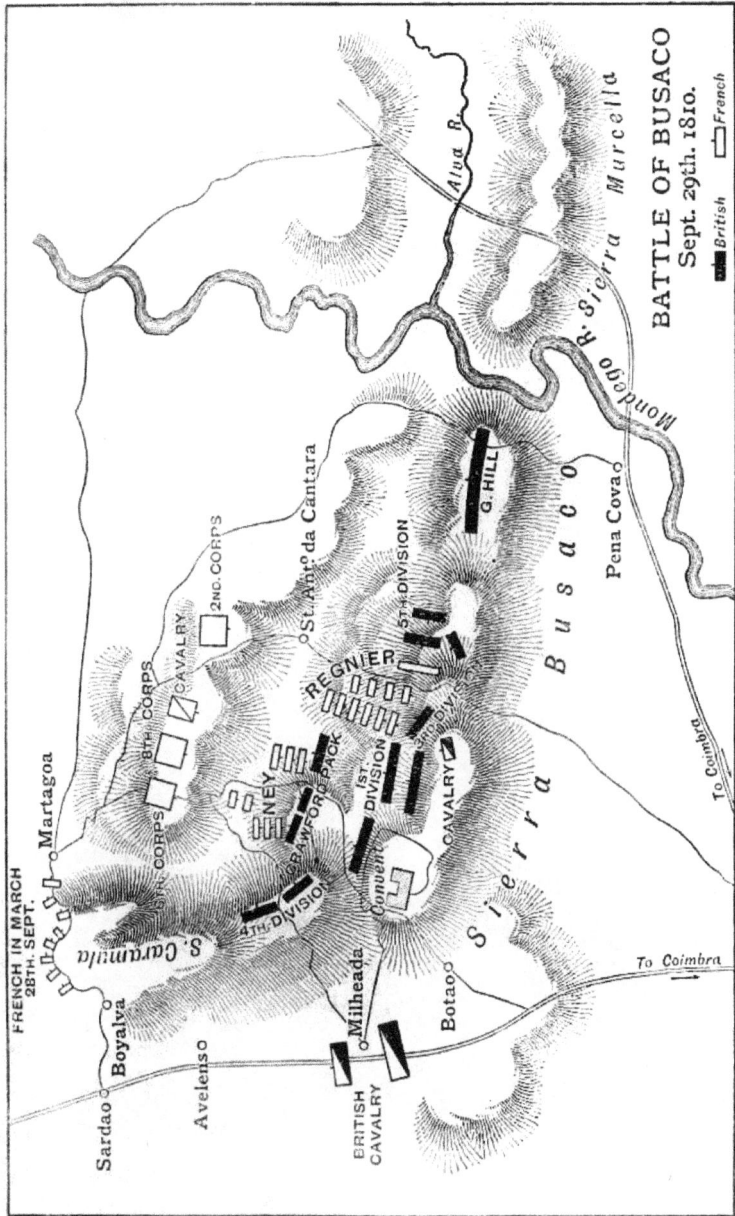

BATTLE OF BUSACO
Sept. 29th. 1810.

British ▨   French ☐

Walker & Boutall sc.

FRENCH IN MARCH
28TH. SEPT.

Martagoa

2ND. CORPS

8TH. CORPS

CAVALRY

St. Ant.o da Cantara

5TH. DIVISION

REGNIER

G. HILL

Pena Covao

Busaco

Mondego R. Sierra Murcella

Alva R.

6TH. CORPS

NEY

CRAWFORD PACK

1ST. DIVISION

3RD. DIVISION

CAVALRY

Sierra

To Coimbra

S. Caramula

4TH. DIVISION

Convent

Sardao

Boyalva

Avelenso

Milheada

Botao

To Coimbra

BRITISH
CAVALRY

BATTLE OF BUSACO

out without following the policy that Pitt had left behind him. The conduct of affairs had passed into the hands of second-rate statesmen like Perceval and Lord Liverpool, but no hesitation was shown, though the National Debt continued to rise with appalling rapidity, and though Napoleon seemed more invincible than ever. The war in Spain was giving England a glimpse of success on land, though her armies had still to act upon the defensive, and to yield ground when the enemy came on in overwhelming numbers. Nation and ministers alike considered themselves irrevocably pledged to the war, and comforted themselves with the thought that Napoleon's empire, built upon force and fraud, and maintaining itself by a cruel oppression of the vanquished, must ultimately fall before the simultaneous uprising of all the peoples of Europe.

The year 1811 had seen the French in Spain checked in their endeavours to resume the invasion of Portugal. Masséna's last approach towards its frontier was stopped dead at the Battle of Fuentes D'Oñoro (May 5). Eleven days later, a bloody fight at Albuera turned back Marshal Soult, who had endeavoured to drive off a part of the English Army that lay further to the south, blockading the fortress of Badajoz (May 16). The French could advance no further, while Wellington, on the other hand, was not yet strong enough to be able to contemplate the invasion of Spain. It was expected in the Peninsula that Napoleon himself would soon appear, to finish the task which his lieutenants had proved unable to carry out. But though he recalled Masséna, he neither came on the scene himself, nor sent any appreciable reinforcements to Spain. He already saw a new war impending over him and had turned all his attention to it.

Russia had not been completely crushed in 1807: her armies had been beaten, but only after a gallant struggle, and it was from a sincere desire for peace, and not from mere necessity, that the Czar Alexander had signed the Peace of Tilsit and accepted the Continental System. Five years' experience of that intolerable burden had convinced him that the friendship of Napoleon was dearly bought by accepting it. His realm was losing more by the complete suspension of its foreign trade than it could lose by open war with France. The great landed proprietors, whose timber, hemp, and wheat had once found a ready market in England, and now could not be sold at all, were furious that they should be ruined to please Bonaparte. Urged on by threats of a conspiracy such as had overthrown his father Paul in 1801, Alexander yielded to the pressure of his nobles, and broke with France.

RUSSIA

TURKEY

CONSTANTINOPLE

AUSTRIAN EMPIRE

GRAND DUCHY OF WARSAW

FINLAND

SWEDEN OR NORWAY

PRUSSIA

CONFEDERATION OF THE RHINE

ILLYRIAN PROVINCES

K. OF ITALY

K. OF NAPLES

FRENCH EMPIRE

SWITZERLAND

ENGLAND

LONDON

IRELAND
DUBLIN

SPAIN

PORTUGAL

LISBON

MADRID

Galicia

Murcia

K. or SARDINIA

SICILY

CORSICA

SARDINIA

Vienna

Marengo

Paris

La Vendée

Toulouse

Bayonne

Boulogne

Brest

Dover

Gibraltar

C. St. Vincent

EUROPE
IN 1811-12.

French Empire.
Naples n's King-
dom of Italy.
Vassal States.
The parts of Spain left
white were not in
French hands in 1811.

This led to Napoleon's great invasion of Russia in 1812—a grandiose scheme, doomed from the first to failure, because its framer had not taken into consideration the difficulties involved in moving and feeding a host of 600,000 men in a thinly-populated land, destitute of roads and great towns. The Russians retired before the invaders, removing all stores of food, and causing the peasantry to migrate along with the army. Half the horses of Bonaparte's army had perished, and a third of his men had been starved or had deserted before the enemy indulged him with a serious battle. He defeated them at Borodino (September 7) and entered Moscow, but only to find it deserted and empty. A great fire destroyed the city soon after his arrival, and he was driven to order his starving army to retreat on Lithuania to take winter quarters. But the first frosts of November slew off the exhausted soldiery like flies; the Russians harassed the melting host on his way, till it broke up in utter disorganisation, and Bonaparte finally fled to Paris to organise new forces, leaving his lieutenants the task of bringing back the 30,000 miserable survivors of the "Grand Army," who had struggled out from the Russian snows.

In Spain, too, 1812 was a fatal year for the French arms. Wellington, having received more troops from England, and having thoroughly re-organised the Portuguese Army, resolved to make a bold push into Spain. Early in the year he took by storm the two great frontier fortresses of Ciudad Rodrigo (January, 19) and Badajoz (April 6), striking so swiftly that the armies of succour could not come up in time to save them. This rapid success was bought at the cost of many lives, for the assaults had to be delivered before the fire of the defenders had been subdued; but time was all-important, and the result justified the lavish expense of blood.

Having secured the frontier of Portugal, Wellington pressed forward into Spain, and won the first great victory in which he assumed the offensive, at Salamanca (July 22, 1812). By a sudden master-stroke he crushed in the flank of Marshal Marmont, and "routed 40,000 men in forty minutes." This victory led to the recovery of Madrid and the flight of Joseph Bonaparte from his capital. But, evacuating the other provinces of Spain, the French armies massed themselves to check Wellington's further advance, and before their superior numbers the English had to fall back on the Portuguese frontier. All southern Spain, however, had been cleared of the invaders, who now only held the northern half of the Peninsula.

The next year (1813) saw the complete ruin of Napoleon. When

THE SAVING OF THE GUNS AT FUENTES D'ONORE

THE BATTLE OF ALBUHERA

Battle of
FUENTES D'ONORE
5th. May, 1811.

■ *Allies*   ▭ *French*

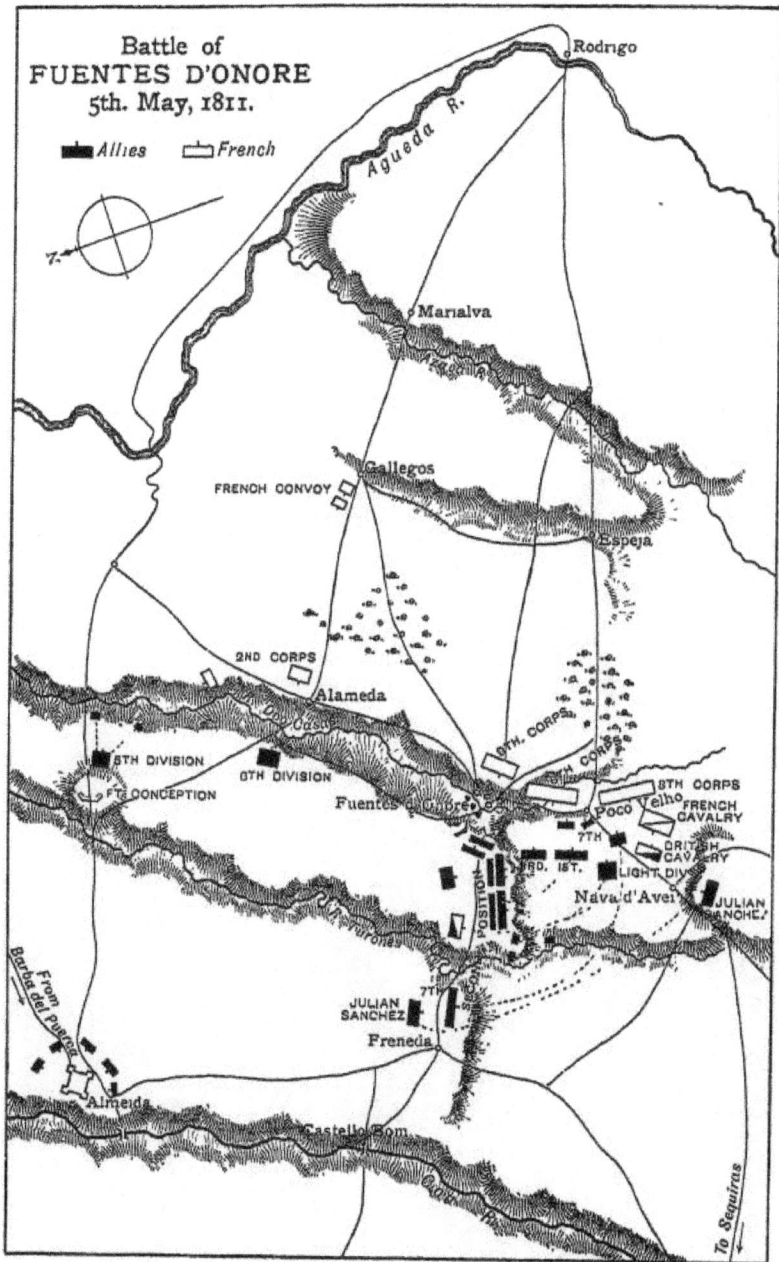

7.

Agueda R.

Rodrigo

Marialva

Gallegos

FRENCH CONVOY

Espeja

2ND CORPS

Alameda

5TH DIVISION

FT. CONCEPTION

6TH DIVISION

9TH. CORPS

CORPS

8TH CORPS

Fuentes d'Onore

Poco Velho

FRENCH CAVALRY

7TH

3RD. 1ST.

POSITION

BRITISH CAVALRY

LIGHT DIV

Nava d'Aver

JULIAN SANCHEZ

JULIAN SANCHEZ

7TH

Freneda

From Barba del Puerco

Almeida

Castello Bom

To Sequiras

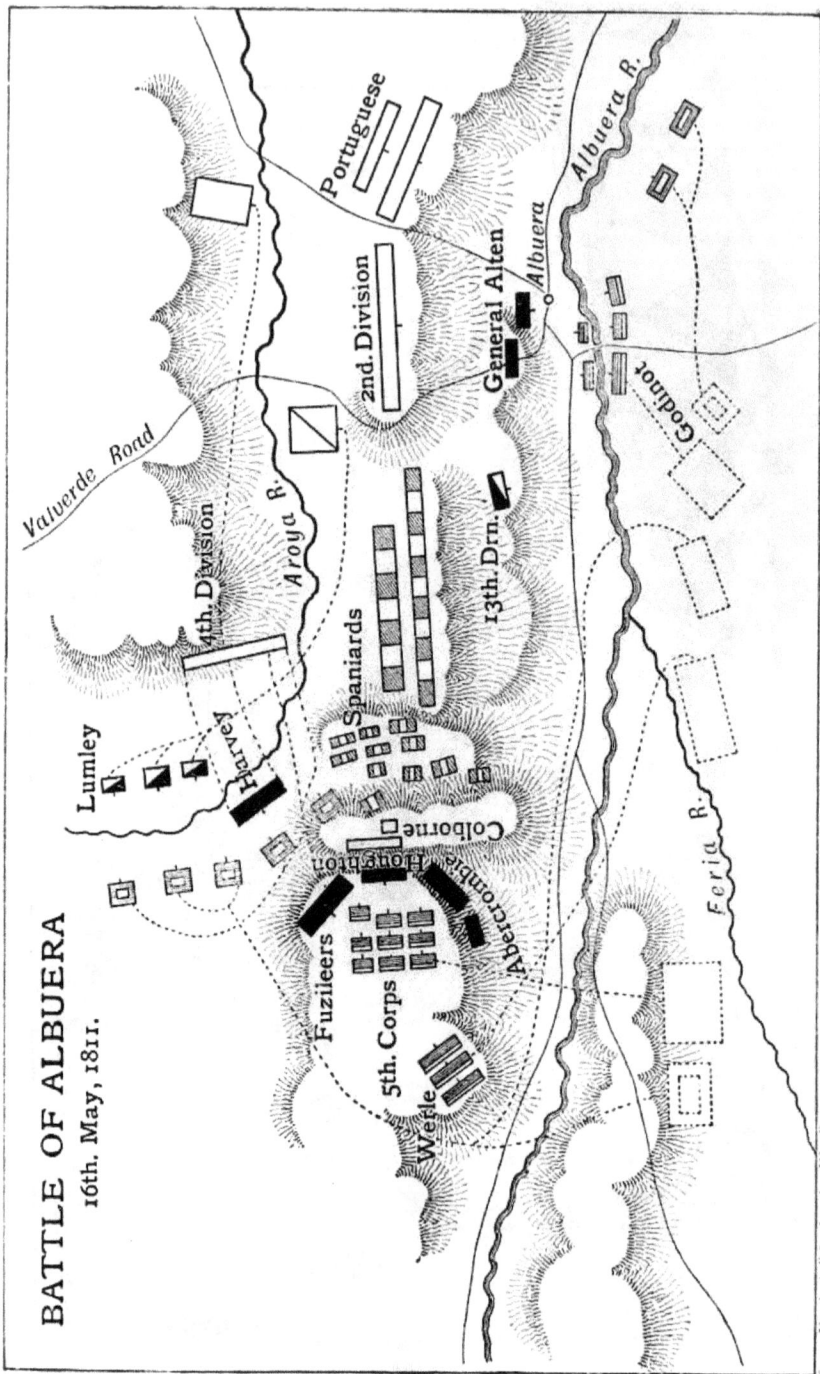

BATTLE OF ALBUERA
16th. May, 1811.

Valverde Road

4th. Division

Portuguese

2nd. Division

General Alten

Albuera

Albuera R.

Aroya R.

13th. Drn.

Spaniards

Godinot

Lumley

Harvey

Colborne

Houghton

Abercrombie

Fuzileers

5th. Corps

Werle

Feria R.

the Russians advanced into Germany, the whole nation rose in arms to aid them. Prussia alone, though she had been mutilated and robbed and oppressed with French garrisons, put 200,000 men into the field. The emperor once more appeared at the head of a vast army, bringing up his last reserves, huge drafts from the army of Spain, and hundreds of thousands of conscripts. But his troops were no longer the veterans of Austerlitz, and his enemies fought with a fury of which he had never before had experience. He gained a few successes in the opening weeks of the struggle, but when his own father-in-law, the Austrian emperor, plunged into the struggle, the odds became too heavy, and at the Battle of Leipzig (October 16-18, 1813) he was overwhelmed by numbers, and suffered a crushing defeat, in which more than half his army was slain or captured.

The enemy pursued him energetically, gave him no time to rally, and entered France at his heels. They had at last learnt to turn his own methods of war against him and knew that a beaten foe must not be allowed time to rally. Crossing the Rhine at midwinter, the allies pushed deep into France. Bonaparte, with the wrecks of his army, made a desperate resistance, but had not a shadow of a chance of success. In spite of his skilful manoeuvring, and of the splendid -endurance of his troops, he was forced nearer and nearer to Paris. At last, while he was engaged with a mere fraction of the allied host, the bulk of it marched past his flank and stormed the lines in front of the French capital (April 4, 1814). On the news of the fall of Paris, Napoleon's own marshals refused to persist in the hopeless struggle and compelled their master to lay down his arms and abdicate. In the rage of the moment the emperor swallowed poison, but his constitution was too strong, and he survived to fall into the hands of the victors. They sent him to honourable exile in the Tuscan island of Elba, whose sovereignty was bestowed upon him.

While the Russians, Prussians, and Austrians had entered France from the north-east, another army of invasion had been pouring into the southern departments. Wellington's campaign of 1813 was the most glorious and successful of all his achievements. In early spring he massed his troops on the north-western frontier of Portugal, and marched rapidly up the valley of the Douro. The French armies, scattered in distant cantonments, could not unite in numbers sufficient to give him battle till he had pushed them as far as Vittoria, at the very foot of the Pyrenees. When they did turn to fight, he beat them, intercepted their line of retreat, captured all their guns and baggage—the

THE BATTLE OF SALAMNCA

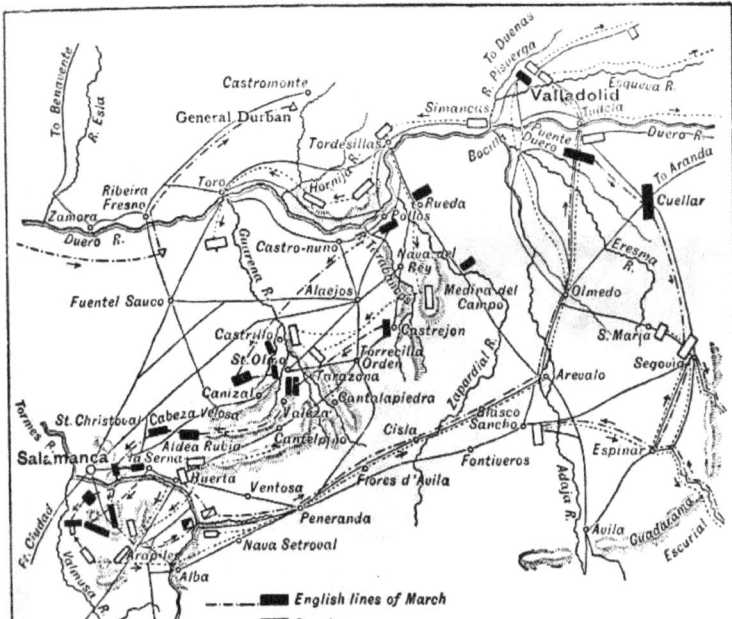

Battle of
SALAMANCA
with operations
before and after the Action.

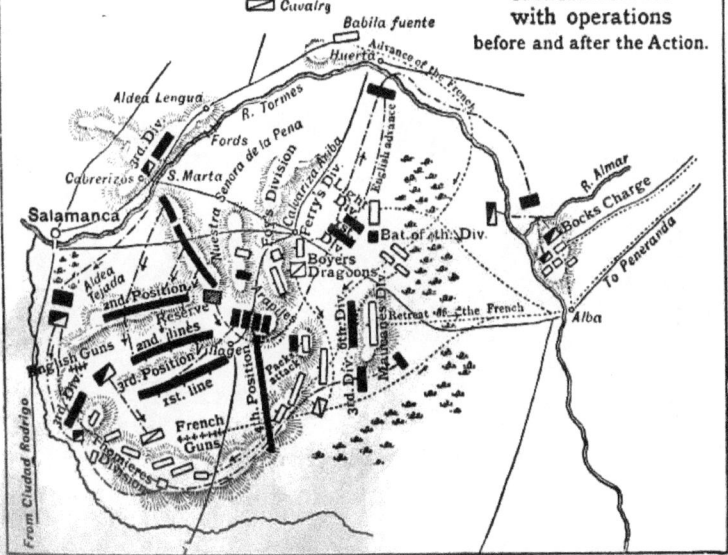

English lines of March
Cavalry
French lines of March
Cavalry

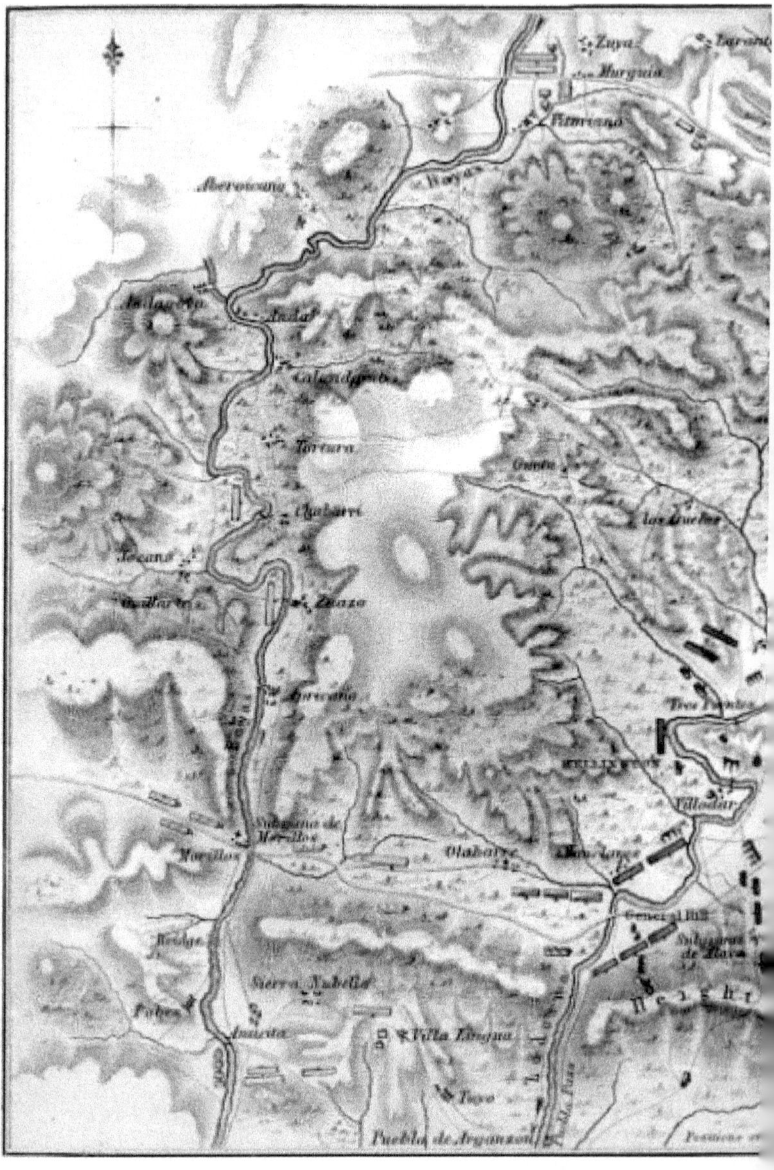

Zuya
Murguia
Tortura
Zuazo
Olabarre
Morillas
Bridge
Sierra Nabelia
Villodas
Tres Puentes
General Hill
Subijana de Alava
Puebla de Arganzon

BATTLE
OF
VITORIA
21ST June 1813.
A. K. JOHNSTON F.R.G.S.

French —— Allies ——
Cavalry — Infantry — Artillery
SCALES
Military Steps 2½ Feet each
English Miles

proceeds of the six years' plunder of Spain—and drove them headlong into France (June 21, 1813).

After having defeated a month later a last endeavour of Marshal Soult to force his way back into the Peninsula (July 27-30, 1813) at the battles of the Pyrenees, Wellington captured the great frontier fortresses of San Sebastian and Pampeluna. He then crossed into France and spent the winter and the early spring of 1814 in forcing Soult back over the rivers and hills of Bearn and Gascony. Just before Napoleon's fall, one division of his army captured Bordeaux, while he himself with the main body evicted Soult from Toulouse, after the last and one of the bloodiest fights of the Peninsular War (April 14). When the news of peace came, he was in full military occupation of eight French departments, and the two largest towns of Southern France.

CHAPTER 7

The Peninsular War, 1808-14

We will now deal with the great conflict in the Iberian Peninsula in some detail. With the political schemes of Napoleon it is not always easy to discover what is end and what is means: whether a particular project is carried out merely for its own sake or is also intended as a step towards some further goal. This is pre-eminently the case with the invasion of Portugal, described in a previous chapter. It has often been maintained that when the emperor launched Junot's corps against Lisbon he was thinking of nothing more than bringing Portugal into line with his other vassal-states in the matter of the Continental System. A careful study of his manoeuvres, however, would seem to make it certain that he was also using the whole affair as a cover for a long-projected attack on Spain.

So far back as 1805 he had muttered to a confidant, "*Un Bourbon sur le trône d'Espagne, c'est un voisin trap dangereux*" ("A Bourbon on the throne of Spain, it is a dangerous neighbour trap"); and with far better justification, after he had received Godoy's bellicose proclamation on the battlefield of Jena, he had vowed to take his revenge in due season on the presumptuous favourite and his imbecile master. "*Je jurai des lors qu'ils me le paieraient, que je les mettrais hors d'état de me nuire.*" ("I swore that they would pay me, that I would put them out of harm's way.")

No one could have blamed him if, after signing the Treaty of Tilsit, he had turned sharply on Spain and demanded the dismissal of Godoy, or even declared war on Charles IV. Ten years later, at St Helena, he acknowledged that this would have been the most expedient as well as

66

the most honest course to take. In place of it he adopted the tortuous and Machiavellian policy of which the first step was seen in the Treaty of Fontainebleau. Godoy, instead of receiving condign chastisement, was promised a kingdom for himself in southern Portugal, on condition that he should allow a French Army a free passage to Lisbon and lend his aid for the expulsion of the House of Braganza.

It is impossible to believe for a moment that the emperor ever intended to call into real existence Godoy's "principality of the Algarves." When he offered a crown and a realm to one who had deserved so ill at his hands, it was clearly with the object of cajoling him into admitting French troops into the Peninsula, and with no intention of carrying out his promise. After Junot had obtained possession of Portugal, no steps were taken to establish the "principality of the Algarves."

Meanwhile, before Junot had reached Lisbon, the domestic troubles of the Court of Spain had at last reached explosion point. On October 27, 1807, Charles IV arrested his son Ferdinand, accusing him of having plotted to dethrone him and to murder his mother and her favourite Godoy. The prince of the Asturias had undoubtedly been intriguing behind his father's back; he had written to Napoleon to beg his protection, and to ask for the hand of a princess of the House of Bonaparte. He had been organising a party of malcontents, who hated the "Prince of the Peace"—such was Godoy's title—as much as he did himself. But his schemes were vague and futile; the most he did was to write obsequious letters to Paris, and to take precautions against Godoy's hardly-disguised intention to exclude him from the succession.

The only compromising documents found in his possession were two drafts of a manifesto denouncing the favourite's designs, and an undated commission appointing the Duke of Infantado (one of his personal *camarilla*) military governor of Madrid and New Castile. He declared, probably with truth, that this last paper was intended to be used only in the case of his father's death or permanent disablement.

But the best proof of Ferdinand's innocence of the grave accusations brought against him is his character. He was very obstinate and a good hater, but he was also cautious in the extreme, and so destitute of courage and proper pride that, though he could resent, he could never revenge an insult, if the least risk was involved. When arrested at the Escorial, he gave up the names of his confederates in the most craven fashion and sent to his parents two letters couched in the most disgusting terms of self-abasement. The king had already written to

MANUEL DE GODOY

FERDINAND VII OF SPAIN

Napoleon stating that his son had been discovered in a plot against his mother's life; he had also published in the *Madrid Gazette* a manifesto to the effect that the prince had been detected in treasonable plots, and that the conspirators were to be tried and punished.

But whether it was that the old man shrank from bloodshed, or that Godoy thought that he had done enough in discrediting Ferdinand in the eyes of the nation, matters were pushed no further. The prince was pardoned by a magniloquent and turgid royal proclamation; and his partisans, *Infantado*, the Canon Escoiquiz, and certain others, were allowed to be acquitted after a formal trial. Nothing could have suited Napoleon's plans better than the publication of this scandalous domestic quarrel; it was indifferent to him whether public opinion regarded Charles IV as an unnatural father or Ferdinand as an unnatural son. In either case the prestige of the Spanish royal family was diminished, and interference in its affairs became more easy.

Meanwhile he was proceeding with his plans for introducing, more French troops into Spain. The Treaty of Fontainebleau had provided that, if the English sent an army to Portugal, the emperor might reinforce Junot's expeditionary corps, after giving due notice to the King of Spain. With this excuse, an army corps of 25,000 men under General Dupont had been collected at Bayonne. On November 22 Dupont received orders to cross the Bidassoa, though no English force had been heard of. No intimation of this movement was sent to the Spanish Government; and Charles IV and Godoy were as much alarmed as they were surprised by the news that the troops of their ally had cantoned themselves in the valley of the Ebro.

On January 8, 1808, they were still further startled by the appearance of a third army-corps under Marshal Moncey, which occupied Biscay and Navarre; whereupon Dupont pushed forward to Burgos and Valladolid. Nor was this all. On February 10 a division of 14,000 men, half French, half Italian, under General Duhesme, began to pour into Catalonia and made its way to Barcelona. As Catalonia is not on the way to Portugal, there was no excuse whatever for the appearance of this fourth army in the north-eastern corner of the Peninsula.

On February 16 the emperor finally threw off the mask and began a series of frankly hostile acts towards his unfortunate ally. On that day the French troops quartered in Pampeluna occupied the citadel of that fortress by a treacherous *coup de main*. On the 29th Duhesme seized the citadel and chief forts of Barcelona. On March 5 the weak-kneed governor of San Sebastian allowed himself to be scared out of that rocky stronghold by threats of force. Finally, on March 18, Figueras, the border fortress of northern Catalonia, was surprised by a French detachment, supposed to be passing peacefully through the town.

The Spanish Court was plunged into wild alarm by the news of the seizure of Pampeluna and Barcelona. Godoy hesitated for a moment whether he should declare war on his treacherous ally or follow the example of the Prince Royal of Portugal and bid the king and queen fly to Cadiz and embark for America. He seems to have thought that there was little use in attempting resistance: a fifth French army corps under Bessières had now commenced to cross the Bidassoa, so that more than 100,000 French soldiers were already south of the Pyrenees. Moreover, the headstrong Murat had appeared at Burgos on March 13 with a commission as "lieutenant for the emperor in Spain." At last Godoy resolved to advise instant flight, without any attempt to defend Madrid or central Spain.

But the Spanish people now intervened. The king and queen had left Madrid for Aranjuez; and their departure for Andalusia had been announced for March 18. On the preceding night a fierce riot broke out in the little town, which was crowded with hangers-on of the Court. Every Spaniard now understood that Godoy had ruined the realm by handing it over to Napoleon, and that his cowardly and obsequious policy had led to far deeper humiliation than could have been caused by the most unfortunate of open wars. He had to pay for nearly twenty years of corrupt and selfish rule, which had led Spain to her ruin; and the explosion of wrath against him was all the more fierce for its long suppression.

A raging mob of soldiers, peasants, and citizens sacked his palace, but sought for him in vain. The crowd then gathered under the king's windows, calling aloud for the favourite's head, and cheering for the Prince of the Asturias. Charles IV was terrified; the queen besought her son to parley with the mob and disperse them on any terms. Ferdinand therefore was able to announce that Godoy had been dismissed from office and banished from the Court. But next day the favourite was detected as he was slinking away; the royal guards rescued him from his first captors in a very battered state and dragged him into the palace. This brought the multitude once more around its gates; and it seemed as if some bloody scene from the French Revolution was about to be re-enacted.

Then came the hour of Prince Ferdinand's opportunity. He told his parents that their personal safety and the life of their favourite could only be secured by an abdication. Without delay the old king wrote a brief statement, in which he announced that his age and infirmities compelled him to resign the crown to his very dear son and heir, the Prince of the Asturias. Armed with this, Ferdinand faced the mob, promised them that Godoy should be imprisoned and brought to trial, and begged them to disperse without further violence. He was hailed as King amid universal rejoicings; the troops took the oath to him as sovereign; and Godoy was sent a prisoner to Villaviciosa (March 19, 1808).

All over Spain, the fall of Godoy was received with feelings of intense relief; and much was hoped from the young king, as if it were likely that the son of Charles IV and Maria Luisa of Parma would prove a hero and a statesman. Ferdinand's first acts proved his unwisdom and timidity; instead of retiring to Andalusia and concentrating what was left of the Spanish Army, he went to Madrid (March 24), though Murat had arrived there on the previous day at the head of Moncey's army-corps. Having taken possession of the royal palace, he wrote a grovelling letter to Napoleon, assuring him of his adherence to the French alliance, and renewing his request for a bride from the Imperial house. It was evident, from the first, that he had taken a false step. The French ambassador refused to acknowledge him as king; while Murat behaved to him in the most discourteous fashion, and, what was more ominous, sent a French escort to guard the person of the former king and queen.

Meanwhile Napoleon had been forced to face the new problems created by the revolution of Aranjuez. Down to this moment he had apparently hoped to scare Charles IV, his queen, and their favourite out of Spain, and then to present himself to the nation as their saviour from the tyranny of Godoy. This was no longer possible when a young and popular king had mounted the throne. It would have been wise to accept the situation, and receive the homage of the new sovereign, whose protestations of obsequious respect to his patron were all that could be desired. But Napoleon resolved to push on his iniquitous plan in spite of the new political situation that had been created by Ferdinand's accession.

The pretext was ready at hand, for Charles IV had no sooner recovered from his first terror, than he drew up a secret protest in which he declared that his abdication had been extorted from him by threats of bloodshed. Long before this document had reached Paris, Napoleon had written to his brother Louis, King of Holland, offering him the

Spanish crown; it is therefore clear that he had been intending in any case to refuse to recognise Ferdinand, and that the protest of Charles IV had nothing to do with his decision. It was, however, welcomed as a useful card in the game; and Murat was directed not only to send the old king to Bayonne, but to forward Godoy in his master's train.

Meanwhile the emperor declared his intention of visiting Madrid in person. He sent before him his *aide-de-camp*, General Savary, who visited the young king, and, as all the Spanish witnesses unite in declaring, informed him that his master intended to take him into favour, and to bestow upon him the hand of the Bonaparte princess whom he had craved as his consort. Unless he had received some such assurance, the cautious Ferdinand would most certainly have refrained from putting himself in the emperor's power. But on April 10 he was persuaded into setting out to meet his mighty guest and was finally induced to cross the Bidassoa into French territory. When he reached Bayonne (April 20) he was put under guard, and informed that Napoleon had resolved to depose him; but that if he would sign an instant resignation of the Spanish crown, he should receive in compensation the kingdom of Etruria.

The king, craven though he was, plucked up courage to refuse this monstrous proposal. Thereupon the emperor produced Charles IV and his queen, whose arrival at Bayonne had been timed so as to follow that of their son by a few days. He confronted Ferdinand with his parents; and a lamentable scene followed in his presence. On being told that his father was still the lawful king, and that he himself was a rebel who had been guilty of high treason, Ferdinand preserved a sullen silence. When he refused to sign a document declaring that he withdrew his claim to the crown, his father tried to strike him with his cane, and his mother burst in with a string of abuse worthy of a fishwife. The emperor put an end to the altercation by thrusting Ferdinand out of the room. He then offered to abdicate if he were allowed to return to Madrid, summon the Cortes of the realm, and execute his renunciation in due form. But this would not have suited Napoleon's scheme; and the offer was refused.

Two days later there arrived at Bayonne the news of the bloody Dos Mayo, the great insurrection at Madrid (May 9). Thereupon the emperor told Ferdinand that if he did not abdicate within twelve hours he should be tried for high treason. Terrified by this threat, the young king executed, on May 6, an instrument restoring the throne to his father. Then appeared the second half of Napoleon's scheme; he produced a treaty, signed on the previous day, by which Charles IV:

> Resigned all his rights to the throne of Spain and the Indies to the Emperor of the French, the only person who in the present state of affairs can re-establish order.

The old king and his wife knew that they could never return to Madrid, and out of revengeful spite had lent themselves to a scheme for disinheriting their son. They received in return certain revenues and estates in France and retired into obscurity in company with Godoy. The miserable trio spent the greater part of their remaining time in Rome, the objects of universal contempt. Ferdinand's enforced abdication could not buy him similar liberty; he was interned in Talleyrand's manor of Valencay and spent six years there under strict military guard. He spoilt his status as martyr by adulatory letters to Napoleon; in one, he even congratulated him on his victories in Spain.

We must turn back eight days from Ferdinand's final abdication, to explain the outbreak at Madrid which had caused Napoleon to apply the last turn of the screw to his captive. Within a short time of the first, arrest of the young king at Bayonne, it had become known in the Spanish capital that treachery was on foot. The effete or cowardly ministers took no action; but the news got abroad in Madrid, and premonitory signs of trouble began to be seen. They were brought to a head by an order from the emperor to Murat, bidding him arrest and send over the frontier all the remaining members of the royal House.

On May 2, when the French escort was preparing to move from the palace the young prince Francis, the last of the sons of Charles IV, an unarmed or half-armed mob fell upon them, broke up the coach, and attacked the soldiers with stones and stilettos. Murat had been warned by his master to be ready for outbreaks, and to treat the *canaille* to a whiff of grape-shot if they should rise. He dispersed the rioters by a couple of volleys from his guard. But this was only the beginning of the trouble: the whole populace of Madrid turned out at the sound of the musketry and flung themselves upon the French with such weapons as they could procure.

The battalions in the city were almost swept away by the furious assault, which was far more formidable than Murat had expected; more than thirty French officers and several hundred soldiers were killed or wounded. But within an hour the brigades of Moncey's corps came marching down from their camps outside the walls and cleared the streets with much slaughter. The Spanish garrison of Madrid took no

FRANCE

Sebastian

Bayonne

Fuenterrabia

Durango

Roncevalles

Pyrenees Mts.

Vitoria Pampeluna

Figueras

gos Calahorra

Gerona

Tudelo Ebro

Saragossa

Lerida

Barcelona

ro Mts Siguenza

Tarragona

ss of Somo Sierra

Tortosa

ADRID

40

Ucles

Majorca

ana

Murviedro

acid I

N

Valencia

na R.

Iviza

orena

Castalla

s dela

olina

Alicante

Murcia

C. Palos

Cartagena

anada

C. Gata

Map of the
SPANISH CAMPAIGN.

English Miles

0 20 40 60 80 100   200

part in the struggle. Only two officers, named Daoiz and Velarde, with a handful of artillerymen, joined the rioters and perished with them.

For a few days after the *Dos Mayo*, Murat at Madrid, and his master at Bayonne, lived in a sort of fool's paradise, imagining that they had made an end of all open resistance to their will. Murat assumed the presidency of a "Junta of Regency," chosen from among the most pliant of the old officials who had been corrupted by twenty years of Godoy's rule. On May 13 he announced to this body that the emperor desired them to ask for a new king, and suggested that the person designated should be Joseph Bonaparte, who for the last two years had been the ruler of Naples. The contemptible *Junta* did as they were ordered, and duly petitioned the emperor that his brother might be granted them as a king. In order that some semblance of national consent might be displayed, Napoleon drew up a list of some 150 magnates, who were directed to present themselves at Bayonne and sue in person for Joseph's acceptance of the throne. Of this body no less than 91 were base and weak enough to obey the mandate. On June 15 the deputation met the emperor at Bayonne and accepted Joseph as their ruler, receiving many promises of liberal reforms and wise governance from that well-intentioned prince, who little understood the unenviable task that his brother had imposed upon him.

But, long ere Joseph Napoleon I had been proclaimed King of Spain and the Indies, the whole country had flared up into insurrection. It took some time for the news of the treachery at Bayonne, followed by that of the *Dos Mayo*, to penetrate to the remoter corners of the Peninsula. But, when the nation began to comprehend the situation, a wild outbreak of patriotic rage followed. It was not led by the lawful and constituted authorities, who for the most part disgraced themselves by a cowardly torpidity. The effervescence came from below; and the leaders were non-official persons, local magnates, street-demagogues, and sometimes clerics. The movement was spontaneous, unselfish, and reckless; in its wounded pride, the nation challenged Napoleon to combat, without any thought of the consequences, without counting up its own resources or those of its enemy. Every province, in many cases every town, acted for itself.

But, though there was no union or organisation, the same spirit animated every region; and all, without exception, rose in arms between May 24 and June 10. It was an unhappy feature of the insurrection that in many places it was stained with massacre. The populace was incensed against its late rulers almost as much as against the

Officier de voltigeurs et Garde national, grande tenue.

GARDE IMPÉRIALE.

Chasseur
1810

Canonnier à pied et Officier d'artillerie légère

GARDE IMPÉRIALE.

Chevau-Légers Lanciers
PREMIER RÉGIMENT. GARDE IMPÉRIALE.

French. Old *protégées* of Godoy, colonels who refused to lead their regiments against Napoleon, officials who had shown zeal in carrying out Murat's orders, were assassinated on all sides. In Valencia a priest led out a band of ruffians who murdered the whole of the French merchants, resident in that great seaport.

It took some weeks for even the rudiments of a government to be formed out of the turbulent and patriotic chaos which prevailed. In every province local *"Juntas"* then emerged and began to call out the strength of the region for the holy war against the treacherous Emperor, the enemy of Church and king. It was unfortunate, but inevitable, that the *Juntas* were largely composed of furious but incapable zealots, ambitious demagogues, and self-seeking intriguers. There was an absolute want of statesmanship and organising ability; and fierce parochial patriotism could not supply their place. No central government whatever was established for some months; and each province fought for itself without much regard for the fate of its neighbours.

The military position at the end of May stood somewhat as follows. The French troops whom Napoleon had pushed down into the Peninsula during the last six months held a narrow triangular wedge of territory, piercing into the heart of New Castile. Toledo and Madrid formed its apex, a line drawn from San Sebastian to Pampeluna was its base. In addition to this there were two outlying French forces, that of Junot, mainly concentrated at Lisbon, and that of Duhesme, which lay at Barcelona. The central army, formed of the troops of Moncey, Dupont and Bessières, was about 75,000 strong: Junot had about 28,000 in Portugal, Duhesme some 14,000 in Catalonia. But the latter two generals were completely cut off from communication with Madrid.

On the Spanish side, the *Juntas* found about 100,000 regulars and militia at their disposal; but these were scattered about in provincial garrisons, badly provided, and wholly unfit to take the field immediately. The main force lay in Galicia and Andalusia, where large detachments had always been kept for the purpose of protecting the seaports from English descents. In each of these provinces there were about 30,000 men available. Of the rest, there were a few battalions in Estremadura, Valencia, and Catalonia, but in mid-Spain hardly a man. Thus, the forces of the insurgents formed a sort of semicircle, extending around the French wedge which ran into the heart of the land. New levies were being hastily prepared on every side, but arms and equipment were hard to find, owing to the depleted state in which

NAPOLEON ON HORSEBACK

Godoy had left the arsenals; while the stores of Madrid, Barcelona, Pampeluna, Figueras, and San Sebastian were in the hands of the enemy. When the fighting began, the remains of the old standing army were the only serious belligerent force on which Spain could count; the rest of the Spanish force consisted of undrilled and ununiformed peasants, officered by untrained and often incompetent civilians.

It was fortunate for the Spaniards that Napoleon at first misconceived the problem that lay before him. He had always nourished the greatest contempt for the fighting power of Spain and was under the impression that the armies which he had already pushed south of the Pyrenees were amply sufficient to hold down the country. But these armies were, as a matter of fact, very imperfect instruments of conquest. When the emperor organised the forces, which worked their way to Madrid, Lisbon, and Barcelona during the winter of 1807-8, he had, not drawn upon the veteran corps which lay in Germany.

Junot's corps, indeed, was of good material, being composed of old battalions picked from the garrisons of western France. But the corps of Moncey, Dupont, and Bessières were a haphazard assembly of second-rate troops and newly-organised provisional units. They included only about 5000 men of old French regiments; but round this nucleus were gathered some 15,000 Swiss, German, and other auxiliaries, and no less than 60,000 conscripts of 1807, hastily organised in "provisional regiments," "legions of reserve," and *bataillons de marche.*

The emperor had collected a very raw and ill-compacted army; he next proceeded to dispose of it on mistaken lines. He had made up his mind that the Spanish insurrection was a mere flash in the pan, the work of monks and *banditti.* The suppression of it would be a mere matter of police; he imagined that a few flying columns would be able to scour the insurgent districts and take possession of the chief strategical points without much difficulty. His orders read as if some isolated *émeutes*, rather than a national rising, had to be suppressed. While Bessières and his corps were to keep open the road from Burgos to Madrid, and to detach a force to subdue the province of Aragon, two expeditions were to be sent out from the capital, the one to reduce Seville and Cadiz, the other to conquer Valencia. The first of these columns, 13,000 strong, was to be led by Dupont; the second, 7000 strong, was given to Moncey. Both were composed entirely of conscript battalions and Swiss auxiliaries, without any stiffening of veteran troops.

The despatch of the two expeditions from Madrid took place on

May 24 and June 4 respectively, and was the last executive order carried out by Murat at his master's behest. He fell ill of a fever a few days later and returned to France; his place was taken by Savary, the betrayer of King Ferdinand, an officer wholly incompetent to face the threatening situation that was gradually developing itself.

Moncey passed the mountains of Cuenca without opposition and met with no resistance till he had reached the borders of the kingdom of Valencia. There he was twice opposed, in the defiles that led down to the shore-plain, by an irregular mass of new levies, which he thrust aside with ease. When he reached the city of Valencia, he found it packed with many thousands of combatants, including some regular troops, and roughly fortified with many batteries and earthworks. He risked two attempts to storm the place (June 28), lost 1000 men, and saw that it could not be taken without a battering train and a regular siege. By a rapid retreat he eluded his adversaries and drew back to the vicinity of Madrid (July 15).

Very different was the fate of Dupont. He too, like Moncey, met with little opposition during the first days of his march. The defiles of the Sierra Morena were not defended against him; and his troops did not fire a shot till they reached the bridge of Alcolea, in front of Cordova, where they dispersed a horde of 10,000 or 12,000 peasants who tried to cover that ancient city. Cordova made no resistance; nevertheless, it was sacked the same evening (June 7). Here Dupont's advance came to an end; he found that between him and Seville lay the Spanish army of Andalusia, nearly 30,000 regular troops commanded by General Castaños. The peasantry of the mountains had risen behind him and cut his communication with Madrid; his conscripts were suffering dreadfully from the summer heat and malaria.

He wisely refused to advance further, and, when Castaños began to move slowly towards him, evacuated Cordova and fell back to Andujar, the point of junction where the routes from the Sierra Morena come down into the valley of the Guadalquivir. He wrote to Madrid for reinforcements, which Savary did not refuse; two fresh divisions of conscripts were sent him, which brought up his force to some 22,000 men. Thus strengthened, he might have defended the passes of the Sierra Morena, though he could not have conquered Andalusia. But instead of retiring to the passes and assuming the defensive, he lingered in the plain at Andujar. He lacked the moral courage to confess to his master that the offensive campaign he had undertaken was hopeless.

At last, a false rumour that the Spaniards were detaching troops to

SIEGE OF SARAGOSSA.

by the

FRENCH ARMY OF ARAGON,

in 1808 and 1809.

A.W. FORBES TOF. F.R.G.S.

The Buildings destroyed by the Bombardment are distinguished by light colouring.

SCALE OF A MILE.

Spanish Feet, 5½ feet each.

RIVER EBRO

LEFT BANK

ATTACK

Inundation

Inundation of the EBRO

Mills

Port of Artillery

Convent of St. Lazare

Suburbs

REDOUBT OF CÆSAR

Convent of St. Joseph

THE CUT OF AYABE

ATTACK

Castle of the Inquisition

Convent of St. Augustine

Convent of the Augustines

Sancho Gate

Carmen Gate

S. Domingo

Portillo

Capuchins Hospital

General Hospital

New Gate

Mount Torrero

close the passes behind his back led him to commit the fatal blunder of dividing his small army into two nearly equal halves, and sending off his lieutenant, Vedel, with 10,000 men to secure the Despeña Perros. Castaños then thrust two divisions under General Reding into the gap, and seized the town of Baylen, halfway between Vedel and Dupont. This was a risky move, as the intervening force might have been crushed if the two French generals had acted in unison. Dupont at once evacuated Andujar, and marched with 11,000 men to clear the road, while Castaños' main body followed him at a leisurely pace. At Baylen Dupont found the road blocked by Reding with 17,000 men. He fought till noon, with much courage but little skill, endeavouring to pierce the Spanish line. But Reding held firm and beat off five partial and successive attacks. When the French were thoroughly exhausted and demoralised, Castaños appeared in their rear and enclosed them. Dupont then offered to capitulate, if his army were granted a free return to France.

Terms were being discussed when, late in the afternoon, General Vedel, with the other half of the French Army, came up in Reding's rear and began to develop an attack upon it. Vedel had shown criminal negligence and torpidity in delaying his appearance; he had refused to hurry, though he knew that Dupont was engaged, and though a distant cannonade had been audible all the morning. When informed that his chief was proposing to surrender, Vedel wheeled off and retired towards the passes. But Dupont nevertheless made a convention with Castaños, whereby he stipulated that not only his division, but that of his lieutenant, should capitulate and be sent back to France. This was unjustifiable conduct; but still more unjustifiable was that of Vedel, who tamely came back and laid down his arms, when he might easily have marched off to Madrid (June 23). In all, 18,000 unwounded men surrendered; more than 3000 had been lost in the fighting. When the French were secured, the Junta of Seville detained them all, and never allowed them to return to France.

This disaster, the worst check that the French arms had suffered since Menou capitulated in Egypt nine years before, had immense effect not only in Spain, but all over Europe. The responsibility for it must be divided between the emperor himself, Dupont, and Vedel. Napoleon, under a false idea of the Spanish strength, had sent out an army too small and too raw to accomplish such a task as the conquest of Andalusia; Dupont had shown both incapacity and want of moral courage; Vedel's torpidity and lack of initiative had doubled the

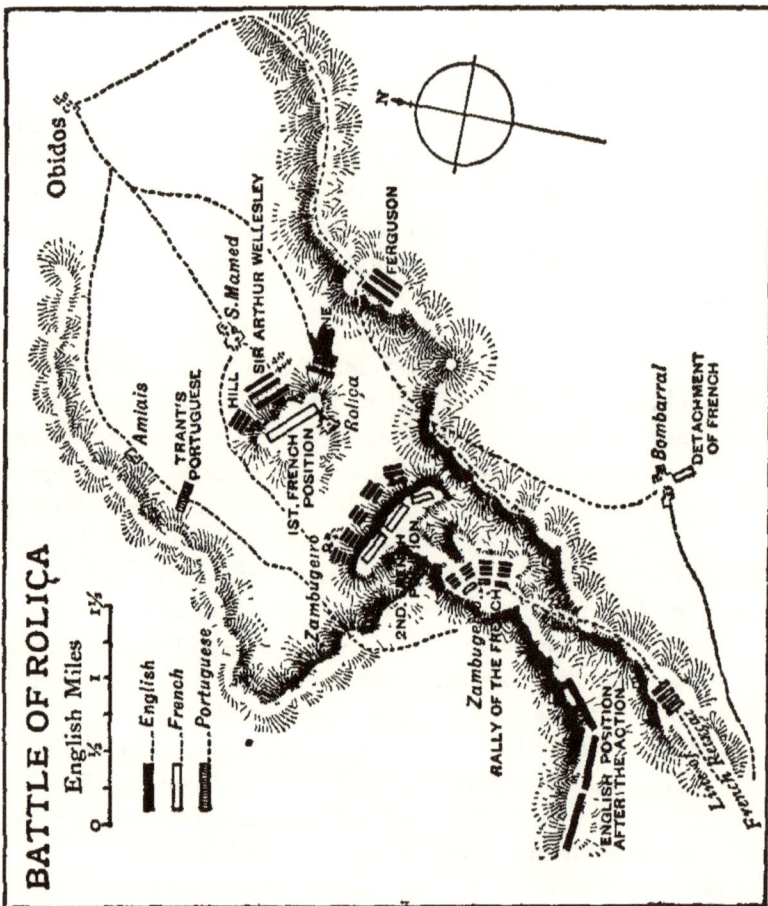

BATTLE OF ROLIÇA

English Miles

English
French
Portuguese

Obidos

S. Mamed
SIR ARTHUR WELLESLEY
HILL
FERGUSON
Roliça
TRANT'S
PORTUGUESE
Amlais
1ST. FRENCH
POSITION
Zambugeiro
2ND
Zambugeira
RALLY OF THE FRENCH
ENGLISH POSITION
AFTER THE ACTION
Bombarral
DETACHMENT
OF FRENCH
French

disaster. The emperor accused them both of cowardice and treason, and had them tried before a military commission, which found them guilty of criminal negligence and of "signing a capitulation containing shameful conditions," but of nothing more. Dupont was imprisoned till 1814; Vedel was pardoned after a few years and again employed.

The first result of Baylen was that King Joseph and Savary, considering their forces insufficient to maintain such an advanced position as the capital, hastily evacuated Madrid (August 1), and did not halt till they had recrossed the Ebro. Meanwhile four other series of operations had been in progress. The Spanish Army of Galicia under General Blake had descended from its mountains into the plains of Old Castile, with the intention of cutting the communications between Madrid and Burgos. Marshal Bessières, whose corps had been told off by Napoleon to protect that line, met him at Medina de Rio Seco on July 14, and inflicted a complete defeat upon the Galicians, though they mustered 22,000 men to his 13,000. This victory, however, had no further effect than to secure for King Joseph a safe retreat from Madrid; Dupont's disaster deprived Bessières of the power of following up his success.

The second independent campaign raging at this moment was that which centred at Saragossa: it was the most creditable to the Spaniards of all the operations of the summer of 1808. The kingdom of Aragon was almost destitute of regular troops; only about 1000 trained men were available when the revolution broke out. But Joseph Palafox, a young and ambitious adventurer, who had led the rising and been saluted as captain-general, collected a considerable body of half-armed peasants and townsfolk at Saragossa, and with them made head against the 15,000 men under Generals Verdier and Lefebvre-Desnouettes, who were detached to subdue Aragon. His defence of Saragossa (June 15-August 13) was an extraordinary feat.

The French having broken through the flimsy medieval walls of the city, Palafox, instead of capitulating, threw up barricades across the streets, defended house after house, beat back many assaults, and was still fighting fiercely inside the town, when the news of the fate of Dupont and the evacuation of Madrid compelled Verdier to retire. The story of Palafox' answer to the French summons, when the *enceinte* had been pierced, "No surrender, and war to the last party-wall" (*hasta la ultima tapia*), seems well authenticated; and the obstinate courage displayed by his Aragonese in the street fighting contrasted strongly with the helplessness of similar levies when forced to give battle in the open.

While Verdier was being held at bay in Saragossa, Duhesme, commanding the French Army in Catalonia, was also brought to a standstill. His troops, concentrated at Barcelona, found their communications with France cut off by the general rising of the province. To open them again, Duhesme delivered two attacks on the fortress of Gerona, which blocked the road to Perpignan. Both were beaten off (June 20-21, and July 22-August 16); and the French general was compelled to shut himself up in Barcelona, where he was blockaded for nearly four months by the insurgents and reduced to great straits.

The fourth local campaign in which Napoleon's expeditionary forces were involved during the summer of 1808 was that of Junot in Portugal. The Spanish rising had isolated the 28,000 French who lay in and about Lisbon; but Junot resolved to defend his conquest without taking any heed of what was going on elsewhere. Fortunately for him, Portugal was completely disarmed; the old army had been disbanded or sent across the Pyrenees; and all the arsenals were in the hands of the French. The efforts of the people, who rose on all sides between June 6 and June 16, were of necessity weak, for there was no nucleus of trained men, and arms were hard to get. Junot's flying columns scoured the whole country and held down central Portugal with success. He was still in good hopes of maintaining his position, when, on August 3, he received the news that on the preceding day a British expeditionary force had landed in Mondego Bay.

CHAPTER 8

The British Army

The arrival of this army marks a new stage in the history not only of the Peninsular War but of Europe at large. The British Government was about to turn aside from that system of sending out small forces to inflict pin-pricks on non-vital spots in Napoleon's empire, which Sheridan wittily called "its policy of filching sugar-islands." Urged on by Castlereagh, who already had in the winter of 1805-6 advocated an interference on the Continent on a large scale, and had hoped much from the expedition to Hanover, and by Canning, who, following Pitt's forecast, was fascinated with the idea of a really national and popular rising against Napoleon, the Portland Cabinet had resolved to strike hard. Even the Whig Opposition could not cavil at the proposal to aid a people so basely betrayed as the Spaniards or make any attempt to defend the morality of Napoleon's late doings. On the arrival in London, on June 4, of deputies from the Asturias asking for help, followed soon after by similar missions from the other *Juntas*, the government promised speedy and ample assistance. In all some 30,000 men were directed to move, and more were to follow.

Lord Castlereagh had intended to place at the head of the whole the young lieutenant-general who commanded the force which sailed from Cork, Sir Arthur Wellesley, the brother of the great Viceroy of India, already known for his victories of Assaye and Argaum. But the Duke of York and the War Office were against the scheme; and there were members of the Cabinet who disliked the Wellesleys. After the first troops had actually set sail, the government resolved to place over Sir Arthur's head two senior officers of no special distinction or ability, Sir Hew Dalrymple, governor of Gibraltar, and Sir Harry Burrard. Sir John Moore also, who was ordered up from the Baltic, would outrank Wellesley, who was thus placed fourth instead of first in command.

Before he was aware that he was superseded, Wellesley had sailed; he landed his 9000 men in Mondego Bay on August 1-2, 1808. The Portuguese welcomed him; but he found that their levies were little more than a useless mob, and that he must depend on his own resources. Four days later he was joined by another British division and set out to march on Lisbon with some 13,000 men. On August 17 he met at Roliça a small force which Junot had despatched to delay his advance and drove it out of a strong position by a vigorous attack. This roused the viceroy of Portugal, who sallied out of Lisbon with his field-army. Having garrisoned Elvas and Almeida and left a whole division to overawe the discontented populace of the capital, Junot only brought 13,000 men to the front. Wellesley, having been joined by two more brigades from England, had over 16,000 British troops in hand, besides some 2000 Portuguese insurgents.

The invading army was encamped at Vimiero, with its back to the sea, when on August 21 it was fiercely attacked by the French. Wellesley had chosen an admirable position on a line of rolling hills, and showed in this, his first European victory, that masterly power of handling troops on the defensive which was to make his reputation. Junot's vigorous but ill-combined assaults were driven back with awful slaughter; and the victor was about to let loose his reserves upon the broken masses of the enemy when his hand was suddenly paralysed. Sir Harry Burrard had landed at this untoward moment, asserted his authority, and forbade a pursuit.

Thus, Junot was able to gather his routed battalion together and to cover the road to Lisbon. Next morning (August 22) Burrard was superseded by Dalrymple, who was much surprised to receive on that same day proposals from Junot that he should be allowed to evacuate Portugal under a convention. The French general was expecting every moment to hear of a revolt in Lisbon; his troops were not inclined to face another general action; and he saw no better way *"pour nous tirer de la souricière,"* ("to pull us out of the mousetrap.")

Dalrymple, overjoyed at finding himself dictating terms ere he had been two days ashore, eagerly accepted the idea of a convention. He was justified in accepting Junot's offer; time was of importance; and the French might, if driven to despair, have ruined Lisbon and made a long and desperate defence. But Sir Hew weakly conceded every demand that was made by the French negotiators, including several that were most offensive to the Portuguese; e.g. he allowed the French to depart laden in the most shameless fashion with the plunder of palaces, museums, and churches, and guaranteed immunity to native traitors. On August 30 this famous Convention of Cintra—falsely so called, for it was neither discussed nor signed in that pleasant spot—was executed. Before the next month was out, 25,000 French troops had been shipped out of Portugal; and the whole kingdom was delivered. It was now possible to think of bringing aid to Spain.

But neither Dalrymple nor Burrard was destined to lead the victors of Vimiero into the uplands of Castile. When the news of the Convention was received in England, universal indignation was expressed. It was thought that Dalrymple had let off the French too easily, and that he might have forced them to unconditional surrender. Letters from officers who complained of the way in which the pursuit at Vimiero had been checked, and complaints from the Portuguese provisional government, added fuel to the flames. All three British generals were recalled and sent before a Court of enquiry. This body reported that, in its opinion, they had all acted according to the best of their judgment and shown proper zeal, and that no further proceedings should be taken. But, while the two senior generals were never despatched on active service again, Wellesley, whose conduct had contrasted so splendidly with that of his superiors, was sent back to Portugal as commander-in-chief in the ensuing spring.

Much had happened before Sir Arthur resumed his place at the head of a British Army. King Joseph and Savary had evacuated Madrid, recrossed the Ebro, and fallen back to the foot of the Pyrenees. This long retreat caused almost as much indignation in Napoleon's breast as Dupont's surrender. He had at first directed Joseph to hold on to Madrid at all costs, then to stay his retreat at Aranda and Valladolid. But both his despatches arrived too late; and, by August 15, the remains of the army of Spain, still nearly 70,000 strong, were concentrated between Miranda and Milagro on the Ebro.

The Emperor, on hearing the news of Baylen, had ordered three veteran corps of the army of Germany, those of Victor, Mortier, and Ney, to march for Spain, and had drawn together other reinforcements from various corners of the Empire. He had hoped that Joseph and Savary would hold out in some advanced position till those succours arrived. But all such hopes were now at an end; and the conquest of the Peninsula had to be begun *de novo*. It was not till the end of October that the heads of the columns from Germany began to cross the passes. While they were marching across France, the emperor went off to Erfurt.

Thus, from the day of Baylen to the opening of the new campaign, the Spanish insurgents had three full months in which to organise their forces. Unfortunately, they did not turn the time to good account. The provincial *Juntas* showed no desire to relinquish their local sovereignty in favour of a new national executive. When they were at last induced to create a supreme authority, it was not a compact regency of a few members but a "Central Junta" of no less than thirty-five delegates. This body was only got together on September 25; and, when it met, it proceeded, like a debating society, to discuss constitutional reforms, instead of turning all its energies to making ready for Napoleon's advance.

The most fatal fault was that it refused to appoint a single commander-in-chief for its armies and tried to direct independently the movements of half-a-dozen captains-general of the provincial armies. These officers became personal rivals, intrigued with the *Junta*, and refused to cooperate with each other. Hence came military chaos and lamentable waste of time. By the end of October, only about 110,000 men had been pushed up to the line of the Ebro to face the French, though about 60,000 more were being drilled and equipped far to the rear. Indeed, the only important addition made to the army at the front after Baylen was that of 9000 of La Romana's troops from Denmark, who landed at Santander.

The Spanish strategy at this moment was hopelessly bad. The *Junta* had allowed their two main armies to drift apart; Blake, with 40,000 men of the Galician Army, had advanced into Biscay, with the inten-

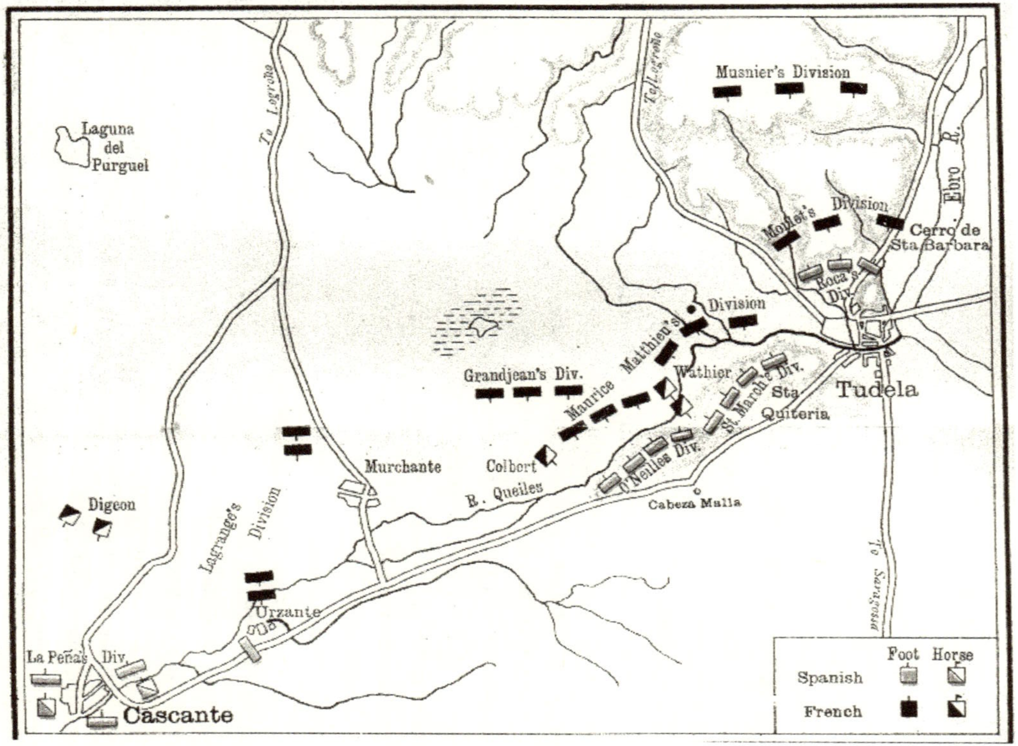

Musnier's Division
To Logroño
Laguna del Purguel
Ebro R.
Morlot's Division
Cerro de Sta Barbara
Roca's Div.
Matthieu's Division
Grandjean's Div.
Manrice
Wathier
St. Marche Div.
Sta Quiteria
Tudela
Murchante
Colbert
O'Neilles Div.
B. Queiles
Cabeza Mulla
Digeon
Lagrange's Division
To Saragossa
Urzante
La Peña's Div.
Cascante
Foot
Horse
Spanish
French

tion of turning the French right; while Castaños and Palafox, with the armies of Andalusia and Aragon, some 60,000 strong, were executing a similar movement far to the east on the side of Pampeluna. To connect these two armies there was nothing but the army of Estremadura, 12,000 strong, which was concentrating at Burgos. Thus, the Spanish array had two powerful wings but practically no centre.

To aid the Estremadurans at Burgos, it was intended that the British Army from Portugal should be brought up. After the departure of Dalrymple, the command of this force had devolved on Sir John Moore (October 6). He had received orders to march into Spain and join British allies; but he found much difficulty in starting his troops, owing to his want of transport and his absolute ignorance of the relative practicability of the various inland roads of Portugal. Receiving false intelligence from the native engineers that it was impossible to move guns over the Serra da Estrella, by the straight road from Lisbon to Almeida and Salamanca, he took the unfortunate step of sending nearly the whole of his cavalry and artillery on a vast detour, by Elvas, Talavera, and the Escorial, while he marched with his infantry columns direct over mountain roads by way of Coimbra and Guarda.

The consequence was that, while 16,000 infantry reached Salamanca in detachments between November 13 and November 23, they could not move till, on December 3, the guns came in from their long turn to the south. Moore's little army at Salamanca was not the only British force which had been sent to aid Spain; a separate division under Baird, 13,000 strong, had been landed at Corunna in the middle of October, and directed to push inland and join Moore in Old Castile. But, much hampered by want of transport, Baird only reached Astorga on November 22. He was still far from his junction with Moore when news arrived that the Spanish armies on the Ebro had received a series of appalling defeats and were retiring in disorder before the French.

Napoleon held back his army in Navarre till the great reinforcements from Germany had arrived, and 200,000 men were under his hand. He then struck with the swiftness and shattering power of a thunderbolt at the weak centre of the Spanish line and opened for himself the road to Madrid. The first battle was fought at Zornosa, in Biscay, on October 29, when Blake's army of Galicia, still bent on its turning movement, was thrust back by Marshal Lefebvre, and had to retire westward. The Galicians were making off, pursued by two French corps, when Napoleon led his main body over the Ebro, and on November 10 dashed to pieces the little army of Estremadura at the combat of Gamonal in front of Burgos.

Next day (November 11) Blake's retreating army, overtaken by Victor at Espinosa in the Cantabrian mountains, received an equally disastrous beating, and was forced to disperse into the hills with the loss of the whole of its artillery. A full month passed before its wrecks, 20,000 strong, were rallied at Leon by the Marquis of La Romana. There remained intact, of all the Spanish armies, only the combined host of Andalusia and Aragon under Castaños and Palafox. On November 23 this force shared the fate of its fellows; its main body, 45,000 strong, was defeated at Tudela by Lannes. Quarrels between Castaños and Palafox were largely responsible for this disaster; their plans were so badly arranged that one-third of the Spanish Army did not fire a shot, while the other two-thirds were being routed and dispersed. Palafox' divisions now drew back to defend Saragossa, while Castaños and the Andalusians made off for Madrid by way of Calataynd. They narrowly escaped falling into the hands of Ney, who had been sent to intercept them, and escaped in wretched plight over the mountains.

Such was the depressing news which Moore and Baird, still far from effecting a junction with each other, received in the last days of November. It seemed that there was no Spanish Army left with which the British could cooperate; and Moore despaired of being even able to meet Baird in safety. Judging himself far too weak to confront Napoleon's main body, he issued orders for a retreat on Lisbon, and directed Baird to fall back on Corunna (November 28). He believed that Spain was ruined and that Portugal was indefensible, and he was prepared to evacuate even Lisbon if the French should push their invasion home.

Meanwhile the emperor, as soon as the news of Tudela reached him, struck straight at Madrid. He was only vaguely aware of Moore's position on his flank and paid no attention to him. The *Junta* had made a hasty attempt to cover the two defiles which lead to Madrid, having drawn to Segovia and the Guadarrama pass the wrecks of the Estremaduran Army, and thrown into the Somosierra pass a force composed of new levies and a few belated battalions of the army of Andalusia. The emperor, leaving Segovia alone, advanced in a single column against the Somosierra, and forced it after a short combat on November 30.

On December 2 he appeared in force in front of Madrid. The Spanish capital was an open town devoid of any regular defences, and had no garrison save some of the fugitives from the Somosierra. But the populace were in a paroxysm of patriotic frenzy, and had sworn to make a second Saragossa of their home. They held out for one day behind extemporised batteries and earthworks; but, when the French stormed the Buen Retiro heights, which command the whole place, and forced their way into the Prado, the enthusiasm died down and the town surrendered (December 3).

From Dec. 4 to Dec. 22 Napoleon remained in the neighbourhood of Madrid, laying down laws and drafting projects for the reorganisation of Spain, and giving his troops a short rest before they should be called upon to march on Lisbon and Cadiz. His reserves and outlying columns were beginning to come in; and he had, in and about Madrid, some 75,000 men. Meanwhile Lannes, with the army which had won the fight of Tudela, was directed to besiege Saragossa and make an end of Palafox; while Marshal Soult, whose corps lay in Old Castile, covering the emperor's flank and rear, was directed to invade Leon and disperse the wrecks of Blake's old army. The Emperor's next move would have been to march on Lisbon, whither he assumed that Sir John Moore would have withdrawn when he heard of the fall of Madrid.

But matters had gone otherwise in the north-west of the Peninsula. Moore had ordered a retreat on Lisbon on November 28; but on December 5 he changed his mind, mainly because he had heard exaggerated reports of the desperation with which Madrid was defending itself, but partly also because he had been at last (December 3) rejoined by his long-lost artillery and cavalry and had discovered that there was nothing to prevent Baird from joining him. In these circumstances, honour required that he should not retire without striking a blow in behalf of Spain. Accordingly, he resolved to execute a diversion in Old Castile, and to make a raid on Valladolid or even on Burgos, with the object of disturbing the emperor's line of communication. In this plan he persisted, even when, on December 9, he received news of the surrender of Madrid. He knew that his move was a dangerous one and wrote to Baird that:

> Both you and me, though we may look big, and determine to get everything forward, yet we must never lose sight of this, that at any moment affairs may take the turn that renders it necessary to retreat.

They must advance "bridle in hand" and ever ready to swerve off to the rear. Moore marched from Salamanca on December 11; two days later, he learnt from a captured despatch that the emperor was unaware of his presence, and that Soult was lying in an isolated position on the Carrion River, with less than 20,000 men. He thereupon resolved to change his direction, and to endeavour to surprise and defeat Soult before he could be reinforced. Turning north, he was joined by Baird on December 20, which raised his force to about 27,000 men. He drove in the French cavalry in several successful combats, and on December 23 lay at Sahagun close in front of Soult. The Marquis of La Romana, Blake's successor, was slowly bringing up the disorganised wrecks of the army of Galicia to his aid.

A battle would have followed next day, had not Moore received from a Spanish source, on the afternoon of the 23rd, the news that Napoleon had at last heard of his whereabouts, and had started from Madrid in pursuit of him with the main body of his army. Without a moment's hesitation, the British general faced his columns to the rear, and slipped off westward on the road to Benavente and Astorga. He had thrown up his base in Portugal and was intending to retreat to Vigo and Corunna. He did not start a minute too soon. Napoleon, on receiving tardy but certain news of the advance of the English Army against Soult, had at once given orders (December 19-20) that the greater part of the troops at Madrid, not less than 42,000 sabres and bayonets, should hasten by forced marches to throw themselves upon Moore's rear, and cut him off from his retreat on Portugal or Galicia.

The sight of the red-coats in the distance had at once drawn him off from all his other plans; and the idea of capturing a whole British Army excited him to almost frenzied exertions. He drove his troops across the snow of the Guadarrama pass in the midst of a blizzard which smote down horse and man and urged them across the plains of Old Castile at a breakneck pace. But Moore was too quick for him. When the cavalry of the emperor's van-guard reached the line of the Esla on December 28, the British were safely across the river and out of danger. As the French pressed on, Lord Paget turned back with his hussars, and cut to pieces the *Chasseurs à Cheval* of the Imperial Guard at Benavente (December 29), capturing Lefebvre-Desnouettes, their commander, and many of his men.

The emperor urged on the pursuit for two days more but threw it up in disgust at Astorga on January 1, 1809. It is usually said that he turned back because of news received concerning the threatening attitude of Austria. This was the official view; but it seems probable that reports of intrigues at Paris, in which Fouché, Talleyrand, and Murat were all concerned, had more to do with the emperor's return. The

CHARGE OF THE HUSSARS AT BENEVENTE

pursuit was handed over to the corps of Ney and Soult. About 45,000 men were ordered to follow Moore and La Romana, whose famishing army had fallen back on Astorga just as the British arrived. The rest of the force that had taken part in the emperor's movement was sent back to Madrid or cantoned in the kingdom of Leon.

The retreat of the British from Astorga to Corunna occupied only twelve days; but an immense amount of misery was compressed into that short space of time. Moore believed that his best policy was to withdraw with such rapidity as to leave the enemy far behind. He had calculated that the pursuers would probably follow him no further than Villafranca, so that he would have a quiet and undisturbed embarkation at the end of his retreat. Accordingly, he made very long marches, not unfrequently by night; the army covered on the average seventeen miles a day, in a rugged mountain country covered with snow and cut up by torrents and defiles. The troops, profoundly disgusted at not being allowed to fight, and wearied out by perpetual marching, got out of hand. Many regiments left multitudes of stragglers behind and plundered the villages by the road. Drunken marauders and footsore stragglers fell by hundreds into the hands of the pursuing French cavalry. But the rear-guard under Paget held together staunchly, and roughly repulsed the enemy when any attempt was made to drive them in.

Yet the French stuck to the heels of the retreating army, and could not, as Moore had hoped, be shaken off. On January 11 the British reached Corunna, in a very dilapidated condition, only to find that the transport-fleet had not arrived. It came up two days later, and the embarkation began. But Soult had also appeared; and, to secure a quiet departure, Moore had to fight the Battle of Corunna (January 16). Four days' rest and the advent of the long-denied opportunity for fighting, had pulled the army together; and, when Soult assailed the British infantry—the cavalry and guns were already on board—he suffered a bloody repulse. Moore was mortally wounded by a cannon-ball in the thick of the battle, or he would probably have attacked in his turn and driven the French into the River Mero, which lay at their backs. But his successor, General Hope, was content with having repulsed Soult, and embarked his troops at leisure next day.

Thus, ended Sir John Moore's celebrated campaign, which undoubtedly saved Spain and Portugal for the moment, by distracting the emperor from his southward advance, and by drawing his field army, which might have marched on Lisbon and Cadiz, into a remote

SECOND
SIEGE of SARAGOSSA
DEC. 1808 TO FEB. 1809

CENTRE ATTACK

The Parts of the City in the
hands of the French at the
moment of the Capitulation
are shown thus.

One Kilometre

RIVER EBRO

SUBURB OF SAN LAZARO

To Barcelona

Artillery Park

Inundation

JESUS CONVENT

COLUSUS CONVENT

SAN LAZARO CONVENT

Inundation

Marsh

BRIDGE

N. S. DEL PILAR

CATHEDRAL

LAS TENERIAS

S. AUGUSTIN
SANTA MONICA
OIL MILL
BATTERY

3-d Parallel

Huerba

SAN JOSÉ

2nd Parallel

RIGHT ATTACK

To Valencia

MONTE TORRERO

1st parallel

PALAFOX GUARD

CHURCH & CONVENT

SANTA ENGRACIA

EL COSO

UNIVERSITY

SEMINARY

EL COSO

SAN PABLO

PLAZA DE LA CONTRATACION

CAVALRY BARRACK

SANTA ENGRACIA GATE

REDOUBT PILAR

3-d Parallel

To Madrid

CARMEN GATE

BATTERY

TRINITARIAN CONVENT

SANCHO GATE

ALJAFFERIA

PORTILLO GATE

AUGUSTINIAN CONVENT

Left or False Attack

and rugged corner of the Peninsula. Moore wrote in his last despatch:

> As a diversion it has succeeded; I brought the whole of the
> disposable force of the French against this army.

And this was absolutely true. The conception was so fine, and the result so satisfactory, that it seems ungracious to criticise the details of the operations. But we may agree with Wellington that "Sir John Moore's error was that he did not know what his men could do," and allow that he drove them too fast in the march from Astorga to Corunna, with great resulting loss. Of 6000 men lost by the way, some no doubt perished owing to their own indiscipline, but more because they were wearied beyond the limits of human endurance. But this was a cheap price to pay for wrecking Napoleon's original plan for the conquest of the Peninsula, just when he himself was on the spot and able to combine the movements of all the French corps in a way that was never again possible.

After abandoning the pursuit of Moore to Soult and Ney, the emperor returned to France. His great *coup de théâtre*, the capture of the British Army, had failed, and the projected invasion of Portugal and Andalusia had been postponed; but, in the main, he was not discontented with the results of his campaign. The spirit of the Spaniards— so he fancied—was completely broken. "*Les affaires d'Espagne sont à peu près terminées,*" ("Spanish affairs are almost complete,") he wrote to one of his ministers; and he returned to suppress intrigues in Paris and to watch Austria. Moore's diversion had, however, allowed time for the Spaniards to rally, and had stopped the French advance for two months. By that time the shattered Spanish armies were once more reorganised, and able to resume their stubborn if too often unsuccessful resistance.

The Spanish affair was far from being "nearly at an end," as Napoleon supposed. He had yet to discover that to defeat a Spanish Army was easy, but to destroy it difficult. The routed force dispersed, took to the hills, and reassembled again to give further trouble. Spain was not the country to be subdued by a single Jena or Austerlitz. The loss of Madrid counted for little or nothing; every province continued to fight for its own hand; and no region could be considered conquered that was not held down by a French garrison planted at every cross-road.

During the midwinter of 1808-9, Moore's diversion had caused the suspension of the French operations in all quarters save two, Aragon and Catalonia, the two regions from which no troops had been withdrawn for the race to Corunna. Lannes had been sent with two corps to take Saragossa, into which Palafox had withdrawn his part of the army that had been routed at Tudela. The siege began on December 20, 1808 and lasted for exactly two months. Palafox was no strategist and made numerous blunders of detail, but he was obstinate and enthusiastic; and his position was far stronger than it had been in the preceding July and August. He had nearly 40,000 more or less organised fighting men; and the flimsy walls of his city had been strengthened by earthworks and batteries since the first siege.

The Aragonese fought with their usual obstinacy; and it was not till January 27, 1809, that the French succeeded in breaking through the outer *enceinte* of Saragossa. Three weeks of deadly street-fighting still remained before them. Lannes only won his way by blowing up house after house, and storming street after street. When the place surrendered, it was because fire and sword, pestilence and famine, had destroyed the garrison. Over 20,000 fighting men, with some 30,000 of the populace, had perished. Desperate but ill-organised patriotism had failed when pitted against military science. But it was clear that the people who could make such a stand were not likely to become the passive subjects of the French Emperor.

In Catalonia matters went no less badly for the Spaniards. Gouvion Saint-Cyr, whom the emperor had sent to relieve Duhesme and his beleaguered army, commenced his operative action by taking Rosas (December 5), and then pushed through the mountains to succour Barcelona. He routed Reding, the victor of Baylen, at Cardadeu on December 16, and cut his way through to join Duhesme. Their united forces then sallied out and beat the army of Catalonia at Molins de Rey (December 21) just outside Barcelona. Even then Reding's spirit was not broken. Rallying his troops, he took the offensive, but he was defeated by Saint-Cyr for a third time at Vails (February 25, 1809). In this last fight Reding was mortally wounded; his broken host shut itself up in Tarragona or took to the hills, leaving Saint-Cyr free to commence the siege of Gerona, the great fortress commanding the road from the French frontier to Barcelona.

Meanwhile the Spanish line of defence was being reconstructed. The wrecks of Castaños' old army had gathered in La Mancha and took their post at the foot of the passes of the Sierra Morena, Under General Cartaojal. The still more dilapidated divisions vanquished at Gamonal and the Somosierra rallied behind the Tagus. They were in a fearful state of indiscipline and had murdered their general San Juan on a wild charge of treason; but their new commander, Cuesta, a morose and incapable but courageous veteran, reduced them to order by a series of military executions. Blake's old army of Galicia, now under La Romana, after parting from Moore's retreating force at Astorga, had retired into the mountains and was reorganising at Orense. Blake himself had been sent to Valencia and was busy in getting together a fresh army in that fertile and well-peopled province. Including other levies in the Asturias and Andalusia, the Supreme Junta, which had now established its seat at Seville, could place some 100,000 men in the field in March, 1809.

But more important, in the end, than the survival of any Spanish Army was the fact that 9000 British troops still remained in Portugal. These were the battalions that had been left in Lisbon when Moore marched to Salamanca in the preceding autumn. Their very cautious general, Sir John Cradock, kept them close to the Portuguese capital, ready to embark if the French should advance in force. Fortunately for Portugal, for Great Britain, and for Europe, the British Government had resolved to continue the struggle in the Peninsula at all costs. In February General Beresford was sent out to reorganise the Portuguese Army, with some scores of British officers to help him, and a great store of new arms and equipment.

On April 2 a far more important announcement was made. Sir Arthur Wellesley, the victor of Vimiero, was named commander of the British forces in Portugal, and ordered to sail for Lisbon at short notice. This appointment was due to Lord Castlereagh, who showed a steady confidence in Wellesley, and always employed him as his chief military adviser. The general had stated that, if granted a British Army of 20,000 or 30,000 men and the control of the native forces, he would undertake to hold Portugal against any French Army not exceeding 100,000 men. This was contrary to Sir John Moore's dictum that Portugal was untenable; but the government, urged on by Castlereagh, resolved to take the risk. Reinforcements began to be sent out; Wellesley himself reached Lisbon and superseded Cradock on April 22, 1809.

Ere he landed, the campaign of 1809 had begun. Before quitting Spain, Napoleon had laid down the general lines that were to be followed by his marshals. Soult, leaving Ney behind him to hold down Galicia, was to march with his own corps from Corunna on Portugal, and to take first Oporto, and then Lisbon. So sanguine was Napoleon that he hoped that the Portuguese capital might fall before February

15. On the other side, Victor, with his corps and certain reinforcements, was to cross the Tagus, crush Cuesta's army of Estremadura, take Badajoz, and then march on Seville. Sebastiani's corps was to deal with the other Spanish Army in the south—that of La Mancha under Cartaojal; but Victor's was to be the decisive blow. Catalonia and Aragon were side-issues of comparatively little importance.

The French columns duly advanced, in obedience to the emperor's orders; but inevitable hindrances—bad roads, bad weather, and difficulty of supplies—caused them to start far later than he had intended. Soult left Corunna with 23,000 men, after turning over the charge of Galicia to Ney. On March 9 he crossed the Portuguese border near Chaves; La Romana, with the wrecks of the Spanish Army of Galicia, had retired northward, wisely refusing battle. Soult's invasion of Portugal was an unbroken series of combats with a half-armed peasantry, backed by a few battalions of disorganised line-troops. They did their best but were utterly unable to stand before the French veterans. At last, on March 27 the marshal forced his way to Oporto, and found in front of the city a line of hastily constructed earthworks manned by 30,000 insurgents, headed by their bishop and uncontrolled by any proper military organisation. He stormed the lines two days later, and made a horrible slaughter of the Portuguese, several thousands of whom were driven into the river.

But here Soult's initiative came to an end; he was unable to carry out the emperor's instructions by advancing against Lisbon. He was cut off from all communication with other French armies by insurgents in his rear. The remains of the Portuguese forces that he had beaten were hanging in a great mass on his left flank; if he left a competent garrison in Oporto, he would not have enough troops for the final advance; and he now knew that there was a British force awaiting him somewhere near Lisbon. Accordingly, he halted, sent out flying columns to open his communication with Galicia, and wrote to the emperor for more troops. Meanwhile he amused himself by assuming quasi-regal state at Oporto and seems to have dreamed of becoming "King of northern Lusitania."

The other French advance had come to a similar standstill at about the same moment. Two Spanish armies, it will be remembered, had been collected for the defence of Andalusia—that of Cartaojal covering the eastern passes, that of Cuesta behind the line of the Tagus. On March 27 Sebastiani beat Cartaojal at Ciudad Real and forced him to take shelter in the Sierra Morena. But the French general had received orders not to press his victory; it was Victor who was to deliver the great blow. On March 15, that marshal crossed the Tagus high up, thus turning the position which Cuesta had taken behind the central course of the river at Almaraz. He had about 22,000 men, a force slightly exceeding that of the Spaniards, who drew back when their flank was turned, and retired across the mountains into the valley of the Guadiana.

Here Cuesta was reinforced by a division drawn from Cartaojal's army and offered battle, for he was as rash as he was unskilful in the field. He took in hand no less a scheme than to surround the French in the open plain near Medellin, and advanced in a line, four miles long and only four men deep. The natural result followed; the French cavalry broke his left-centre by a furious charge, and then rolled up his isolated wings in detail. The slaughter was awful, for there was no friendly mountain or ravine to shelter the routed troops; more than 7000 were cut down, and nearly 2000 made prisoners (March 28). Nevertheless, Victor's offensive was exhausted at Medellin, just as that of Soult had been at Oporto. Insurrection had burst out in his rear; his army was enfeebled by detachments and suffering from want of food. He could hear nothing of Soult, whose advance on Lisbon was to synchronise with his own on Seville. He declared that he was not strong enough to besiege Badajoz, much less to invade Andalusia, and halted in the valley of the Guadiana, clamouring for reinforcements, which King Joseph at Madrid was too weak to send him.

Such was the condition of affairs when Wellesley landed at Lisbon. The French invasion had come to a standstill. Soult would not move without reinforcements from Ney, nor Victor without reinforcements from Madrid. Wellesley at once grasped the situation; he had at his disposal, counting the newly-arrived regiments from England, some 25,000 British and 16,000 Portuguese troops. This was enough to enable him to deal a crushing blow at either Soult or Victor, while leaving a detached force to "contain" the other. Without a moment's hesitation, he resolved to deal with Soult first, and, leaving 12,000 men at Abrantes to watch Victor, marched with the rest on Oporto. If successful in the north, he intended to rush back to Estremadura and deal with the second French Army.

Everything favoured Wellesley's enterprise. Soult had dispersed his army to hunt down the Portuguese insurgents and was attacked before he could concentrate. At the moment when the blow fell, he was more intent on suppressing a republican conspiracy among his own officers

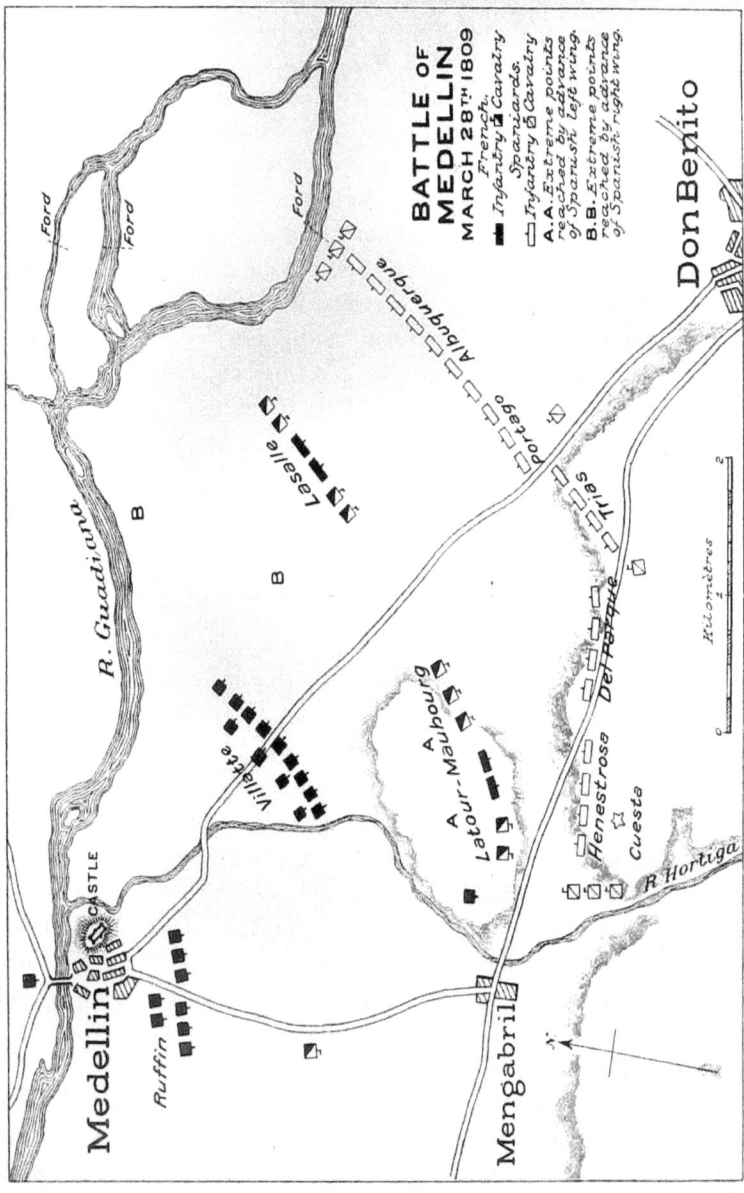

BATTLE OF
MEDELLIN
MARCH 28TH 1809

French.
▬ Infantry ◾ Cavalry
Spaniards.
▢ Infantry ◇ Cavalry
A.A. Extreme points
reached by advance
of Spanish left wing.
B.B. Extreme points
reached by advance
of Spanish right wing.

Ford

Ford

Ford

Ford

Alburquerque

Portago

Trias

Don Benito

R. Guadiana

CASTLE

Medellin

Ruffin

Villatte

Lasalle

Latour-Maubourg

Henestrosa

Del Parque

Cuesta

R. Hortiga

Mengabril

B

B

Kilomètres

than on watching for any advance on the part of the British. On May 12 Wellesley was in front of Oporto, while Soult was hurriedly assembling his troops and preparing to retreat. Noting the confusion in the French ranks, Wellesley carried out at midday his astounding passage of the Douro, throwing his advanced guard across a broad river edged with precipitous cliffs, when he noted that the enemy had neglected to guard all the passages. The move was completely successful, and Soult was hunted out of Oporto and driven eastward, in search of the divisions of his army which had not yet been able to join him.

But Wellesley had thrown a Portuguese force under Beresford across the line of retreat by which the enemy could retire up the Douro into Spain. Thus intercepted, Soult rallied his missing columns, but found that he was shut in between Wellesley, Beresford, and the inhospitable and roadless mountains of the Serra de Santa Catalina. Burning his baggage and destroying all his artillery, he escaped by goat-tracks over the hills towards Galicia. Hotly pursued by Wellesley, and harassed by the peasantry, he finally got off with the loss of 5000 men and led his corps in a disorganised mass to Orense. He found that Galicia was no safe harbourage for him; the whole province was up in arms, and the detachments of Ney's corps were fighting for existence against La Romana's army and the local guerillas. With some difficulty Soult and Ney ultimately concentrated at Lugo and resolved to devote themselves to crushing the Galician insurrection.

As they were thus engaged, Wellesley had ample time for a blow at Victor in Estremadura. But, while he was hurrying his victorious troops from Oporto to Abrantes for a rapid stroke at the 1st corps, the French Army of the south was enduring such dire starvation that Victor at last resolved to retire towards Madrid, before the whole force should become ineffective from sheer exhaustion. He evacuated Estremadura about the middle of June, and retired to the valley of the Tagus, fixing his headquarters at Talavera. Thus, he abandoned all that he had won at Medellin. This rearward movement of the 1st corps compelled Wellesley to revise his plans, since Victor was no longer isolated, but had fallen back to a position where he was in close touch both with Madrid and with Sebastiani in La Mancha.

After taking counsel with Cuesta and the *Junta* at Seville, Wellesley consented to embark in the first and only campaign which he ever undertook in company with a Spanish colleague and without supreme control over the whole conduct of affairs. The scheme was ambitious, yet not unpromising if the details had been properly car-

PLAN OF THE PASSAGE OF THE DOURO.

British
French

A Sherbrooke's Passage
B Paget & Hills do
C Murray's

Brigade Avintas
Murray's Division
AVINTAS
French Retreat
Storned by Soult March 1809
Candal Point
SEMINARY
OPORTO
To Braga
To Penafiel Av.
Entrenchments
To Condo
Portuguese
Soult's Position
From Minho
De Foz
R. DOURO
VILLA NOVA
From Ovar
From Grijo

ried out. The *Junta* undertook that Venegas, now in command of its army of La Mancha, should distract the attention of Sebastiani and King Joseph by a cautious demonstration against Madrid. Meanwhile Wellesley was to march up the Tagus, unite his forces with those of Cuesta, and endeavour to catch and crush Victor's corps while still isolated. He did not fear interruption from the other French armies, believing Ney and Soult to be occupied with the Galician insurrection.

On July 18 the British troops, just 20,000 strong, joined Cuesta's Estremaduran Army, which had been raised to a strength of 35,000 men, near Almaraz; and the two bodies marched in company against Victor. The marshal drew back before them, evacuated Talavera, and retired towards Madrid. Matters looked fairly well, though Cuesta had proved a very perplexing colleague. It was, however, not he, but Venegas, who ruined the campaign. That officer, instead of detaining Sebastiani in his front, remained inactive, and allowed the enemy to march away unperceived. Thus Victor, Sebastiani, and King Joseph, who had brought up the last reserves from Madrid, were able on July 26 to mass nearly 50,000 men in front of Wellesley and Cuesta, ignoring completely the army of La Mancha.

There followed the bloody Battle of Talavera, extending over the two days (July 27-28). Wellesley and Cuesta had taken up a position extending from the Tagus to a bare hill, three miles north of it. The Spaniards held the right in the town of Talavera and its suburbs and olive-groves, the British the left, partly in the plain, partly on the isolated hill which marked the end of the line. Victor, overruling King Joseph and Jourdan, who were theoretically in chief command, delivered three desperate attacks on the British position, leaving only a few thousand cavalry to contain the Spaniards. He had never before met the British, and, looking on the thin line opposed to him, exclaimed, "*si on n'enforce pas ça, il faudrait renoncer à faire la guerre*," ("if we do not enforce this, we should give up the war.")

Practically the whole of the French infantry threw themselves upon Wellesley's half of the line, with a superiority in numbers of nearly two to one. The fighting was desperate, and at one moment the British left-centre was broken. But Wellesley saved the day with his single reserve brigade; and the French drew back, leaving 17 guns and 7200 killed and wounded upon the field. The British had suffered even more heavily in proportion, losing 5300 men out of 20,000 present. The Spaniards were but slightly engaged, and their casualties were trifling.

Both armies were exhausted; and when, during the night, the

French retired from the field, Wellesley was unable to pursue them. King Joseph's position was now a dangerous one, for Venegas and the army of La Mancha had at last come up and were beginning to threaten Madrid in his rear. But an interruption from a new quarter suddenly changed the whole face of the campaign. On July 30 the news came in that Soult with a considerable force—how great no one yet knew—was marching from Salamanca on Plasencia and the middle Tagus, so as to cut the British communications with Portugal.

A few words are necessary to explain the appearance of this army upon the scene. When Soult had been driven back into Galicia in May, and had there met Ney, the two marshals had agreed to cooperate; Ney was to clear the coast-land, Soult to sweep the interior. But they were jealous and suspicious of each other's loyalty; and the joint movement was a failure. Ney was checked by the insurgents at the estuary of the Oitaben; Soult, disregarding his colleague's difficulties, made off to the south-east, and ultimately descended into the plains of Leon.

Therefore Ney, declaring that he had been betrayed and abandoned, suddenly evacuated Galicia, withdrew all his garrisons, and returned into the plains by another route. Thus, by June 30, Galicia was delivered from the French; but, on the other hand, two corps, 35,000 strong, which had been locked up in this remote corner of Spain, had returned to the valley of the Douro, and were now available for the main central operations of the summer campaign of 1809.

It was this fact that ruined Wellesley's plans for the recovery of Madrid. On hearing of the advance of the British and Estremaduran armies along the Tagus, Soult had written to King Joseph (July 19), asking for leave to fall upon the rear of the Allies, while the troops of Victor and Sebastiani were detaining them in the front. He had been given permission so to do, and had received, in addition to the two corps lately arrived from Galicia, a third, that of Mortier, which had recently been drawn back from Aragon into Old Castile. With this large body of troops, about 50,000 strong, he marched from Salamanca on July 27, the first day of the Battle of Talavera.

On July 30 Wellesley was warned that French troops were descending upon Plasencia and threatening his communications with Portugal. On August 2 he started off to fight them, believing that Soult was raiding in his rear with no more than a few divisions. But, on the following day, an intercepted despatch revealed to Wellesley and Cuesta the real strength of the approaching enemy. They at once

BRITISH GUARDS

BRITISH INFANTRY 1814

95TH RIFLEMAN

BRITISH INFANTRY SERGEANT

saw the danger of their position and retreated behind the Tagus by the bridge of Arzobispo, abandoning at Talavera 4000 wounded, for whom no transport could be procured. There was still some danger that Soult might anticipate them at Almaraz, the main passage of the Tagus; but Wellesley seized this important strategical point by a forced march (August 7), and the situation became comparatively safe. The Anglo-Spanish armies had now a broad river in front of them, and a fair line of retreat behind; and the French could no longer hope to surround them.

On August 8 Soult forced the passage of the Tagus at Arzobispo, driving off the Spanish division which tried to defend the bridge; but this was his last forward move. The only remaining incident of the campaign was that on August 11 Venegas gave battle to the king and Sebastiani at Almonacid near Toledo. He was beaten and forced back into La Mancha, with a loss of 5000 men. It is difficult to say whether he was more to blame for his culpable slowness at the commencement of the campaign, when he failed to detain the 4th corps in his front, or for his culpable rashness at the end of it, when he courted and suffered a wholly unnecessary defeat.

No further active operations occurred in central Spain till the autumn. The French Army dispersed in order to get food; and Wellesley, in equal danger of starvation at Almaraz, retired on August 20 to the valley of the Guadiana, where he remained quiescent for several months recruiting his army. Thoroughly disgusted by his experience of cooperation with Cuesta, he refused to lend himself to any of the plans for offensive action in company with the Spanish armies which the *Junta* proposed.

While the Talavera campaign was in progress, there had been sharp fighting in Aragon and Catalonia, regions in which the war always took a course wholly unaffected by the main struggle in Castile and Portugal. General Blake, having raised a new army in Valencia, had advanced in May with the object of recovering Saragossa. He was attacked (May 23) by Suchet, the new commander of the French Army of Aragon, but repulsed him in a sharp fight at Alcañiz. Continuing his advance, Blake pursued Suchet and brought him to action again at Maria just outside the gates of Saragossa. But on this occasion the Spanish Army was beaten (June 15); and, after suffering a second and more decisive defeat at Belchite (June 18), the Valencians dispersed in disorder, leaving Suchet master of the plains of Aragon.

Meanwhile, in Catalonia, Saint-Cyr had been occupied during the whole summer and autumn in the siege of the fortress of Gerona, a place of very moderate strength, but held by a gallant and resourceful governor, General Mariano Alvarez, and a garrison whose courage and endurance surpassed even the level that had been attained by the defenders of Saragossa. From May 6 to December 10, 1809, the French lay before its ramparts, keeping up an incessant bombardment and making assault after assault upon the breaches. They won the outworks, but could not penetrate into the town, till sheer starvation and incessant fighting had practically annihilated the garrison.

Blake came up from Valencia with the wreck of his army to disturb the siege but was too weak to drive off Saint-Cyr, and only succeeded in prolonging the agony of Gerona by throwing in a few convoys and some trifling reinforcements. On December 10 the place surrendered, the governor and nearly the whole of the surviving defenders being prostrate in the hospitals. From first to last the siege had cost the French 20,000 men. This was undoubtedly the most brilliant piece of service performed by the Spaniards during the whole Peninsular War.

Long before Gerona fell, the lull in the main operations in Castile, which followed upon the Battle of Talavera, had come to an end. Seeing the French passive, the Spanish Junta resolved to take the offensive again in October. They asked, but asked in vain, for the cooperation of Wellesley (now Viscount Wellington), who warned them that if their armies tried to fight general actions they would be beaten and besought them to confine their efforts to the defence of Andalusia.

Nevertheless, the *Junta* ordered a new advance on Madrid. Two forces were to take part in this scheme, starting from two remote bases. The larger consisted of the old army of La Mancha, formerly commanded by Venegas, to which had been added the greater part of the army of Estremadura. Cuesta had been invalided in August; Venegas had been disgraced after his defeat at Almonacid; and the united force was entrusted to General Areizaga, an officer more rash and decidedly more incapable than either of his predecessors. He was ordered to march on Madrid with some 50,000 men and to bear down all opposition. At the same time, del Parque, with La Romana's old army of Galicia, now counting over 20,000 bayonets, was ordered to advance into Leon, and to move on Salamanca and ultimately on Madrid.

Del Parque started first, pushed boldly forward, and met the French 6th corps, commanded by General Marchand in the absence of Ney, at Tamames near Salamanca. Taking a strong position, he awaited the attack of the enemy, and beat them off, the assailants losing an eagle and

BATTLE
OF
OCAÑA
19th November 1809.

French   Spanish
Cavalry   Infantry   Artillery
SCALES
English Miles

Ontigola

OCAÑA

First Position

Convent of San Francisco

Retreat of the Spanish Army

Dos Barrios

Cabañas

Valley of the Gigela

1500 men (October 18). Marchand was forced to evacuate Salamanca, which the Spaniards occupied. After a pause, del Parque advanced again, but found that the enemy had received reinforcements, which made him too strong to be faced. The Spanish general began to fall back but was surprised and beaten at Alba de Tormes (November 28). His army fell back, with a loss of 3000 men, partly on Galicia, partly on Ciudad Rodrigo.

The fate of Areizaga in the south was far worse. Starting from the passes of the Sierra Morena on November 3, he made a sudden dash for Madrid, driving before him at first the small French detachments which occupied La Mancha. But, having reached Ocaña near Aranjuez, only three marches from the capital, he found heavy forces gathering in his front, was stricken with sudden irresolution and indecision, and waited to be attacked by the enemy. King Joseph, having collected the corps of Mortier and Sebastiani and the Madrid reserves, fell upon him with 30,000 men on November 19, and inflicted on him a defeat less bloody, indeed, than that of Medellin, but even more disastrous. The French made no less than 18,000 prisoners; some 4000 Spaniards were killed or wounded. It took five weeks to collect the wrecks of the army in the Sierra Morena; and, even then, only 25,000 out of the 50,000 men with whom Areizaga had started could be rallied.

The rout of Ocaña sealed the fate of southern Spain. Napoleon was now free from the Austrian troubles which had absorbed his attention during the summer of 1809 and was at liberty to turn his whole attention to the Peninsula. He sent up huge reinforcements, and ordered a general advance, before the enemy should have recovered from the effects of Alba de Tormes and Ocaña. It was in his power to throw the great mass of his troops either on Seville or on Lisbon; in other words, to break the centre of the Spanish line of defence and occupy the fertile Andalusia, or to overwhelm Wellesley and drive the British out of Portugal. Fortunately for Great Britain and for Europe, the emperor chose the easier enterprise, and ordered Soult, with the corps of Victor, Sebastiani, and Mortier, to force the Sierra Morena, occupy Andalusia, and drive the Spanish Army of the south into the sea.

The conquest of Portugal was to be postponed till the next year. Accordingly, Soult led out some 70,000 men at midwinter, threw himself upon Andalusia, and in less than a fortnight overran the whole kingdom. On January 20, 1810, the passes of the Sierra Morena were forced at three points; Seville fell on January 31; and by February 4 the French advance-guard was in front of Cadiz, the only town that had

Leiria

From Coimbra and Busaco

R. Zezere
From Busaco

Ovrem

Thomar

Alcobaça

Torres Nova   Barquina

Gollega

Alcanhede

Pernes

Chamusca

Caldas

Rio Mayor

Peniche

Obidos

Azambugeira

Roliça

Rio Mayor

Santarem

El Valle

Cercal

Lourinha

Alcoentre   Cartaxo

Mte. Junto

Vimiero

R. Tagus

Torres Vedras

S. Barannueda

NEY

Otta   Villada

R. Zizundre

Runa   Alemquer

JUNOT   Carregada

Sobral   Cacafaes

Zibreirao   Enxara

REYNER   Villa Franca

ROMANA   Aruda

Alhandra

Mafra

Bucellas

S. Lorenzo

S. Seures   Quintella

Cintra

LISBON   Aldea Gallega

R. Tagus

LINES OF EMBARCATION

Almada

FORT ST. JULIAN

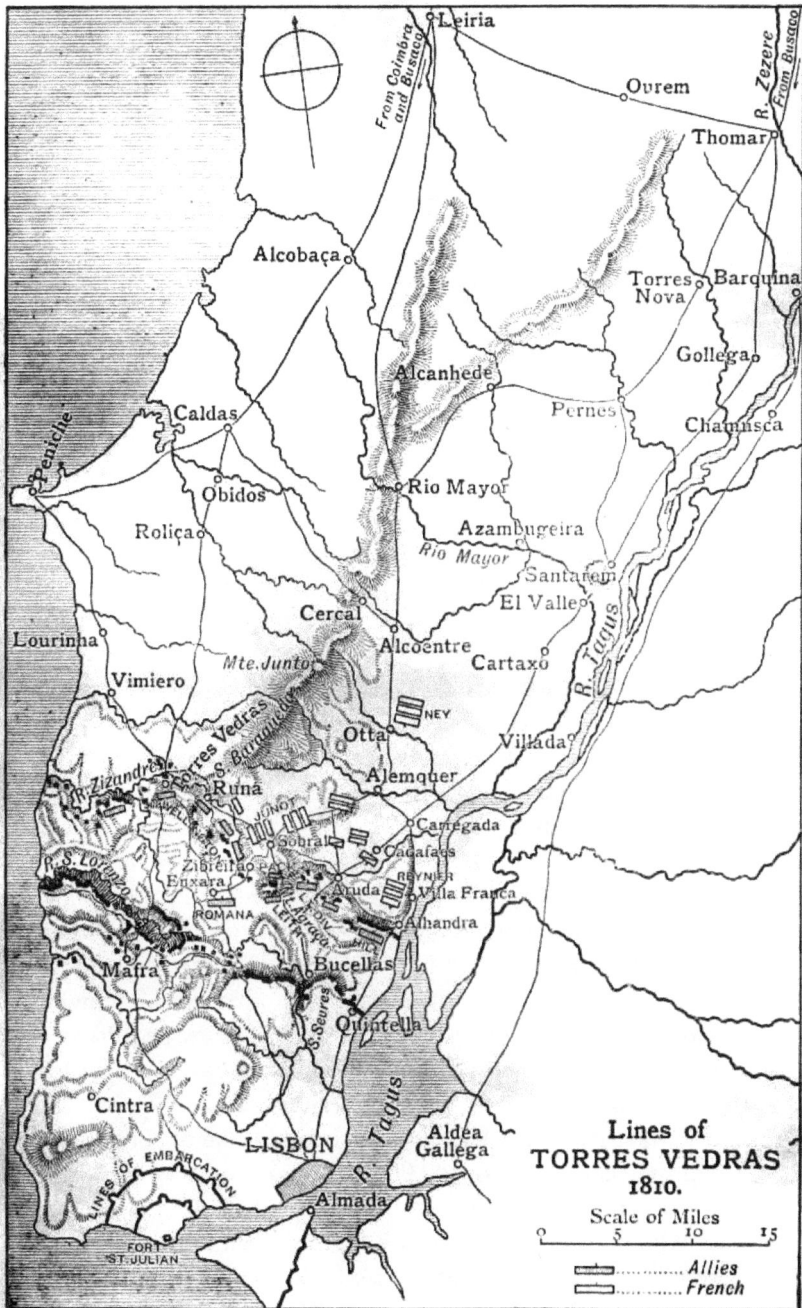

Lines of
TORRES VEDRAS
1810.

Scale of Miles
0   5   10   15

Allies
French

not been submerged by the flood of invasion. The demoralised troops of Areizaga had dispersed or fled into Murcia; and Cadiz itself was only saved by the Duke of Albuquerque, who threw himself into the town with 10,000 men from Estremadura just before Victor arrived.

CHAPTER 9

Wellington

The loss of Andalusia appeared the crowning disaster of the whole war; and many observers, both French and English, thought that the end was at hand. But it was really a blessing in disguise; the whole Imperial field-army available for offensive operations was absorbed by the tasks of garrisoning the newly conquered kingdom and of besieging Cadiz. No surplus troops remained for an attack on Portugal; and meanwhile Wellington was preparing the defence of that realm with a thoroughness which no one suspected. He had completed its regular army, drilled and armed some scores of thousands of militia, and got well to work on the famous lines of Torres Vedras, against which the advancing wave of French invasion was to surge in vain during the ensuing year. In short, the seven additional months of preparation which were granted for the organisation of the defence of Portugal were all-important.

There was a long gap in the offensive operations of the French between the conquest of Andalusia and the commencement of the invasion of Portugal. The former enterprise had been completed in February, 1810; the latter did not begin till August. The reason of this delay was that the emperor waited till the spring before sending across the Pyrenees the reinforcements from Germany, which were to form the bulk of the army destined for the march on Lisbon. Nearly 100,000 troops were ultimately poured into the Peninsula for this purpose, including two new corps, the 8th and 9th, under Junot and Drouet, 20,000 men of the Imperial Guard, and many other smaller units. For the command of the whole, Marshal Masséna, lately created Prince of Essling for his services on the Danube, had been selected. The Emperor's choice was good, for despite his personal faults—he was selfish, greedy, and quarrelsome—Masséna was more capable of conducting a great campaign at the head of 100,000 men than any other of the marshals. He took up his command at Valladolid on May 15, 1810.

Meanwhile Soult, in the far south, was busy with the siege of Cadiz. It was an unpromising enterprise; for the town, situated at the point of a peninsula projecting far into the sea, and separated from the mainland by a broad creek, is almost impregnable without the assistance of a fleet. It was to little purpose that the French bombarded the outlying defences at long range. Cadiz was "observed" rather than besieged; and Victor's corps had always to be left in front of it. That of Sebastiani lay at Granada and Malaga, charged with the duty of keeping down the insurgents of the Sierras and watching the Spanish army of Murcia. For further offensive operations Soult could only count on Mortier's corps; the emperor had directed that he was to use it, when Masséna was ready to start the main attack on Portugal, for the reduction of Badajoz and Elvas, and finally for an invasion of the Alemtejo which would take Lisbon in the rear.

But Masséna was long in moving; and Soult waited for the signal without impatience, being well content to devote himself to organising the civil government of Andalusia—a profitable vice-royalty for one who loved money and was an indefatigable and unscrupulous collector of works of art.

In the eastern parts of the Peninsula the war during the spring of 1810 did not stand still, as in the south; but it was inconclusive in its results. Suchet, having reduced the plains of Aragon to obedience, risked an advance against Valencia with a column of 12,000 men, a force too small for the enterprise. He was repulsed (March 5-10) and forced by the news of fresh revolts in Aragon to retire to Saragossa. Warned by this check that he must not go too far afield till he had made all safe in his rear, Suchet now turned his attention to the reduction of the fortresses on the borders of Aragon and Catalonia, and speedily captured Lerida (May 14) and Mequinenza (June 8).

He had now won his way far down the Ebro valley; and one further push would take him to the sea and enable him to cut the communications between Valencia and Catalonia. Meanwhile Augereau, who had replaced Saint-Cyr in Catalonia in time to receive the surrender of Gerona in December, 1809, fared far worse in the new year. His only success was the capture of the petty mountain fortress of Hostalrich (May, 1810), while his failures were many; for the Catalans were obstinate and enterprising, and their general, O'Donnell, was a man of resource. So many of Augereau's outlying detachments were cut off, and so many of his enterprises proved fruitless, that early in the summer the emperor recalled him to France in disgrace, sending Macdonald, Duc de Taranto, to supersede him.

But events in Aragon and Catalonia were unimportant compared with the great invasion of Portugal, which was just about to commence. At no period of the struggle did matters look so hopeful for the French as at this moment. Masséna had under him 130,000 men, of whom three corps (the 2nd, 6th, and 8th), over 70,000 strong, were to form the actual field-army; while the 9th corps and other troops guarded the plains of Leon in his rear, and the Imperial Guard came up to occupy Navarre and Old Castile. This seemed an overwhelming force to turn against Wellington, who had less than 30,000 British bayonets and sabres, about the same force of Portuguese regulars, and a mass of native militia useless in the field and only fit for raids and bickerings in the mountains.

Moreover, the British general had always to guard against the chance of a separate invasion of the Alemtejo by Soult, far in his rear. To aid him there were two weak Spanish armies, the remnants of del Parque's old force—one in Galicia, the other in Estremadura near Badajoz; together these forces did not muster 25,000 men, and they were much demoralised by their late defeats. Neither gave any profitable assistance during the campaign in Portugal.

When Masséna began his advance, the two Castiles, with Aragon and Andalusia, were quiet. The guerilla bands which afterwards troubled them had not yet developed their strength; and the French garrisons were so strong that no corner of central Spain was left unguarded. In this summer there were no less than 370,000 French troops in the Peninsula—a larger number than was ever seen before or after. Everywhere, save in Catalonia, the Spaniards seemed discouraged; and it appeared probable that one further effort would drive them to despair and surrender. The Supreme Junta, which had hitherto conducted the war, had become so unpopular that it resigned its powers to a Regency of five members on February 2. But the new government, if not so arrogant and unteachable as the old, inspired little confidence. Had the invasion of Portugal proved successful, there would have been no power of resistance left in Galicia, in Cadiz, in Valencia, or even in Catalonia; and the war would have ere long flickered out.

Masséna had resolved not to start on his great enterprise till all the troops from Germany were nearing the front; and some of them, especially the 9th corps, were still far in the rear. He had also resolved to secure his base of operations in Leon, by capturing the fortresses of north-western Spain, before he crossed the frontier of Portugal. Astorga, the outer bulwark of Galicia, had fallen on April 22, after an honourable defence. The greater stronghold of Ciudad Rodrigo made an even more creditable resistance, its governor, Herrasti, holding out from April 25 till July 10 against all the efforts of Ney.

His laudable tenacity caused the invasion of Portugal to be postponed till August, to the satisfaction of Wellington, who needed every moment that he could gain for the organisation of his defence. He had refused to risk a battle for the relief of Ciudad Rodrigo, though pressed to do so both by the Spaniards and by some of his own officers; his forces were not yet strong enough to face the French in the plains, and lay distributed along the hills of the Portuguese frontier, observing the enemy from a distance.

It was not till August 24 that Masséna crossed the Coa at the head of the main body of his army. He then laid siege to Almeida, the fortress which protects north-eastern Portugal against attacks from the side of Spain. It was defended by a good native garrison under an English governor, Colonel Cox; and Wellington had expected it to delay the enemy as long as Ciudad Rodrigo. But on the third day of the siege a shell exploded the main powder-magazine; nearly the whole town was destroyed; and Cox was forced to surrender next day (August 27). Having mastered Almeida with such unexpected ease, Masséna called up all his columns, 63,000 strong, collected his stores and provisions, and advanced into Portugal on September 15.

On plunging into the interior of Portugal, Masséna was surprised to find the whole country-side, and even the larger towns, completely deserted by their inhabitants. This was the first intimation that he received of Wellesley's new and original scheme of defence. He had obtained from the Portuguese Regency permission to order all the people of the invaded districts to retire from their homes after destroying all their food-stuffs. The wealthier classes were to make their way to Lisbon or Oporto; the rest to take refuge in the mountains, or in regions to which the French columns could not easily penetrate. Knowing that Napoleon's armies relied chiefly on local requisitions, he rightly supposed that such a device would soon reduce the invader to great distress.

Meanwhile he had prepared a secure refuge for his own army, by constructing across the neck of the peninsula on which Lisbon stands the celebrated lines of Torres Vedras. These were not mere field entrenchments, but solid closed works connected by ditches and palisades, and furnished with ample provision of heavy guns from the Lisbon arsenal. Skilled engineers, aided by the whole of the able-bodied peasantry of Estremadura, had been at work on them for more than half a year; and they were now perfectly complete. The first line was

29, the second 22 miles long from sea to sea; they included 126 closed redoubts, defended by 427 pieces of artillery. The ground in front of them had been cleared of all cover, and on the more exposed points the slopes had been scarped away.

Finally, to provide against the possible but unlikely contingency of the lines being pierced, a third series of fortifications had been built at the mouth of the Tagus, to allow the army to embark in safety in the event of disaster. A very large force would be required to man so long a front. Wellington had arranged that the whole British Army, nearly 30,000 strong, five-sixths of the Portuguese regulars (a force of about the same strength), and some 20,000 Lisbon and Estremaduran militia should hold the lines.

He even borrowed during the autumn 7000 Spanish troops from the army of La Romana, which lay at Badajoz, so that, in the end, he could count on nearly 100,000 men for the defence, though a large proportion of them were of inferior material.

But this was not the whole of Wellington's plan. The militia of northern and central Portugal were not taken inside the lines but were ordered to wait till the French Army should have passed on into the interior, and then to cut its communications, harass its rear, and enclose it in a net of mobile columns. They were directed to avoid all serious fighting with large forces, but to destroy stragglers and de-tachments, cut off convoys, and prevent the enemy from foraging far afield. If Masséna dropped small garrisons to guard the more impor-tant points on his line of advance, they would be cut off and destroyed. If he kept his whole army in a mass, he would move on in a sort of perpetual blockade, with an active but intangible enemy hemming him in on all sides.

When he reached the lines of Torres Vedras and was forced to stop, he would find himself the besieged rather than the besieger. The main difficulty in Wellington's plan was the dreadful sacrifice imposed on the peasantry of central Portugal, who were asked to quit their houses and destroy their provisions in the face of approaching winter. But a combination of patriotism and wholesome fear of the marauding propensities of the French sufficed to cause the orders of the Regency and the commander-in-chief to be carried out.

Masséna was entirely unprepared for the tactics used against him. He imagined that he had but to win a battle somewhere in front of Lisbon, and so to compel the British to embark; the capital and the whole kingdom of Portugal would then be his own. He advanced through northern Beira for ten days, while the army of Wellington re-tired before him, refusing to commit itself to a fight. The route which he had taken, to the north of the Mondego, by way of Vizeu, at last brought him in front of the position of Busaco, where the main road to Coimbra and Lisbon crosses a range of precipitous heights.

On this commanding ridge, which overlooks all the upland of cen-tral Portugal on one side, and the plain of Coimbra on the other, Wel-lington stood at bay; he did not intend to make a permanent defence of the position, well knowing that it could be turned on the left, but merely to check the French if they should venture on a direct attack. His troops were eager for a fight, and he was anxious to indulge them if it could be done without risk. It would be useful too, from the po-litical point of view, to retire to the lines of Torres Vedras only after having won a victory which should impress public opinion.

Masséna acted much as Wellington had hoped. He had never be-fore seen a British Army in battle, and thought that this might be driven, by a vigorous attack in column, even from such ground as that which lay in front of the convent of Busaco. He had a distinct superi-ority in numbers—about 59,000 men to 50,000—and knew that half his opponent's army was composed of Portuguese, for whom he had a supreme contempt. Accordingly, on September 27, he launched Ney's corps against Wellington's left-centre, and Reynier's against his right-centre, keeping Junot's in reserve to clench the victory. The two great columns of assault were directed against the least precipitous parts of the English position; but even here the slope was steep; and, when the French had toiled to the summit under heavy musketry fire, their order was broken and their impetus spent.

Charged vigorously by Craufurd's light division on the left, and by Picton's 3rd division on the right, they were rolled down the hill in fearful disorder and with great loss. The actual clash of battle hardly lasted an hour, but the French lost five generals and 4400 men killed and wounded. Wellington's casualties were less than 1300; and only a third part of his army had been engaged. It was a matter of im-mense relief and encouragement that the Portuguese line regiments had stood perfectly steady and had contributed their fair share to the victory. After this Wellington knew that he could safely trust them in line of battle—a piece of knowledge which well-nigh doubled his fighting power.

Having suffered this well-earned punishment for trying to "rush" a British Army securely posted in a good position, Masséna took the obvious step of turning Wellington's left wing by the circuitous road through Boialva. His opponent had expected this move, and promptly resumed his retreat, evacuated Coimbra, and fell back towards the lines. The marshal occupied the deserted town, where he found foodstuffs, that had not been properly destroyed, in quantity sufficient to enable him to resume his advance (October 1).

Now that he had reached this point, prudence seemed to demand that he should establish a new base at Coimbra and leave a division to guard it and to care for the 5000 sick and wounded who now encumbered his march. But Masséna felt that he would require every available man for the battle in front of Lisbon which he believed to be impending. Accordingly, he took the rash step of leaving all his sick and wounded at Coimbra under the guard of half a battalion, and with the remainder of his army hurried on in pursuit of the British (October 4). The nemesis for this blunder was not long in coming. On October 7 Colonel Trant, the commander of the nearest militia brigade, learning of the smallness of the force at Coimbra, surprised the place at dawn, and captured both the garrison and the men in hospital, 5000 in all.

Wellington's army passed within the lines on October 11, escorting the whole population of northern Estremadura, which moved down to take refuge in and about Lisbon. On the following morning Masséna's columns came up; the marshal had only heard of the existence of the lines five days before and was even now unaware of their strength. But when he had surveyed them with his own eyes and had made one or two tentative attacks on some of the outlying positions, he recognised the hopelessness of his situation. He had now not much over 50,000 men left and saw that it would be insane to risk an attack with such a force.

His provisions were running out, and the Beira militia had closed in upon his rear, so that he commanded no more ground than that on which his three army corps were encamped. His communications with Almeida and Ciudad Rodrigo had long been cut; and he had not the least idea what was going on in Leon, or whether his reserves were on their way to join him. Nevertheless, he remained for a month in front of the lines, hoping against hope for some chance to make a successful assault, and then retired to Santarem, thirty miles up the Tagus. He despatched, meanwhile, letters to the emperor begging for instant aid, lest all the results of his campaign should be lost.

In and about Santarem the French Army abode from November

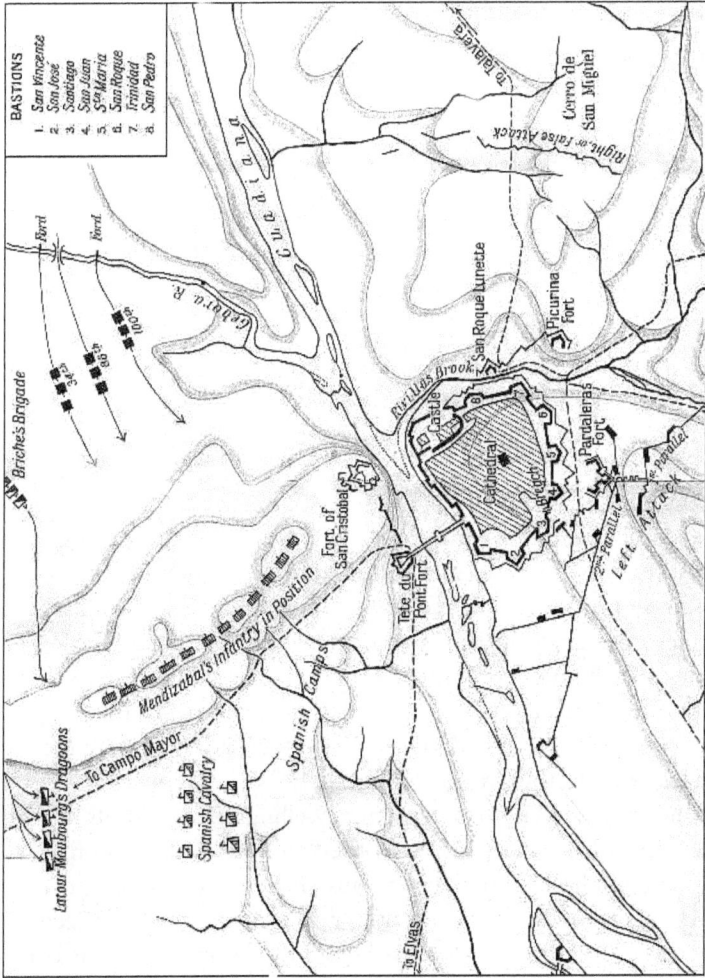

FIRST SIEGE OF BADAJOZ AND GEBORA

15, 1810, to March 5, 1811, obstinately refusing to retire, though by the end of that time it was suffering from sheer starvation. When the resources of the region had been eaten up, the army had to live by pushing marauding columns into the surrounding districts—columns which were always opposed and often destroyed by the Portuguese militia. Wellington refrained from attack; for hunger was doing the work of the sword, and the invading army dwindled day by day.

Masséna had hoped for more effective assistance from Soult, who, according to the emperor's orders, was to cooperate in the attack on Lisbon by advancing into the Alemtejo and threatening the Portuguese capital from the south. But Soult's, movements were begun too late; he had no love for Masséna and refused to hurry. He came up with a single corps, the 5th under Mortier, into Estremadura, and prepared to capture Badajoz as a preliminary to the advance into Portugal. On February 19 he destroyed the Spanish Army of Estremadura at the Battle of the Gebora, and then began to press the siege of Badajoz. The place made a weak defence and was surrendered by its cowardly or treacherous governor Imas on March 10.

Five days earlier Masséna had in despair abandoned Santarem and started on his weary retreat to Ciudad Rodrigo across the mountains of central Beira. The army of Portugal would have perished if it had remained a fortnight longer in its advanced position. It was now in a desperate plight; nearly all the horses were dead; the men, demoralised by long privations, left the colours in thousands and hunted the Portuguese peasantry in the mountains in the search for food. The atrocities which they committed on these marauding tours surpass description and brought about horrible retaliation on all French parties surprised by the natives. Prisoners on either side who were merely shot were thought to have got off lightly.

On hearing of Masséna's departure, Wellington started off in pursuit with five divisions, giving two others to Beresford, with orders to march through the Alemtejo into Spanish Estremadura, and, if possible, to relieve Badajoz. Beresford's march, however, was made fruitless by the surrender of Badajoz two days before the army of succour could reach its vicinity. Masséna's retreat from Santarem to Ciudad Rodrigo occupied just a month (March 5—April 4), and was conducted with great skill. Ney, who took charge of the rear-guard, fought a long series of partial actions to detain the British van, but nearly always drew off just in time to escape serious loss. The only occasion on which the French were severely punished was at Sabugal (April 3), where the

British light division surprised the 2nd corps in a fog and killed or wounded more than 1000 men.

The French Army had entered Portugal on September 15, 1810, with some 63,000 sabres and bayonets, and had received some 6000 or 7000 men in reinforcements while at Santarem. When it recrossed the frontier on April 5, it mustered only 45,000 men. Masséna therefore had lost some 25,000 men during the seven months of his campaign—far more by sickness and starvation than by the sword, for he had fought only one general action, that of Busaco, and a dozen combats, in none of which (save Sabugal) the casualty list was heavy. He had been dislodged from Portugal, not by force but by Wellesley's use of the terrible weapon of hunger. The price that the Allies had paid for their success was no insignificant one; a broad strip of central Portugal had been reduced to a desert, and many thousands of its inhabitants had perished.

But thereby the rest of the realm had been saved; and the end was well worth the sacrifice. For the moral effect of Masséna's defeat was enormous; the emperor had sent forth his lieutenant, with much pomp and circumstance of war, to "drive the leopards into the sea." The whole of Europe had been summoned, as it were, to look upon the spectacle of the punishment of the English for their rash attempt to defend a section of the Continent against the invincible French arms. For many months the fall of Lisbon had been prophesied; and Masséna's checks and miseries had been carefully concealed. When the wrecks of the army of Portugal fell back on Ciudad Rodrigo, the facts could no longer be kept secret. The offensive power of the French hosts in Spain was spent; and it may be said that the retreat which began at Santarem only ceased at Toulouse.

During the six months which Masséna spent in Portugal, the course of the war in the other regions of the Peninsula was on the whole favourable to the French. The successful operations of Soult, described above, were carried out in spite of a strong diversion which the Allies conducted on the side of Cadiz. That place was full of troops, including an Anglo-Portuguese division of nearly 5000 men under General Graham. The Spanish Government was anxious to make what use it could of this accumulation of forces.

Power at Cadiz was no longer in the hands of the Regency which had been appointed in February, 1810: a Cortes, or national parliament, had been summoned to meet on September 24. It was not a very representative body, since many provinces were in the hands of

BATTLE OF

BARROSA.

5th March 1811.

A M. SPENCER R.E. C.E.

REFERENCES.

Cavalry ▭ Allies. Infantry ▬ Artillery ▬ French ▬

SCALE.

Military Steps 75 Feet each.

English Mile.

Miles.

Positions before and after the battle coloured light

BATTLE OF BARROSA

the French, and the delegates who sat for these regions had not really been chosen by the people. But it was energetic and vigorous, if too much given to ill-timed discussions. The Spanish Liberals had a predominance in it; and the "*serviles*" or partisans of absolute monarchy were in a decided minority.

When the news of the departure of Soult and the 5th corps for the siege of Badajoz became known at Cadiz, the Spaniards were eager that something should be done to disturb the small army under Victor which was blockading the city. Accordingly, in February, 1811, a Spanish force of 9000 men under General La Peña, accompanied by 4000 British under Graham, was sent down the coast to Tarifa on shipboard, and put ashore with the object of attacking the French lines from the flank and rear. The expedition was not quite large enough for the end in view; for Victor had nearly 20,000 men dispersed along his front, and, without entirely evacuating his redoubts and batteries, could gather a force sufficient to turn back La Peña and Graham. The Anglo-Spanish Army marched for three days along the coast, and on March 5 reached the heights of Barrosa, overhanging the southern extremity of the French lines.

Here Victor, aware of their approach, had gathered all the available troops of the 1st corps. He sent one of his three incomplete divisions to demonstrate against the Spaniards, who formed the head of the Allies' long column of march, and fell with the other two upon the British, who formed its rear. La Peña allowed himself to be overawed by the few thousand men on his flank, and sent no aid to Graham, who had to fight a battle of his own, with about 4500 men opposed to 7000. Nothing daunted, the British general turned about, and fell upon the advancing columns with desperate resolution, though he had to attack uphill. Once more the line proved too strong for the column; and Graham's musketry shattered and drove off the French with a loss of 2000 men, six guns, and an eagle, his own casualties amounting to 1100 killed and wounded.

La Pena, in spite of his colleague's urgent entreaties, refused to send him cavalry or reinforcements, or even to take up the pursuit of the routed force. Indignant at this desertion, Graham led his troops back to Cadiz. La Pena followed two days later. The two generals entered on a campaign of wrangling; and the expedition, which might have wrecked half the French lines, came to an ignominious end. No more was attempted on the side of Cadiz for some months.

Meanwhile, in eastern Spain, Suchet was cooperating with Macdonald, who had superseded Augereau in command of the army of Catalonia. Their main object was to capture Tortosa, and so to block the communications between Catalonia and Valencia and cut the Spanish defence in two. In December, 1810, Macdonald, though much harassed by the indomitable Catalans, succeeded in pushing southward, and placed himself in a position from which he could cover the siege of Tortosa, while the actual attack was confided to Suchet and the army of Aragon. The operations were conducted with Suchet's usual decision and activity; the defence was so feeble as to cause not unnatural suspicions of treachery; and Tortosa fell on January 1, 1811, after holding out for less than three weeks.

This was a serious blow to the patriotic cause; Catalonia was henceforward isolated, and only kept in touch with the other unsubdued Spanish provinces by means of the British ships ever hovering about its coast. Yet it showed no signs of weakening in its defence; indeed, the most daring exploit of the Catalans during the whole war was carried out in the spring following the fall of Tortosa.

On April 9 the bands of its northern border took by surprise the great fortress of Figueras, which commands the road from France to Gerona and Barcelona. Macdonald had at once to depart with the larger half of his army to attempt the recovery of this important place. Meanwhile the emperor ordered Suchet to take charge of the conquest of southern Catalonia and assigned to him the remainder of Macdonald's troops. Thus strengthened, he was ordered to lay siege to Tarragona, the one great seaport of that region still in Spanish hands, and the rallying-point and arsenal of the Catalan Army.

Suchet, leaving Macdonald to shift for himself in front of Figueras, concentrated every man for this enterprise, and sat down before Tarragona on May 4. Contreras, the governor, made an honourable defence; but the place was stormed on June 28, and sacked from cellar to garret, with much unnecessary bloodshed among the civil population. The loss to Spain was great; and the surviving Catalan divisions had to take to the hills since the last of their seaports was gone. Yet still they held out, and the province remained unsubdued.

We must now return to the operations of Masséna and Wellington. When the Prince of Essling recoiled across the Spanish frontier on April 5, the only fruits remaining to him from his nine months' campaign were the two fortresses of Ciudad Rodrigo and Almeida. While the French Army was refitting in the neighbourhood of Salamanca, Wellington laid siege to Almeida. The marshal had to make his choice between allowing it to fall unsuccoured or leading forward his exhausted army once more in the hope of raising the siege.

As might have been expected from his indomitable temper, he chose the latter alternative. But, seeing that his cavalry was almost destroyed, and that he could not horse half his guns, he made a desperate appeal to his colleague Bessières, the commander of the army of the north, to aid him with all his artillery, and as many squadrons as he could concentrate. The younger marshal showed no great zeal for the enterprise but brought 1500 horse and a single battery to Ciudad Rodrigo on May 1. With this small auxiliary force, and the whole surviving strength of the army of Portugal, some 39,000 sabres and bayonets, Masséna marched on Almeida.

On May 3 he found Wellington's army, about 34,000 strong, arrayed across his path on the heights of Fuentes d'Oñoro. On the first day of battle Masséna endeavoured to force back the British line by a frontal attack; he failed, and after waiting a day despatched half of his troops to turn Wellington's right flank by a *détour* to the south. On May 5 the struggle was resumed; again, the assault on the British front was repelled, but the turning column forced back the extreme southern wing of the allied army and compelled its general to throw back part of his line on to new ground. Here he stood to receive a third attack; but Masséna dared not deliver it. His ammunition had run short; his troops were exhausted; and his colleague Bessières and his corps-commanders were unwilling to persevere with the attempt to relieve Almeida. He was forced to abandon the place to its own resources and drew off on May 8.

In the two fights he had lost nearly 3000 men, Wellington not more than 1800. Brennier, the commandant of Almeida, on hearing of the result of the battle, blew up the walls of his fortress and sallied out at midnight (May 11) with his garrison, to cut his way through the lines of the besiegers. His courage was rewarded by success, and he escaped with two-thirds of his force to Masséna's outposts. But Almeida, the last hold of the French in Portugal, was lost; and Masséna had fought to save the place, not the garrison.

The marshal's career had now come to an end. Napoleon, dissatisfied with his conduct of the campaign of Portugal, observed that "Masséna had grown old," and superseded him by the young and ambitious Marmont, who had still his spurs to win as the commander of a large army. The new chief arrived at the front on May 6 and took over the charge of the army of Portugal on the 12th. His first action was to disperse his exhausted divisions into cantonments in the province of Salamanca, where they began to repair the losses they had suffered during the late campaign.

The state of the French Army was not concealed from Wellington, who resolved to utilise the enemy's enforced leisure for a raid into Estremadura, and an attempt to capture Badajoz. Leaving four divisions on the Portuguese frontier opposite Marmont's army (May 15), he marched with two to join Marshal Beresford and the force which had been detached against Soult at the moment of Masséna's retreat from Santarem. But, before he could arrive, matters had come to a head in this quarter, and a battle had been fought. Beresford had marched from Lisbon into Estremadura at the end of March. His operations were dilatory; and it was not till May 5 that he succeeded in driving off the 5th corps, which Soult had left on the Guadiana, and in investing Badajoz. The remains of the Spanish Army which had been crushed at the Gebora, and other troops sent from Cadiz, now came to his aid, under Castaños and Blake.

On May 10, after receiving news of the investment of Badajoz, Soult marched from Seville with the reserves of the army of Andalusia, and on May 15 presented himself with 23,000 men in front of the position of Albuera, where the allied army stood prepared to dispute his passage. Beresford had drawn off his army from the trenches three days before and had concentrated nearly 32,000 men; but of these less than 8000 were British. Nor was his fighting-ground well-chosen; his front was covered only by a brook everywhere fordable; and dense woods on the further bank prevented him from discerning the enemy's movements.

At dawn on May 16 Soult delivered his attack against the flank and not the front of the Allies. Crossing the stream high up, under the cover of the woods, he fell unexpectedly upon Beresford's right wing, which was composed entirely of Spanish troops. While endeavouring to change their front, Blake's regiments gave way; but Beresford came up with the British 2nd division and attacked the head of the French column. At the moment when the troops were closing, a furious rain-storm swept over the hill-side; and, under cover of it, a brigade of French light cavalry charged in upon the flank and rear of the British and absolutely annihilated the three leading battalions.

The surviving seven battalions of the 2nd division maintained for a long time a desperate musketry-battle with the 5th corps, in which neither side gained an inch. Soult's rear brigades were coming up, and

Beresford flinched and thought of retreat; but he was persuaded by Colonel Hardinge to throw into the fight his last troops, three British and three Portuguese regiments of the 4th division. Myers' fusiliers thrust aside Soult's reserve, and falling upon the flank of the 5th corps drove it off the field. This struggle was the most bloody incident of the whole Peninsular War; on both sides the infantry had maintained the battle at close quarters, and had fallen by companies and battalions as they stood.

Over 6000 French were killed or wounded; but their proportion of casualties was as nothing to that of the British, who lost 4100 men out of less than 8000 present. The Portuguese had about 400 killed and wounded, the Spaniards 1000, so that the total casualties among the Allies were not much less than those of the enemy. They had also lost a gun, five standards, and 500 prisoners. But the object of the battle had been achieved, in spite of Beresford's unskilful management; after lingering for another day in front of his adversary's position, Soult retreated towards Andalusia, leaving 1000 of his severely wounded to the mercy of the Allies. The victors therefore were able to resume the siege of Badajoz on May 20.

When Wellington arrived from the north and assumed command in Estremadura, he resolved to press the siege with vigour. But his engineers were unskilful; his Portuguese battering train was both small and weak; and two assaults were beaten off with loss.

On June 12 he was obliged to retire from before the well-defended fortress, for Marmont had united his whole army and marched southward to join Soult. The British divisions left near Almeida had executed a march parallel to that of the French Army of Portugal; but, even when they had been united to the force in Estremadura, Wellington had not the numbers to face the two marshals combined in the open field. He therefore retired to the Portuguese frontier, and took up a position behind the Caya River, which he strengthened with fieldworks; here he waited with 50,000 men in line, inviting an attack. Soult and Marmont had brought 62,000 men to relieve Badajoz, but only by stripping Leon and Andalusia of their garrisons, and leaving their rear exposed to the incursions of the Spaniards.

From June 22 till July 4 the two marshals lay in front of the Caya, threatening an attack. These twelve days were the most critical period of the campaign, for hardly ever again were the French in a position to assail Wellington with superior numbers and force him to fight for the safety of Portugal. But they held back, and on July 4 Soult marched

Spanish Entrenchment

St.Domingo

St.Francisco

Light
Division

Pack's
Portuguese

Fausse Braie

Salamanca gate

St Jago gate

Spanish Teson

Great Teson

Small Breach

3rd.Division

Grt.Breach

Castle

Fort
Francisco

Sap

Colonel O'Toole
Cazadores

Santa Cruz

4th

A g u e d a   R i v e r

77th.

5th.

Siege of
CIUDAD RODRIGO
1812.

away to save Seville from an attack by Blake. Marmont, too weak to fight without his colleague's assistance, drew off to the valley of the Tagus; and the crisis in Estremadura came to an end.

Seeing no immediate hope of resuming the siege of Badajoz, for a movement against it would have brought back both Soult and Marmont to the Guadiana, Wellington resolved to transfer his main force back to the north, and to threaten Ciudad Rodrigo. On Aug. 1 he set out for Almeida and Sabugal with six divisions, leaving two in Estremadura. Beresford was not again trusted with the command of this independent corps; and the detachment placed to observe Soult was committed for the future to the charge of a cautious and steady general, Sir Rowland Hill. On arriving near Ciudad Rodrigo, Wellington began preparations for the siege; but the battering train, which was to come from Oporto, was still far off, and for some weeks he could do no more than blockade the fortress from a distance.

This demonstration, however, was enough to call Marmont out of his cantonments; assembling his whole army, he left the valley of the Tagus and called to his aid Dorsenne, who had lately succeeded Bessières in the command of the army of the north. More zealous than his predecessor had been at the time of Fuentes d'Oñoro, Dorsenne came up with four strong divisions; and, when the two armies joined near Salamanca on Sept. 21, they mustered 60,000 sabres and bayonets. Against such a force Wellington could do nothing, as he was inferior in numbers by nearly a third. Without firing a shot, he allowed Ciudad Rodrigo to be relieved (Sept. 25), and retired into the Portuguese mountains.

The enemy followed hard upon his steps; and he was forced to cover his retreat by two rear-guard actions, at El Bodon (Sept. 25) and Aldea de Ponte (Sept. 27). On the 28th Wellington had concentrated his army in a strong position in front of Sabugal, where the ground was so much in his favour that he dared to offer battle. Marmont and Dorsenne, being without the provisions and transport which would have justified them in commencing a serious invasion of Portugal, refused to attack. They retired after revictualling Ciudad Rodrigo and dispersed their armies into winter quarters. Wellington at once came down again from the heights and resumed the blockade of the fortress. But he was not in a position to press it closely so long as the roads and the weather were favourable to the reconcentration of the enemy; he lay for two months awaiting the moment when a *coup de main* would be practicable.

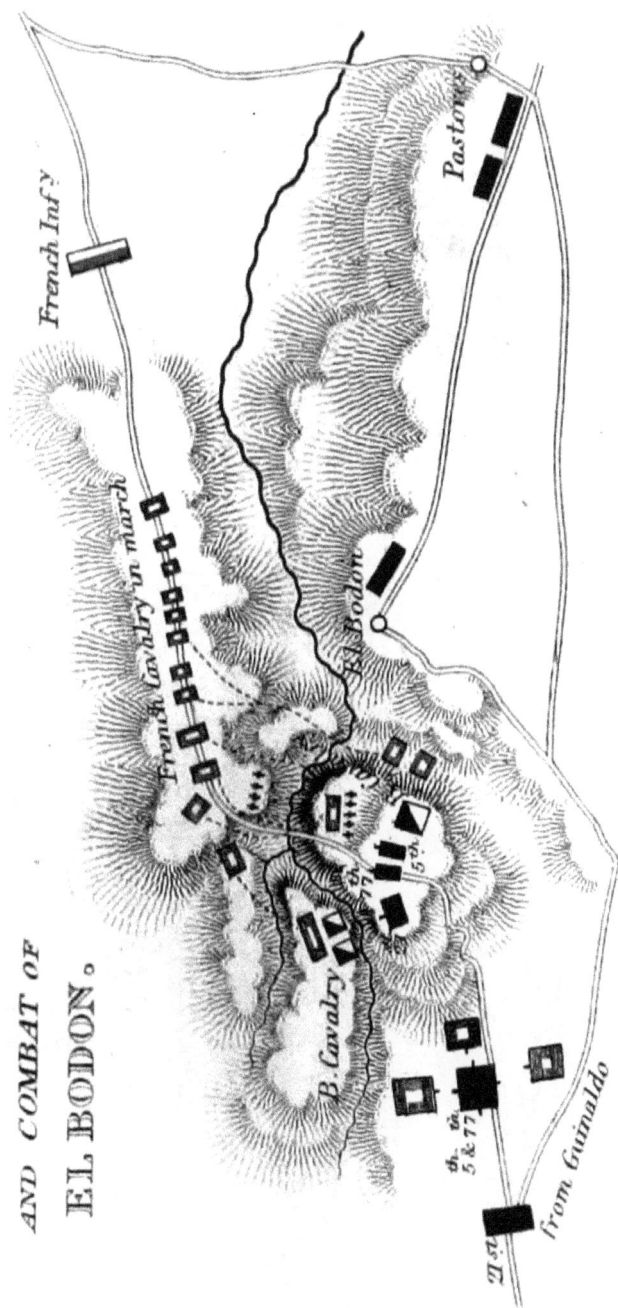

EXPLANATORY SKETCH
AND COMBAT OF
EL BODON.

French Inf.ª

Pastores

French Cavalry in march

El Bodon

B. Cavalry

77.ᵗʰ

5.ᵗʰ

th. th.
5 & 77

71.ˢᵗ

from Guinaldo

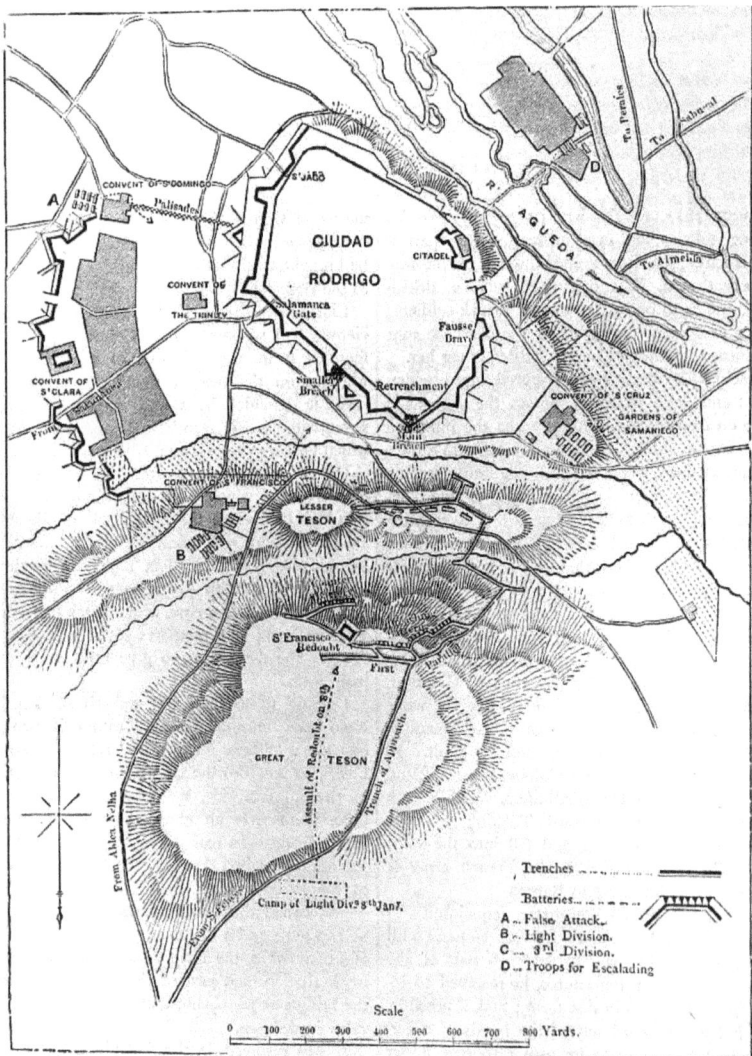

PLAN OF THE ASSAULT ON CIUDAD RODRIGO.

THE SECOND SIEGE OF CIUDAD RODRIGO

THE SECOND SIEGE OF BADAJOZ

Thus, the main series of operations in Spain came to an end in October. The French offensive was spent; neither north nor south of the Tagus had their commanders dared to resume the invasion of Portugal, even when they had collected an imposing force and greatly outnumbered Wellington's field-army. To concentrate such masses for a serious campaign, they were forced to strip the provinces in their rear; and, when those regions were left ungarrisoned, they lapsed at once into insurrection. Soult could not quit Andalusia, nor Marmont Leon and the Tagus valley, for more than a few weeks, under pain of seeing the country behind them aflame. Enormous as was the force—over 300,000 men—which the emperor had thrown into Spain, it was still not strong enough to hold down the conquered provinces and at the same time to attack Portugal.

For this fact the Spaniards must receive due credit; it was their indomitable spirit of resistance which enabled Wellington, with his small Anglo-Portuguese Army, to keep the field against such largely superior numbers. No sooner had the French concentrated, and abandoned a district, than there sprang up in it a local *Junta* and a ragged apology for an army. Even where the invaders lay thickest, along the route from Bayonne to Madrid, guerilla bands maintained themselves in the mountains, cut off couriers and escorts, and often isolated one French army from another for weeks at a time.

The greater partisan chiefs, such as Mina in Navarre, Julian Sanchez in Leon, and Porlier in the Cantabrian hills, kept whole brigades of the French in constant employment. Often beaten, they were never destroyed, and always reappeared to strike some daring blow at the point where they were least expected. Half the French Army was always employed in the fruitless task of guerilla-hunting. This was the secret which explains the fact that, with 300,000 men under arms, the invaders could never concentrate more than 70,000 to deal with Wellington.

There is little that needs description in the operations in eastern and southern Spain during the latter months of 1811. On August 9 Soult defeated an attempt of the army of Murcia to invade the kingdom of Granada, but was unable to push his advantage, having to keep a watchful eye on Cadiz and Badajoz. His only offensive movement in the winter was an attempt to take the small fortress of Tarifa, near the Straits of Gibraltar, which was handsomely repulsed by the British garrison of the place (Dec. 1811). Macdonald in Catalonia was occupied by the long siege of Figueras till September had almost arrived; and, even when it had fallen, he accomplished little against the

BREACHES

French Retrenchment

Sword blades

St. Maria

Trinidad

Holes

Cunette

Cunette

Light
Division

4th. Division

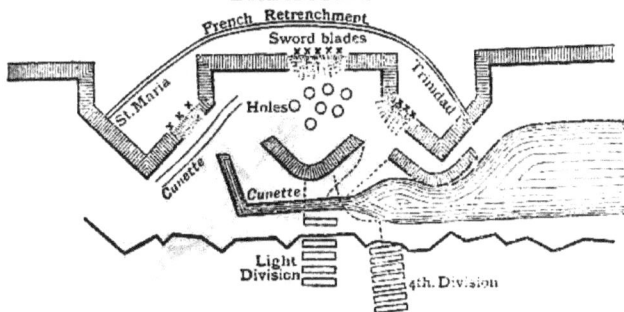

Siege of
BADAJOS
1812.

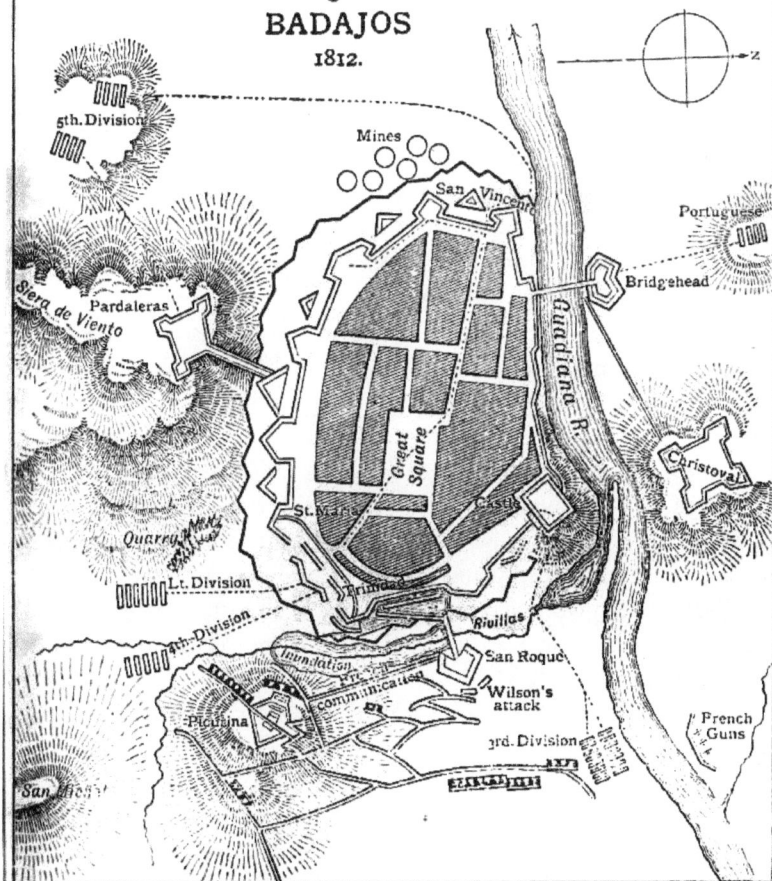

Mines

5th. Division

San Vincent

Portuguese

Bridgehead

Sierra de Viento

Pardaleras

Guadiana R.

Great
Square

Christoval

St. Maria

Castle

Quarry

Metz

Lt. Division

Trinidad

Rivillas

4th. Division

Inundation

San Roque

communication

Wilson's
attack

Picurina

French
Guns

3rd. Division

San Diego

indomitable Somatenes of the mountains.

Further south, however, matters went differently. After capturing Tarragona, Suchet had resolved to leave Catalonian affairs to his colleague Macdonald, and to strike at Valencia, the largest and wealthiest city in the whole realm which still remained in the hands of the patriots. In September he led the greater part of the army of Aragon down into the Valencian coast-land, and laid siege to the rock-fortress of Sagunto, which forms the chief bulwark of the fertile *Huerta*. It was well defended by General Andriani; and, when it had beaten off two assaults, Blake came to raise the siege with the whole of the armies of Murcia and Valencia. Suchet turned to meet him, and on the plain south of Sagunto was fought (October 25) the last pitched battle of the war in which a Spanish Army, unaided by British troops, attempted to face the French. Blake, though he attacked vigorously, was defeated with a loss of 5000 men. But his disasters did not end here.

Sagunto surrendered next day; and Suchet then pushed on against Valencia itself. He had obtained leave from the emperor to draw on the army of the north for reinforcements; and, when he had been joined by Reille and two divisions from Navarre, he advanced on a broad front, sweeping Blake's army before him. On December 26 he fought a long, running fight with the Spaniards, and drove two-thirds of them, with their commander-in-chief, into the city of Valencia; the remainder escaped towards Murcia.

Blake had not intended to be shut up in this fashion; the place had no regular modern fortifications, nor had it been properly provisioned. He made two futile attempts to break out, and was forced on Jan. 9, 1812, to surrender at discretion. This was the last and not the least of the disasters of the Spanish armies; 16,000 men laid down their arms, and only a remnant was left in the field to maintain the struggle in Murcia. Suchet was now at the height of his fortunes; he had been made a marshal for capturing Tarragona and was now created Duke of Albufera and given vice-regal power over all eastern Spain. But the capture of Blake's force was to be the last, as well as the most striking, of his exploits.

Even before Valencia fell, the fortune of war was beginning to turn on the more important theatre of war, along the Portuguese frontier. Wellington had been watching his opportunity for a renewed attack on Ciudad Rodrigo, and found it at midwinter, when the armies of Portugal and the north were dispersed in distant cantonments. He calculated that he might count on three weeks before they could concentrate in such force as to drive him off. Hence, he was forced to work in haste, under pain of seeing his scheme fail if the place had not fallen within that time. But all went well; on January 8 he invested Ciudad Rodrigo and brought up his battering train.

On the 13th he had begun to breach the walls; on the 19th the 3rd and light divisions stormed the place. This was sharp work, for, by the strict rules of siege-craft, the attack should have been held back some days longer, till the fire of the defence had been subdued and the breach had been made more practicable. But speed was necessary, and Wellington's happy audacity was justified by the result. The splendour of the success was somewhat tarnished by the misconduct of the victorious troops, who sacked the town in the most scandalous fashion.

Marmont had called out his army from its cantonments on receiving the news that Wellington had invested Ciudad Rodrigo; but bad roads and worse weather prevented him from concentrating at Salamanca before January 25; and by that time, he had received news that the place had fallen. Seeing no profit in a winter campaign, he sent back his divisions to their old quarters. Wellington, thus left undisturbed, proceeded at once to carry out the second half of his great plan. As soon as he was certain that Marmont's army had dispersed, he marched with six divisions on Estremadura, there to join the detached corps of Hill. Starting on March 6, he reached the gates of Badajoz on the 16th.

The moment was even more favourable than he could have expected for a great offensive movement; Napoleon had now the Russian war looming clearly before him, and had begun, for the first time since the war began, to draw troops from Spain. In February he had recalled 13,000 men of the Imperial Guard from the army of the north and had directed Soult and Suchet to send him their two Polish divisions; he had also ordered off some German troops; so that, as a net result, the army of Spain was 30,000 men weaker than it had been in the autumn of 1811. This diminution was most important, as it was now far more difficult for the enemy to concentrate superior numbers against the Anglo-Portuguese, either in the valley of the Guadiana or in that of the Douro.

Badajoz, like Ciudad Rodrigo, had to be besieged "against time"; for it was clear that Soult and Marmont might unite to relieve it, as in June, 1811, if the siege were long protracted. Accordingly, Wellington pushed matters as fast as he could. On the twentieth day after the investment had begun, he ordered the place to be stormed,

Map 1 (top):

To Benavente
To Duenas
To Piuerga
R. Pisuerga
R. Esla
Castromonte
Simancas
Esquena R.
General Durban
Valladolid
Tudela
Tordesillas
Bocill
Puente
Duero
Duero R.
To Aranda
Ribeira
Fresno
Toro
Hornija
Cuellar
Zamora
Duero R.
Rueda
Eresma
R.
Fuentel Sauco
Guarena R.
Castro-nuno
Pollos
Navo del
Rey
Olmedo
Alaejos
Medina del
Campo
S. Maria
Castrillo
Castrejon
Segovia
St. Olmo
Torrecilla
Orden
Arevalo
Canizal
Tarazona
Cantalapiedra
Zapardial R.
Valesa
St. Christoval
Cabeza Velosa
Cantelpino
Blasco
Sancho
Espinar
Salamanca
Aldea Rubia
Cisla
Fontiveros
La Serna
Huerta
Ventosa
Flores d'Avila
Adoja R.
Avila
Guadarrama
Fr. Ciudad
Peneranda
Escurial
Valmusa R.
Arapiles
Nava Setroval
Alba

Legend:

▬ English lines of March
▭ Cavalry
···· French lines of March
▱ Cavalry

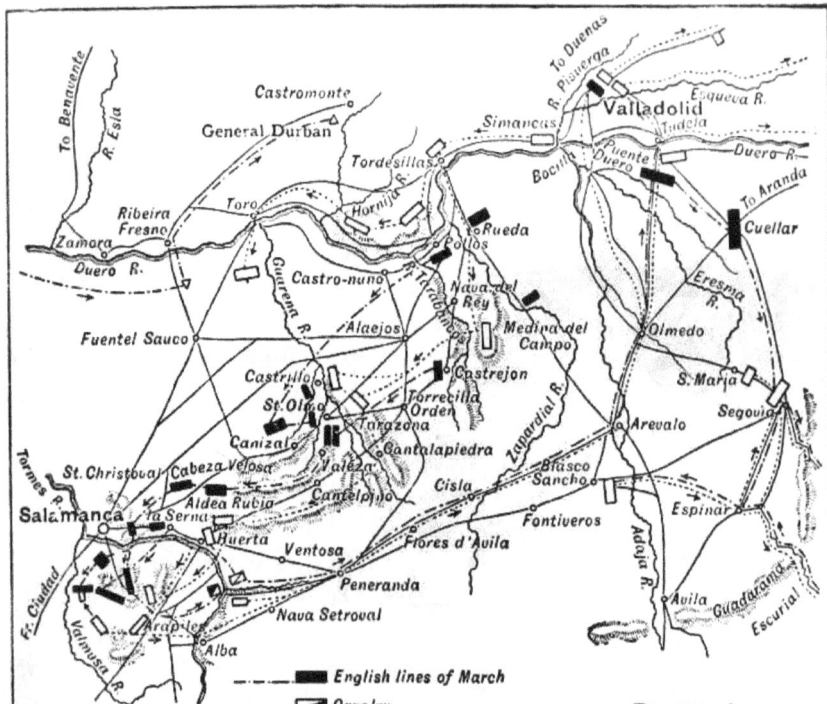

**Battle of
SALAMANCA
with operations
before and after the Action.**

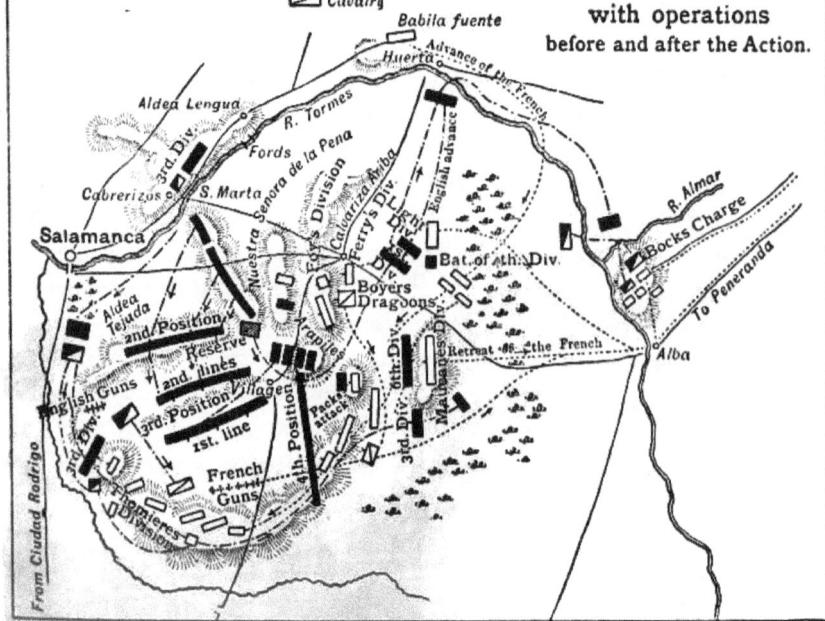

Map 2 (bottom):

Babila fuente
Advance of the French
Huerta
Aldea Lengua
R. Tormes
3rd. Div.
Fords de la Pena
Cabrerizos
S. Marta
Salamanca
Nuestra Senora de la Pena
Cavarizo Ariba
Foy's Division
Ferry's Div.
Bat. of 4th. Div.
R. Almar
Bocks Charge
To Peneranda
Boyers
Dragoons
Aldea
Tejuda
2nd. Position
Arapiles
3rd. Div. 6th. Div.
Retreat of the French
English Guns
Reserve
2nd. lines
3rd. Position
Village
Maucanes Div.
Alba
Packt attack
1st. line
Position
French
Guns
From Ciudad Rodrigo
Leopieres Division

though his preparations were still incomplete and the defence was still strong. Badajoz was taken, though at the cost of dreadful bloodshed: nearly 5000 men were killed or wounded, and the main assault on the breaches failed. But Picton and Leith, with the 3rd and 5th divisions, penetrated into the town by escalade; and the French were forced to surrender. Excesses far worse than those committed at Ciudad Rodrigo disgraced the storm; the troops got entirely out of hand, and fell to plunder, rape, and arson, in the most desperate fashion. It was three days before they could be restored to discipline.

Soult arrived in Estremadura with the bulk of his army a few days after Badajoz fell; he refused to fight when he heard that the place was lost and retired to Seville. Marmont, instead of marching straight to the Guadiana, had taken the unwise step of trying to draw off Wellington by a foray into central Portugal. But the British general disregarded this diversion, believing himself quite capable of dealing with the marshal when Badajoz should have fallen. He was justified in his belief; for, on hearing of the disaster, Marmont hastily withdrew from Portugal and fell back to the middle Douro.

On learning that Marmont had retreated, the British general determined to pursue him, and to push matters to a decisive issue in Leon. But, before marching on Salamanca, he resolved to strike a blow which should make the united action of the armies of Portugal and Andalusia even more difficult than it had recently been. Their sole line of communication was by the boat-bridge of Almaraz on the central Tagus: if this were destroyed, they had no way of keeping touch with each other save the circuitous route through Madrid. Accordingly, Hill was directed to send a lightly-equipped expedition through the mountains and to break the bridge. This feat he accomplished on May 19, surprising and storming the two forts which guarded the structure and burning its pontoons.

Having thus secured himself from the danger that Soult might come up in time to succour the army of Portugal, Wellington challenged Marmont to battle by marching straight on his headquarters at Salamanca and laying siege to the forts which dominated the town (June 17). The marshal, having concentrated the greater part of his divisions, appeared three days later in front of the British Army; but he found that he was somewhat outnumbered by the allied forces, and instead of attacking, retired behind the Douro (July 2). The Salamanca forts fell ere he had completed his retreat.

The campaign then stood still for a fortnight, while Marmont was

THE BATTLE OF SALAMANCA

THE SIEGE OF SAN SEBASTIAN

waiting for reinforcements. He called in the French garrison of the Asturias, and besought aid from the army of the north, in command of which Caffarelli had now superseded Dorsenne, and from King Joseph at Madrid. Both promised him help, but both were tardy in carrying out their promise; and Marmont was impatient. When he had been joined by the Asturian division alone, he recrossed the Douro and assumed the offensive. Wellington fell back before him, till he had reached the immediate vicinity of Salamanca, and then drew up his army on the heights to the south of the town (July 22).

The contending forces were very nearly equal in numbers, each having about 42,000 men in line; but Wellington was handicapped by the fact that more than a third of his army was composed of Spanish and Portuguese troops. Over-eager to press his adversary, and to cut him off from the direct road to Portugal, Marmont took the dangerous step of pushing his left wing forward to turn Wellington's right and extended his forces on a much longer front than was safe. While he was executing his flank-march across the front of the British position, Wellington came down upon him with the speed and fury of a thunderbolt. The isolated French left wing was suddenly assailed in front by Wellington's right, which descended from the heights, while the 3rd division under Pakenham, which had been concealed in woods and had escaped Marmont's notice, fell upon its flank and rear.

Three French divisions were routed and dispersed in half-an-hour, and, Marmont himself was grievously wounded by a round-shot as he was hastening to repair his fault. The remainder of the army of Portugal, the centre and right of its line, massed themselves in a defensive position, and fought hard to save the day; but they were gradually pushed off the field by a concentric attack from front and flank. They lost 8000 killed and wounded, 7000 prisoners, two eagles and 12 guns; and Clausel, who had succeeded to the command, was unable to rally the wrecks of the army for many days. The disaster would have been still greater, if a Spanish force which Wellington had placed to block the ford of Alba de Tormes, over which the routed host retreated, had not left its post without orders before the battle.

The victory of Salamanca shook the French domination in Spain to its very foundations; and its results were felt to the remotest corners of the Peninsula. King Joseph and his army of the centre had started from Madrid on the day before the battle, and would have joined Marmont, had he only waited three more days before fighting. As it was, the King and his 15,000 men had to retreat in haste, as soon as it

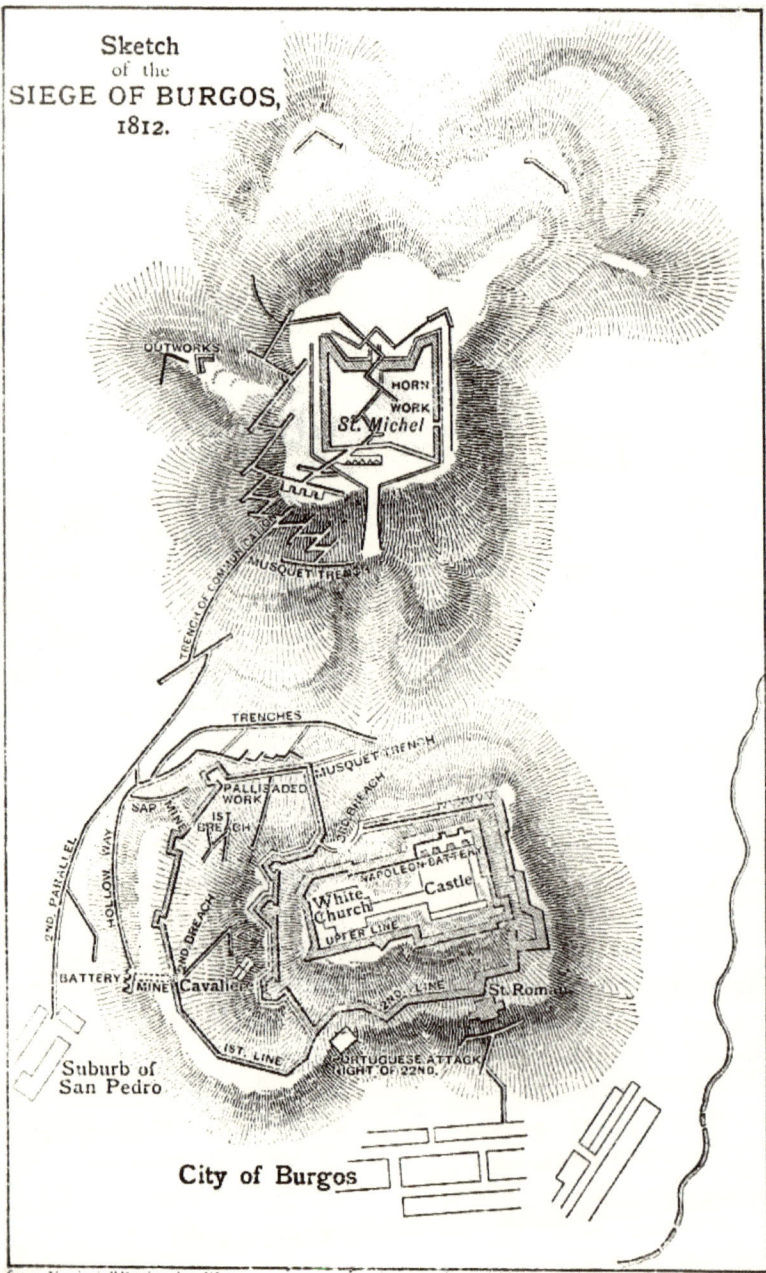

Sketch
of the
SIEGE OF BURGOS,
1812.

OUTWORKS

HORN
WORK
St. Michel

TRENCH OF COMMUNICATION

MUSQUET TRENCH

TRENCHES

MUSQUET TRENCH

PALLISADED
WORK
1ST
BREACH

SAP

2ND PARALLEL

HOLLOW WAY

3RD BREACH

2ND BREACH

NAPOLEON BATTERY

White
Church

Castle

UPPER LINE

BATTERY

MINE

Cavalier

2ND LINE

St. Roman

1ST LINE

PORTUGUESE ATTACK
NIGHT OF 22ND

Suburb of
San Pedro

City of Burgos

from Napier's "Peninsular War"

was known that Wellington was moving on Madrid. The victor had sent one division and his Spanish auxiliaries to pursue Clausel, while with the rest he marched upon the capital. Joseph was forced to fly, with his Court, his officials, and the Spaniards who had sold themselves to his cause, a mixed multitude of 10,000 souls. Fearing that, if he retired towards France, he would be taken in flank by the British, the king ordered a retreat on Valencia, where he could take refuge with the victorious army of Suchet.

On August 12 Wellington entered Madrid in triumph, and next day compelled a garrison of 1200 men, which Joseph had left in the Buen Retiro forts above the city, to lay down their arms. Leon and both the Castiles were thus delivered from the power of the enemy. Nor was this all; Soult in Andalusia now found himself cut off from all the other French armies and saw that he could no longer maintain his position in the far south. Evacuating with bitter regret the splendid provinces where he had reigned as viceroy for three years, he concentrated his whole army, some 55,000 sabres and bayonets, and marched to join Suchet at Valencia. The Spanish troops thereupon emerged from the long-blockaded Cadiz and reoccupied Andalusia; while Hill, left with no enemy before him in Estremadura, moved up the Tagus to Madrid.

The very completeness of Wellington's success had led to a dangerous concentration of the French armies, which, giving up the attempt to hold down the provinces of the south and centre, had gathered in two threatening masses. Soult, Suchet, and the king had nearly 90,000 men at Valencia; the army of Portugal had fallen back to join the army of the north; and 40,000 men were assembled about Burgos and on the upper Ebro. It was clear that Wellington, with some 60,000 men concentrated at Madrid, could not face these overwhelming numbers if they acted in unison. But he hoped to keep them apart, and he had just received from the Cortes the chief command of all the native forces of Spain, which gave him the power of ordering diversions from many quarters against the enemy.

Unfortunately, the Spanish generals were dilatory and even disobedient; and comparatively little profit accrued to Wellington during the autumn of 1812 from this quarter. Only the Galician Army, some 11,000 men, was at this moment actively engaged in his support. The forces which had come out of Cadiz made little attempt to distract Soult; and the Murcians and Valencians were completely cowed by Suchet. A British force of 6000 men from Sicily landed at Alicante on August 7 but was far too weak to have any effect on the general course of operations on the eastern coast.

Trusting, however, that the great accumulation of French troops at Valencia might not be immediately dangerous, Wellington left Madrid on September 1 with four divisions, and joined the troops whom he had left in the Douro valley, with the intention of pushing back the French force in the north. Hill, with three divisions, remained at Madrid to guard against any movement on the part of Soult and the king. On September 19 the British main army appeared in front of Burgos; and Clausel retired before it to the Ebro, after having thrown a garrison into the forts above the city. Wellington was of opinion that Burgos must be reduced before he could venture to pursue the French into Alava or Navarre; he therefore invested its citadel. The siege lasted just a month (September 19—October 19). It was the most unfortunate operation which he ever conducted. The place, though small; was strong; and the material provided for the attack was lamentably insufficient, only eight heavy guns being available. For want of transport, a sufficient train was never brought to the front; and Wellington was foiled. Though the outer works were captured, four successive attempts to storm the castle failed; and a whole month was wasted.

This respite enabled the French to combine and arrange for a general forward movement against the allied armies. Souham, who had succeeded Clausel in command, led the armies of Portugal and the north to relieve Burgos; while Soult and the king, leaving Suchet to hold down Valencia, marched upon Madrid with 60,000 men. Wellington would probably have fought Souham if he had not been aware that even a victory in this part of the field could not save Hill from being crushed by the superior numbers that were moving up against Madrid. He was compelled to fall back in order to unite the two halves of his army, and, while retiring slowly from Burgos along the valley of the Douro, sent Hill orders to abandon New Castile and join him at Salamanca. The two retreats were carried out with complete success; and the whole allied army was concentrated on the Tormes by November 3.

But the two armies of Soult and Souham had also combined; and nearly 100,000 men were facing Wellington on his old battlefield south of Salamanca; during the whole war the French had never before gathered so large a force upon a single line. The British general had hoped that the dearth of provisions and the miserable autumn weather would arrest the further progress of the enemy. But Soult pressed on, always turning the right of the allied army; and Wellington was forced to fall back for three marches more till he had reached Ciudad Rodrigo (November 18). This last stage of the retreat was made in drenching rain over roads that had become almost impassable and cost the retreating host several thousand men in sick and stragglers, who were left behind to perish or fall into the hands of the enemy. But the French also were in a desperate state of exhaustion, and at last desisted from the pursuit.

In spite of the failure at Burgos and the losses in the subsequent retreat, the net results of the campaign of 1812 had been most satisfactory. Though the French had reoccupied Madrid and Toledo, they had been compelled to evacuate all southern Spain. Estremadura, Andalusia, and La Mancha had been completely freed from the invaders; and the casualties of the Imperial armies had exceeded 40,000 men. They were now thrown upon the defensive and had lost confidence in their ultimate success. But this was not the worst of their misfortunes.

At midwinter arrived the news of the emperor's awful disasters in the retreat from Moscow; and shortly afterwards he began to requisition troops from Spain to reconstitute the Grand Army. Soult was summoned off to Germany, and with him many other generals, a number of complete regiments, and a still greater proportion of *cadres* composed of picked officers and non-commissioned officers, who were to train the mass of conscripts which was being levied for the next campaign. Yet so enormous were Napoleon's resources that, after deducting men in hospital or detached, there were still nearly 200,000 French troops left in the Peninsula in the spring of 1813.

Of these, 63,000 men were under Suchet in Valencia, Aragon, and Catalonia; the remainder—the armies of Portugal, the south, the centre, and the north—were still facing Wellington. Yet the British general was able to commence the operations of the new year with a greater prospect of success than he had ever before enjoyed. He had about 75,000 fighting men of the best sort in his own Anglo-Portuguese Army; and with these the main blow would have to be delivered. But he was also in a position to utilise all the scattered Spanish forces as he had never done before. Ballasteros and some other generals who had disobeyed orders in 1812 had been removed in disgrace; and in 1813 Wellington could rely upon obedience.

There were about 60,000 Spanish regular troops available in Galicia, Estremadura, and La Mancha; but quite as important were the *guerilleros* who had been stimulated to redoubled activity by the successes of the previous year. Indeed, it may be said that these bands were of greater profit to the cause of Spain in 1813 than were her armies; for their daring and ceaseless raids during the spring diverted the attention of the French from the early operations of Wellington and caused them to spread their divisions far and wide in regions remote from the real point of danger. So harassed were the French that Marshal Jourdan, who directed King Joseph's armies since the departure of Soult, determined to make a desperate attempt to hunt down the main bands before concentrating in face of Wellington.

This fatal error was committed in March, when the whole army of the north and four divisions of the army of Portugal were drawn up into the northern mountains and devoted to the sole task of exterminating the *guerilleros*. Dispersed in numerous columns, and cut off from each other by the active insurgents, these 40,000 men were no longer available for the main operations upon the Douro.

While Clausel and Foy were hunting Mina and his compeers to little effect, the line of battle from Salamanca to Toledo was too thin for safety. The French armies were dispersed over an immense front; and, to draw together in any strength, they would be forced to fall back far to the rear and to abandon vast tracts of territory. Meanwhile the campaigning season had arrived; and Wellington saw his advantage. It was clear that the French would expect his main attack to be delivered from the direction of Ciudad Rodrigo and Almeida, as in previous years. Their defensive position had been taken up to guard against this eventuality. But, instead of repeating his old move, Wellington secretly passed up five British divisions to the north of the Douro into the Portuguese province of the Tras-os-Montes. Braganza, not Ciudad Rodrigo, was to be his real base; and the larger half of his forces was thus placed in a position from which it overlapped the extreme French right wing and could turn its flank whenever it attempted to make a stand.

Jourdan had forgotten to guard against this possibility, since this north-eastern extremity of Portugal was so rugged and so badly furnished with roads that it had never before been used as the starting-point of a large army. Graham, the victor of Barrosa, was placed in command of this corps; while Wellington remained in person at Ciudad Rodrigo, with three divisions, lest the news that he had gone northward should arouse the suspicions of the enemy.

It was not till May 16 that Graham had struggled through the defiles of the Tras-os-Montes and commenced his descent into the plains of Leon behind the French flank. Wellington himself therefore

Attack of
SAN SEBASTIAN
between 11th. July & 9th. September 1813.

MONTE OLIA

Passages del Calzada

Artillery Depôt

Right of the Attack

March of Portuguese Columns

Battery of St. Elmo

Mirador

Bateria del Principe

MONTE ORGULLO

Convent. (Hospital)

Castle of La Mota

Low water mark

Low water mark

River Urumea

Sta. Catalina (turret)

Bridge (burned)

Parallel

Horn and Drum Work

Cast. Redoubt

Suburb of St. Martin

Convent & Heights of St. Bartolomeo

Left of the Attack

Convent of Antigua

Santa Clara

Reference.
1. Convent of Sta. Teresa
2. Arsenal
3. Great Square
4. Flat or Cavalier Bastion
5. Mine spring by the besiegers
6. Mine spring by the garrison

Scale of Yards
0   100   200   300   600

only set out on the 22nd; but, when once the advance was begun, the results were startling. The enemy's van-guard retired from Salamanca without offering resistance, for Jourdan proposed to concentrate and fight in Old Castile. But, every time that he thought that he might stand to resist Wellington, he discovered that Graham had marched onward and was behind his right wing.

The British attack had been directed so far to the north that the French could not concentrate within any reasonable space of time. Orders had to be sent to evacuate Madrid and Toledo in hot haste, and to direct every available man on Burgos. The isolated divisions engaged in guerilla-hunting in Navarre and Biscay were also called in to join the main army. But Wellington gave the retreating army no leisure; and, when he had reached the ground in front of Burgos, the enemy had only 50,000 men collected.

Joseph and Jourdan saw that to offer battle with such inferior numbers would be ruinous, and reluctantly fell back beyond the Ebro, after blowing up the citadel of Burgos (June 12-13). The king had vainly hoped to defend the line of the Ebro; but, instead of attacking him in front, Wellington once again pushed forward Graham and his left wing, which crossed the river far to the west of the French headquarters. Once more Joseph had to draw back, till he reached a strong position in front of Vittoria, where he was covered both in front and in flank by the stream of the Zadorra. Here at last he stood to fight, having collected some 65,000 men. But Wellington had nearly 80,000 men in line; with such a numerical superiority, he naturally attacked at once.

The essential part of Wellington's tactics in the battle of June 21 was to push forward, once more, his left wing under Graham, so as to turn the French right, and cut them off from their line of retreat, the great high road to San Sebastian and Bayonne. This was accomplished early in the day; but the enemy, drawing back his exposed wing behind the Zadorra, kept Graham for many hours from advancing further. Yet the loss of the power to retreat on Bayonne was fatal. For Wellington, attacking vigorously with his centre and right, crossed the lower course of the Zadorra at several points, and drove in the main body of the French towards the town of Vittoria. If the road behind them had been open, Joseph and Jourdan might have retired without any ruinous losses.

But Graham was blocking the way; and the defeated host had to retreat by the only route left to them, a rough mountain track to Salvatierra and Pampeluna, unsuited for the passage of an army encumbered with heavy impedimenta. The king had with him not only a vast train of artillery, but a great convoy of Spanish refugees— his partisans from Madrid—and countless carriages and waggons laden with treasure, pictures, state archives, and valuable property of all sorts, the accumulated spoil of six years of conquest. The whole of this heterogeneous mass of vehicles was thrown upon the narrow Pampeluna road, and hopelessly jammed within a few miles of its starting-point.

The defeated army abandoned everything and fled over the hillsides. In actual casualties it had not lost heavily—some 6000 killed and wounded, and 1000 prisoners; while the Allies had 5000 men *hors de combat*. But the French had saved nothing but their persons; the whole equipment of the army of Spain was captured by the victors, 143 guns, 500 caissons, nearly £1,000,000 sterling in the military chest, besides several thousand carriages laden with valuables. Seldom has an army shared such plunder as fell to the Allies that night.

The vanquished host reached Pampeluna in complete disorder; and Jourdan, after strengthening the garrison of that place, ordered the retreat to be continued beyond the Pyrenees. On June 26 the whole force re-entered France, and only halted at Bayonne, where desperate measures were taken to rally the regiments, and to refit the army with artillery drawn from the arsenal of that fortress and from the depots at Toulouse and Bordeaux. The pursuit had not been vigorous, for Wellington had turned aside the greater part of his army to hunt the columns of Foy and Clausel, which had not succeeded in joining Joseph in time for the battle. Both were hard pressed, but ultimately escaped to France by devious roads.

When he found that they had eluded him, the British general told off his Spanish auxiliaries to invest Pampeluna, and two of his own divisions to besiege San Sebastian. With the rest of his army he advanced to the frontier but refused to cross the Bidassoa till the two great fortresses had fallen. Their leaguers began simultaneously on July 1, 1813. Thus, ended this brilliant and skilful campaign, which had lasted only forty days (May 22—July 1), and had cleared all northern Spain of the enemy. If the four French armies of Portugal, the centre, the south, and the north, could have been concentrated on a single position, they would have outnumbered the allied forces. But Wellington never allowed them to gather, hurried matters to a crisis with unswerving determination, and finally drove the enemy over the Pyrenees, at a cost to himself of not more than 6000 men in the whole series of operations.

The campaign of Vittoria is separated by a gap of some three weeks from the second campaign of 1813, that of the Pyrenees. During this space, Napoleon had time to send Soult from Dresden, to reorganise the army of Spain. Joseph and Jourdan were recalled to the interior of France in disgrace; and the emperor expressed his opinion that, with a change in leadership, his hosts would be able to resume the offensive and deliver Pampeluna and San Sebastian. Though four divisions of cavalry left for Germany, the French still counted more than 100,000 men. Some 3000 were in Pampeluna, about the same number in San Sebastian, 1500 in Santoña. After deducting a garrison for Bayonne, Soult had some 85,000 with which to take the field.

Before proceeding to relate the campaign of the Pyrenees, it is necessary to cast a glance at eastern Spain. So long as King Joseph held Madrid and Toledo, Suchet had been able to retain Valencia He even assumed the offensive, and on April 11 beat Elio's Murcians at Yecla and Villena. Two days later he attacked the Anglo-Sicilians on the heights of Castalla, and was beaten off with loss. But Sir John Murray, the officer who commanded this force, made no attempt to profit by his victory, and remained passive throughout May. On the last day of that month, acting under orders from Wellington, Murray put his troops and a Spanish division on board ship at Alicante, and sailed for Catalonia. He was directed to join the Spanish Army in that province and to lay siege to Tarragona.

The purpose of this move was to give Suchet full occupation during the campaign in Old Castile. When the news of the landing arrived, the marshal hurried north with part of his troops, and, joining Decaen, the officer left in command at Barcelona, marched against Murray. That general fled with unseemly haste on hearing of the approach of the French, abandoning his siege artillery while he hurriedly embarked his troops (June 12). He was superseded five days later by Lord William Bentinck, and afterwards tried for cowardice and disobedience to instructions. The court-martial ended in an acquittal, though he was censured for gross errors of judgment.

On July 5 Suchet received the news of Vittoria, which compelled him to evacuate Valencia, since the garrison of that province would have been in a perilous position when New Castile and Aragon had fallen into the hands of Wellington. He retired beyond the Ebro, and a little later abandoned Tarragona, after blowing up its fortifications (August 17). The Anglo-Sicilian army, with the Spaniards of the Murcian force, advanced along the coast and took up positions whence they could observe Barcelona from a distance. On September 12, Suchet, thinking that they were pressing him too close, advanced against them, and routed Bentinck's van-guard at the combat of Ordal. But, as he did not use his advantage, the Allies continued to hold Tarragona, and to push the siege of the garrisons which Suchet had left behind him at Tortosa, Lerida, Monzon, and other places.

The marshal would have done far better to have evacuated them; for he lost the services of 10,000 good troops, whom he was never in a position to succour. The emperor began to withdraw troops from his army for use in Germany during the autumn; and, as Suchet's main body grew feebler, it became increasingly clear that he would never be able to relieve his outlying garrisons. In the winter of 1813-4, the struggle in Catalonia dwindled down into a mere war of demonstrations and affairs of outposts.

Far otherwise had matters gone on the shores of the Bay of Biscay. On July 23, Soult, in accordance with his master's orders, resumed the offensive. The allied army was now ranged on a long line upon the Franco-Spanish frontier, so as to cover the sieges of San Sebastian and Pampeluna. Soult's opportunity lay in the fact that the hills impeded the lateral communications between the British divisions. He secretly moved 60,000 men far inland to his extreme left and fell upon the troops under Picton and Hill who were guarding the passes of Roncesvalles and Maya. He hoped to overwhelm them, by a twofold superiority of numbers, before Wellington could bring to their aid the corps cantoned nearer to the sea. He would then push on, relieve Pampeluna, and force the allied army to quit the frontier by a general attack on their flank and rear.

This ingenious plan miscarried, partly owing to fog and rain, which delayed the French advance, but more because of the long and vigorous resistance of the British outlying brigades. Maya and Roncesvalles were both forced in the end (July 25-26); but their defence gave Wellington time to concentrate in front of Pampeluna a force which, though much smaller than that of Soult, was yet strong enough to hold him at bay. At the Battle of Sauroren (July 27-28) the marshal strove in vain to storm the heights held by the allied troops. Reinforcements were hurrying up from the west to join Wellington; and the marshal had no alternative save to fall back on France. This series of fights, generally called the battles of the Pyrenees, had cost him 10,000 men.

Wellington now pressed the sieges of San Sebastian and Pampeluna,

Combat of
RONCESVALLES
July 25ᵗʰ 1813
Scale of Miles
0 1 2

Val Haira

Lamartinière
Maucune
Foy
Ross
Campbells

Chateau Pignon
Vandermaesen
Taupin
Morillo
Byng
Roncesvalles
Anson
Stubbs
Espinal
Burguete

Val Carlos

Ibañeta Pass
Mendichur Pass

To Pampeluna

Loredo
Orbaiceta

British   Spanish and Portuguese   French

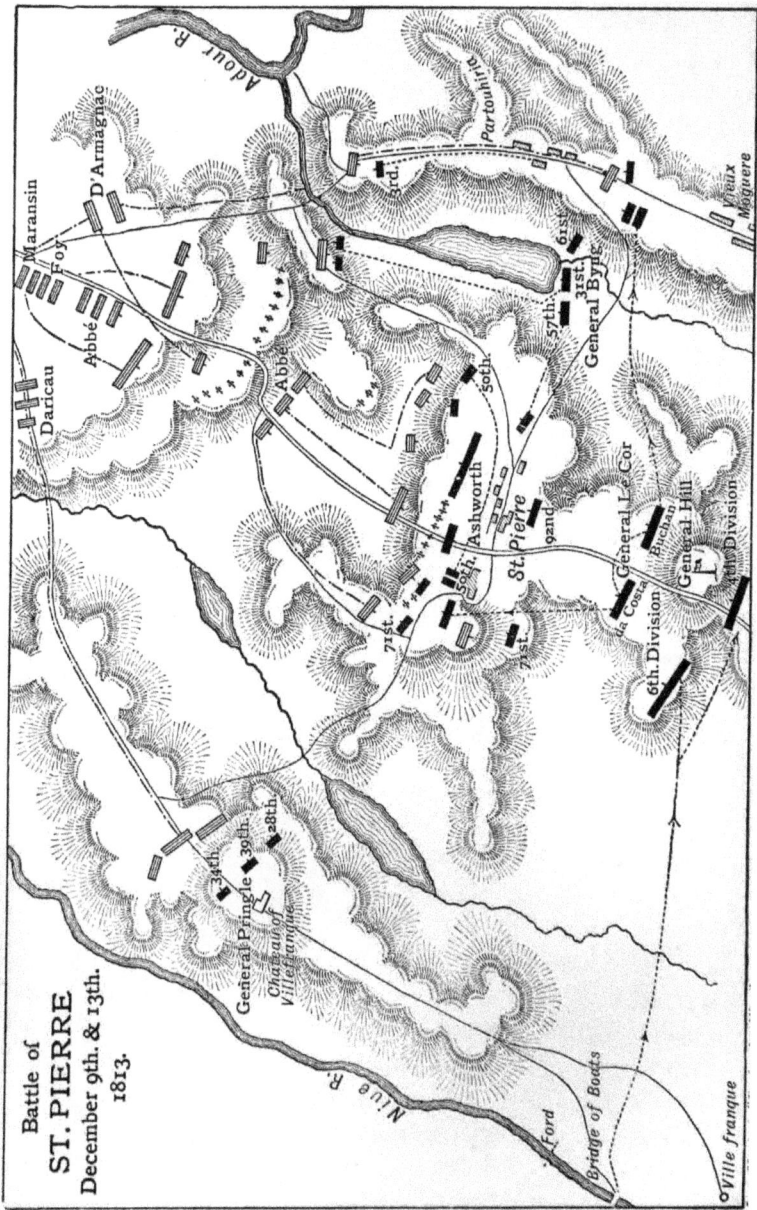

Battle of
ST. PIERRE
December 9th. & 13th.
1813.

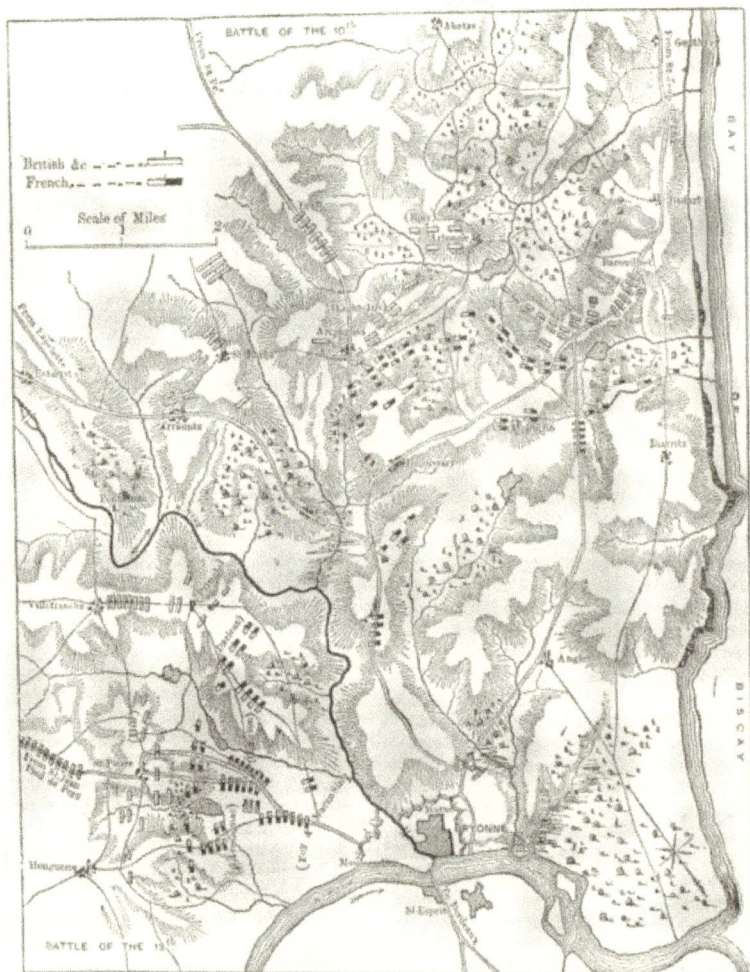

PLAN OF THE BATTLES ON THE NIVE.

ATTACK OF THE
FRENCH ENTRENCHED POSITION
ON THE
NIVELLE
10th Nov.r 1813.

French
Cavalry   Infantry   Allies
                                                   Artillery

SCALES
Military Yards   British Yards
English Miles

hoping to secure both places in time to allow him to advance into France before the winter came. But his efforts were not at first successful. British siege-craft was seldom efficient in these years; and San Sebastian beat off two assaults. The town was finally stormed on August 31, and the castle surrendered nine days later: but the success cost 2500 men. Soult, on the very day of the storm, made a last attempt to raise the siege, but was heavily repulsed at the combat of San Marcial by the covering force, consisting mainly of Freyre's and Longa's Spaniards. Pampeluna fell on October 31, by starvation, not by assault. Thus, Wellington's entry into France was delayed for four months.

But, on October 7, the British general had already begun his preparations for advance by forcing the lines of the Bidassoa, which Soult had strengthened by a long chain of redoubts. Fording the broad river at low tide, the British divisions swept all before them and captured all the enemy's works. The French then fell back on a second and stronger line behind the River Nivelle. This series of positions was carried on November 10, after a series of desperate assaults on almost inaccessible peaks and defiles, where the storming columns had to crawl and climb up the cliffs of the Rhune and other lofty mountains.

A third line of positions now faced the British, formed by the River Nive and the fortress of Bayonne behind it. A month of heavy rain and cold delayed the attack on this new line of defence; but, with the return of fine weather, Wellington forced the passage of the Nive (December 9) and advanced close to the outworks of Bayonne. His army was now divided into two halves by the Nive, a fact of which the indomitable Soult tried to take advantage. He first massed his whole field-force against Wellington's left and strove to crush it before it could be succoured by his right, which had to cross the river by a single distant bridge.

After severe fighting, this attack failed (December 10); whereupon the marshal shifted his main army to the east bank of the Nive and repeated his experiment against the British right. At the battle of Saint-Pierre (December 13), the entire French Army was repelled by one British and one Portuguese division under Sir Rowland Hill; and Soult was already foiled, when the appearance of the reserves from beyond the river forced him to beat a precipitate retreat. The Battles of the Nive had cost the marshal some 6000 or 7000 men and would have sufficed by themselves to discourage him from making any further attempts to assume the offensive. But his position was rendered utterly hopeless when, shortly after, he received orders from the

BATTLE OF ORTHEZ
Feb. 27th. 1814.

■ Allies   ▱ French

Emperor directing him to send two divisions (10,000 men) to aid in the defence of the eastern frontier. His army was now reduced to less than 50,000 men, little more than half the strength which Wellington could put into the field. If he lingered much longer at Bayonne, he ran a chance of being shut up.

When, therefore, Wellington manifested an intention of surrounding Bayonne, by casting a great bridge of boats across the Adour below the city, and transporting several divisions to its northern bank, Soult was driven to retire into the interior and to leave the stronghold to its fate (Feb. 26, 1814). He retreated, not directly northward along the road to Bordeaux, as might perhaps have been expected, but eastward in the direction of Toulouse, so as to place himself upon the flank of the allied army.

This move made matters more difficult for Wellington, who could not push forward and leave Soult in his rear but was constrained to turn aside and pursue him along the roots of the Pyrenees, moving every day further from the sea, from which alone he could receive supplies and reinforcements. He was forced also to leave 30,000 men to besiege Bayonne.

The first stage of Soult's retreat was marked by the Battle of Orthez (February 27). Knowing that the British Army had been enfeebled by the large force left before Bayonne, the marshal offered a defensive battle on the heights above the town but was driven out of his position after a hard day's fighting and forced to resume his retrograde movement to the east. After the battle, Wellington detached two divisions under Beresford to march on Bordeaux, where the partisans of the Bourbons, had promised to hoist the white flag as soon as British aid came in sight. Beresford's detachment reached Bordeaux on March 12; and the royalists were as good as their word, opening the gates to him and proclaiming the Duc d'Angoulême, who had come out in the wake of the British Army, as Prince Regent.

This movement was not without its inconveniences, for, if the allied sovereigns had made peace at Châtillon, as was quite possible, the Bordelais would have been left exposed to terrible punishment at the hands of the emperor. Wellington had given them fair warning of this, but they nevertheless carried out their agreement. All the neighbouring departments were practically on the same side; and the invading army was readily supplied with information and provisions by the peasantry. Soult's attempts to raise a partisan warfare in the rear of the Allies met with no success. Still less fruitful was Napoleon's last des-

BATTLE OF ORTHEZ

FIGHTING IN THE SUBURBS OF TOULOUSE

Sketch Map of the
Country round Bayonne.
showing the Passage of the Adour,
& the events of December & February 1813-14.

■ Allies ☐ French

To Orthez

To Navarrenx

Gave d'Oleron

Gave de Pau

Peyrehorade

R. Adour

Port de Lanne

Hastingues

Oyregave

Bidouze

Guiche

Came

Bidache

Labatte

Leren

Sndos

Hastingue
Bastide
de Bearn

Bergoney

R. Bidouze

Esperaute

Ithere

Sombrail

Garris

St. Palais

Heights of La Montagne

BATTLE OF LA MONTAGNE
FEB. 15TH. 1814

St. Martin

Mcharin

Oreg

Isturitz

St. Estèben

R. Bidouze

Ayerre

Bardos

Bastide
Hireen

Ballon la Hoquin

Banloc

To St. Jean P. de Port

Hasparren

R. ARAN

R. URT

URT

Mendionde

Macaye

Mt. Ursuia

To St. Jean de Port

R. Nive

Izalzu

R. Lahoussoa

To St. Jean P. de Port

River Adour

BAYONNE

Briscous

Lahonce

Urcuit

Halsou

Bas Cambo

Urguray

Cambo
Bridge

Château Villefranque

Lormentioa

Bridge of boats

Villefranque

R. Nive

Ustaritz
Bridge

Arauntz

Mousserolles

St. Etienne

St. Pierre
DEC. 13TH. 1813.

Wellington's
Bridge

Bar

PASSAGE OF THE
ADOUR FEB. 23RD. &
24TH. 1814.

Anglet

Marac

Boucaut

Jubiains

BATTLE OF
Arcangues
DEC. 10TH. 1813

Arbonne

Biarritz

Bidart

Gelos

St. Pée

R. Rhune

R. Nivelle

St. Pée

PASSAGE OF THE
NIVELLE NOV. 10TH. 1813.

Espelette

R. Nivelle

To St. Jean de Luz

Walker & Boutall sc.

N

Battle of TOULOUSE.

Allies · French

perate device. On March 13 he released Ferdinand VII from Valençay, having made him sign a treaty of peace, which the Spanish Cortes very properly ignored.

Soult's retreat did not end till he had fallen back under the walls of Toulouse (March 24), where he once more stood at bay in lines which he had caused to be thrown up outside the city. He had some 39,000 men left. Wellington, owing to the detachments at Bayonne and Bordeaux, was not greatly superior in force, having only six Anglo-Portuguese divisions and a Spanish corps, less than 50,000 sabres and bayonets. In spite of the strength of Soult's entrenchments, he resolved to attack (April 10). The business turned out more formidable than had been expected.

The assault of Freyre's Spaniards upon the French centre failed; and it was only after desperate efforts that the 4th and 6th divisions succeeded in storming the lines upon Soult's left, and driving the enemy back into the town, which was commanded by the captured heights. The victors lost 4600 men, far more than the vanquished, who, protected by their entrenchments, suffered only 3200 casualties. But the result of the battle was sufficiently clear, when Soult on April 12 evacuated the town, and retired still further east, to join Suchet, who was coming up to his aid with the small remnant of the army of Catalonia. Toulouse, if the combatants had but known it, was an unnecessary battle; for Paris had capitulated to the Allies on March 30, and Napoleon had abdicated on April 6. Unnecessary also was the bloodshed before Bayonne on April 14, when the French garrison made a sortie, which cost each side 800 casualties.

So, ended the great struggle which sapped Napoleon's strength, though it was not the direct cause of his fall. He called it himself "the running sore"; and such indeed it was, considered from his point of view. For it was the constant drain of men and money to the Peninsula which rendered him too weak to fight the Powers of central Europe. What might not have happened in Saxony in 1813, if the emperor had been able to dispose of the 200,000 veterans locked up behind the Pyrenees?

If, with the raw army that he actually commanded, he almost achieved success, the experienced troops of Soult and Suchet must certainly have turned the balance in his favour and have enabled him to impose on the Allies a peace that would have left his Empire intact, even if his prestige had lost some of its ancient splendour. He paid in 1813 the price for his iniquitous doings at Bayonne in 1808. The never-failing, if often ill-directed, patriotism of the Spaniards, and the skill and firmness of the much-enduring Wellington, had detained for six years in the Peninsula the army with which he might have dictated peace to Europe.

CHAPTER 10

The Emperor Returns

After the fall of Paris, and the abdication of Napoleon, the allied powers placed on the throne the representative of the long-exiled house of Bourbon, Louis XVIII.—the best choice perhaps that they could make, yet in itself an unsatisfactory experiment. Louis, though not destitute of a certain shrewdness, was elderly, and a confirmed valetudinarian; he left the conduct of affairs to ministers whose XVIII. unwise actions made the French complain that "the Bourbons had learned nothing and forgotten nothing"—they behaved, in short, as if the whole Revolution and its consequences had passed over their heads unnoticed.

Meanwhile the allies met in congress at Vienna to redistribute Europe and to make an end of the relics of the Napoleonic *régime*. There were many conflicting interests, for the desires of Prussia, Russia, and Austria crossed each other on a dozen points, and a long period of friction was inevitable before a settlement could be reached. But the powers commenced to disarm and thought nothing less probable than a new French war.

England alone was unable to disband her troops or dismantle her navy. She was still engaged in a struggle which had broken out in 1812. One of the consequences of the Continental System and the "Orders in Council" had been to inflict grave hardships on the trade of the United States, the one great neutral power in the world. France and Great Britain had done them equal damage, but it was natural that the Americans should resent more the action of the power which lay nearer to them and domineered over the seas. They were specially vexed at the harsh exercise of the right of search, and the frequent impressment of British seamen found serving on American ships, whose change of nationality British Government refused to recognise.

To these sources of irritation was added a notion that while England was locked in her death-grapple with Bonaparte, it would be easy to overrun and annex Canada. Hence it came that the United States declared war in the summer of 1812. This "stab in the back," as the English called it, had no effect whatever on the general course of the European war. The small garrison of Canada, gallantly aided by the lo-

165

cal militia, beat off every attempt to invade the great colony, and even compelled two small American armies to surrender. It did not prove to be necessary to distract troops from Europe for their aid.

On the other hand, the English navy had an unpleasant surprise when, on three separate occasions, the large and admirably-handled American frigates took or sunk British ships of slightly inferior force in single combat—a thing which no French, Spanish, or Dutch vessel had ever accomplished. The American ships had to be hunted down by superior numbers—a fact very galling to the pride of their opponents.

A considerable amount of damage was also done to British mercantile marine by American privateers. On the other hand, a strict blockade sealed up Boston and all the other ports of the United States, whose commerce was for the moment absolutely annihilated. When Napoleon was at last disposed of, the British Government began to pour Wellington's Peninsular veterans into America. One expedition took Washington, the capital of the United States, though another sent against New Orleans was beaten back with fearful loss. But before serious pressure had been applied, a peace was signed at Ghent (December 24, 1814), which left all matters—territorial and other—just as they had been before 1812. The end of Napoleon and his Continental System had removed the cause of war, and both parties gladly brought it to an end.

Meanwhile, in March, 1815, a new and unexpected crisis had arisen in Europe. While the envoys at Vienna were engaged in parcelling out the spoils of Napoleon, they received the unwelcome news that the ex-emperor had escaped from Elba, landed in Provence, and called his old followers to arms. The Bourbons had made themselves so profoundly unpopular that no one would fight for them; whole regiments and brigades tore off their white cockades and came to join the great adventurer.

In a few days he was at the head of 100,000 men. Louis XVIII. fled to Flanders, and ere he had been gone more than a few hours Napoleon was again installed in the Tuileries. He trusted that his sudden success might impose on the allies, and that the dissensions which had divided the Congress of Vienna might keep them from united action. But he was woefully mistaken. Every state in Europe promptly declared war on him.

BATTLE OF NEW ORLEANS,
Jan. 8th 1814.

Explanation

1. Detachment Blauveque Drag.
2. Cap.t. Chauveau's Horse Comp.t.
3. Beale's Rifle Comp.t.   5. Pyrowder's
Howitzer.
No. 1. Lt. Norrie 1.24 pr.
No. 3. Cap.t. Domingue. &
Bluche.t. 2 24. pr.
No. 4. Lt. Crawley 1.32 pr.
No. 5. Lt. Perry. 2. 6 pr.
No. 6. Lt. Spotts. 1.18 & 1. 4 pr.
No. 7. Col. Harpersr. 1.12 & 1.6 pr.
No. 8. Lonall. howitzer. 9½ inches.

Cypress Swamps

Cypress Swamps

Gen. Coffee's Command

Canal Rodriquez

Here
Col. Packenham fell

British supposed to be
9000 strong

Main attack of ☞ ☞
between 8 & ☞

Batteries erected on the
1st of Jan. & silenced

on the same day by the
American Artillery

Longuille's Plantation

L. Reg.t. 1 Bn.

Gen. Adairs Comm.t.
7.th Jan.t at night

MACARTY'S

Cap.t. P. Ogden's
Horse Company

Canal Rodriquez
Major Gen.l Iackson
Gen. Carrolls Command

Ba.Depigny.
4.th Reg.t

M.
Daquin's
Bn.

M.
Lacoste's
Bn.

Line Iackson

Batteries erected on 1st
Jan. & silenced by

Amer. Art. & put up
again on the 7.th at night

Head Quarters

Powder Mag.

Public Road

Levee   Mortar   Left column of British supposed to be 1200 strong   Levee

Battery erected on the
28. Dec. 1814.

MISSISSIPPI RIVER

DEATH OF PAKENHAM

CHAPTER 11

The Hundred Days (1815)

On the very night of his arrival at the Tuileries, Napoleon found himself able to reconstruct the official machinery of the Imperial *régime*. Most of his former ministers hastened to place themselves at his disposal, Maret took up again the post of Secretary of State; Decrès returned to the ministry of Marine; Gaudin to the ministry of Finance. Cambacérès was put in temporary charge of the department of Justice; Caulaincourt, with some show of reluctance, consented to become once more Minister for Foreign Affairs. There were, however, two new appointments of first-rate importance. Davout was placed at the War Office, where it was hoped that the talent for organisation which he had shown during his pro-consulate at Hamburg would display itself once more.

Carnot became Minister of the Interior; Napoleon had not forgotten the patriotism which the old republican had evinced in 1814 and saw that it would help him to rally the Liberals to his side, if he could once more exhibit their strongest man taking service under the Empire because France was in danger. Carnot in office was a surprise; but it was still more surprising to see Fouché once more Minister of Police. He had presented himself, with his usual cynical impudence, at the reception held at the Tuileries on March 20; and, ignoring his former disgrace, had offered himself as the only man capable of satisfactorily filling the post from which he had been degraded in 1810. Remembering how inadequately Savary had worked the machine after the removal of the Duke of Otranto, Napoleon gave the old intriguer the place, though he had no confidence in his honesty or his good intentions.

The emperor had reconstituted his government before he had been two days in Paris; it only remained that he should force France to recognise it. Except in the south, no serious opposition was made to the restoration of the Empire; the whole of northern, eastern, and central France adhered to the new *régime*. But things went otherwise on the banks of the Rhone and the Gironde. In those districts the royalist party was in a clear majority among the civil population; and, though the regular troops were known to be disaffected, the partisans of the Bourbons hoped to hold their own.

At Toulouse the prefect, the Baron de Vitrolles, kept the white flag flying till April 4, when he was seized and imprisoned by General

Delaborde, his levies refusing, at the critical moment, to fire upon the troops of the line. At Bordeaux the Duchesse d'Angoulême and Lynch, the mayor who had opened the gates to Beresford in 1814, gathered several thousand men and defended the passage of the Dordogne against General Clausel (March 29). Civil war would have begun, had not the garrison of the city declared, in unmistakable terms, that it would join Clausel and attack the volunteers if matters went further. The duchess rode from barrack to barrack, making desperate appeals to the linesmen; they received her with sullen silence, and their officers besought her to fly while there was yet time. Convinced that it was hopeless to resist, she bade her army disband, and sailed for England (April 2).

Only on the Rhone was there any serious fighting. Provence was wholly royalist in feeling; and the Duc d'Angoulême had gathered more than 10,000 volunteers and National Guards at Nimes, a force which overawed the few regular battalions which remained in the district. Having boldly resolved to march on Lyons, he beat two small forces of imperialists at Montélimar and Loriol (April 1, 2), and reached Valence; but here his expedition came to an inglorious close. He found General Grouchy in front of him, while news reached him that the regular troops, whom he had left behind, had proclaimed the emperor at Avignon, Montpellier, and Nîmes. His men began to melt away; and on April 8 he signed the Convention of La Palud, by which he and his officers were granted a free departure, and his volunteers were to be pardoned on laying down their arms.

Thus ended, for the moment, the resistance of the royalists to the restoration of the Empire. The Vendée remained quiet for a while, though the old leaders were doing their best to stir up the peasantry; and the ministers at Paris deluded themselves with the idea that the west, no less than the south, was pacified. It was not till May 15 that the Vendean insurrection broke out in force.

But, though Napoleon seemed master of all France on April 10, it was not in France but at Vienna that his fate was to be settled. On the news of his landing, the plenipotentiaries of the Eight Powers had signed a declaration, by which they bound themselves to aid Louis XVIII with all their strength, and announced that Bonaparte, having broken the convention signed by him on April 1, 1814, had placed himself in the position of an outlaw, and, "as the enemy and disturber of the peace of the world," was given up to the vengeance of Europe (March 13). Four days later, a practical turn was given to this rather turgid piece of declamation, by a treaty in which Great Britain, Russia, Austria, and Prussia bound themselves each to put 150,000 men in the field, and to keep them under arms "till Bonaparte should have been rendered absolutely incapable of stirring up further troubles," By a supplementary clause, the British Ministry engaged to place £5,000,000 at the disposal of her Continental allies, in order to aid them in the rapid mobilisation of their armies.

The emperor had some hope that these warlike intentions would be affected by his having recovered possession of France with such rapidity and ease. His first care, therefore, was to address pacific overtures to Austria and Great Britain, the two Powers which he had some hopes of detaching from the Coalition. He declared that he adhered to the terms of the Treaty of Paris, wished for nothing but peace, and was anxious to give every guarantee of his good intentions. But Metternich dismissed his agent Montrond with a blank refusal; and the Prince Regent sent back unopened a letter addressed to him in Napoleon's own illegible handwriting. The temper of Great Britain was shown by the fact that, when Whitbread and other leading Whigs raised a protest against war in the House of Commons, only 72 votes were given in favour of their resolution, while 273 were against it.

Before April was out, Napoleon had to acknowledge to himself that war against united Europe was the only course open to him. Even while he was sending out the olive-branch to Vienna and London, he had been hurrying forward his military preparations. He was quite aware that he could not face his enemies with an army such as that which had won Austerlitz and Jena, still less with a force so great as that which had invaded Russia in 1812 or defended Saxony in 1813. He was shorn of the numerous auxiliary corps which had been wont to double the strength of his hosts. Was it possible to raise, within the boundaries of France alone, men enough to withstand the victors of 1814?

Napoleon could count on the aid of a mass of veterans who had been shut up in the prisons of England and Russia during his last two campaigns and had not witnessed the disaster of Leipzig or the fall of Paris. But, of the levies of 1813 and 1814, an enormous proportion had perished during the campaigns in Saxony and France; and those who remained had little cause for zeal. The actual army which Napoleon took over from Louis XVIII numbered not more than 200,000 men under arms. Of the 114 infantry regiments, some were reduced to one, most to two battalions, and all were weak. Officers to train new units could be found in plenty, among the thousands of veterans on half-pay who were offering themselves; but time to collect, embody, and arm the men would be wanting, if the Allies struck quickly.

Moreover—and this shows how the position of Napoleon in 1815 differed from that which he had enjoyed in earlier years—the emperor hesitated long before he dared let fall the odious word conscription; the one popular act of the restored monarchy had been its abolition. In April and May, the veterans and the men on leave were called back to their standards, but no call for conscripts was made. It was only a few days before fighting actually commenced that the emperor ventured to take the step of calling out the class of 1815. This is the reason why, in spite of all his efforts for three months, the regular troops, who had numbered 200,000 in March, had only risen to 284,000 in June. It was the finest army that Napoleon had commanded since Friedland, for it was purely French, and was composed almost entirely of veterans; but it was too small for its purpose.

The emperor was well aware of this and endeavoured to supplement it by auxiliary troops of a different kind. The organisation of the National Guard existed all over France; and, theoretically, all citizens from twenty to sixty years of age were liable to service in it. By a series of decrees, issued in April, it was directed that 326 battalions of this levy should be mobilised and sent to the frontier fortresses. But it was only in the east and the centre of France that the emperor could carry out this plan; in the north and west the men refused to come forward. The decrees had contemplated the placing in the field of 234,000 National Guards: on June 15 only 135,000 had been collected. In many departments, the *prefects* reported that an attempt to enforce the levy would lead to open insurrection.

Napoleon had formed some other units of secondary value, by embodying, as battalions for land service, the greater part of the men of his navy, by enrolling 26,000 *gendarmes* and *douaniers*, and by arming, under the name of *fédérés*, some thousands of the workmen of Paris and Lyons. But in June the total of his auxiliary forces did not exceed 250,000 men; and very few of the corps could have been relied upon for efficient service.

The whole army indeed, line and National Guard, was not numerous enough for the task of resisting the united hosts of Europe. Napoleon calculated that, if he had been left alone till October, he might have raised 600,000 or even 800,000 men. But he was well aware that this leisure would not be granted him. It was useless to demonstrate that in October, by the aid of conscription, the regular army might have shown 400,000 men under arms, and the force of the National Guard might have been doubled. Time was everything; and of this his enemies were as well aware as himself.

But military problems formed only part of the cloud of cares which beset Napoleon in April and May, 1815. He saw that, if he was to obtain solid support from France, he must abandon his old autocratic methods and pose as a liberal sovereign, ready to consult his people and to meet their desires. Even Louis XVIII had granted the country a Charter and a Constitution. The warmth with which the Emperor had been at first received cooled down unmistakably when it became known that his return meant war with all Europe. He saw that he must put forth some programme which would rouse enthusiasm; and he determined with small hesitation that this programme must take the form of an appeal to the Liberal section of the nation.

He must try to rouse the old Jacobin zeal for the rights of man and the liberty of France, to raise the cry of "the country in danger," to present himself as a dictator elected to save the republic, no longer as the successor of Charlemagne or the anointed of the Pope. Hence the genesis of the *Acte additionel*, a supplement to the former Imperial Constitution, which gave France a Parliament of two Houses—a nominated Chamber of Peers and an elected Chamber of Representatives; It also proclaimed the liberty of the press, and announced that the ministers would, in some degree at least, be responsible to the Chambers. The Representatives were not to be chosen directly by the people, but by small boards of electors previously nominated by the constituencies.

The *Acte additionel* was laid before the people for acceptance by means of a plebiscite. Registers were opened in every commune; but only 1,500,000 citizens took the trouble to record their suffrages. The number of votes was less than half of those received when the project for the Life Consulate was laid before the nation in 1802. Such as they were, however, they sufficed; and on June 1 the new Constitution was proclaimed, at a ceremony which the emperor designated as the *Champ de Mai*, a term borrowed from Merovingian phraseology. It was a gorgeous, interminable, and hollow affair. The emperor swore to obey the Constitution; the newly-elected Chambers and the army vowed fidelity to the emperor. To one of his confidants Napoleon (at a later date) confessed that his intention had been to abolish the House of Representatives as soon as this could safely be done.

Meanwhile he found himself, to his disgust, saddled with a Lower House of the temper which he least desired. Among 629 deputies there were some 40 Republicans, 80 pure Bonapartists, ready to revive autocracy when the favourable time should come, and about 500 Liberals of all sorts, whose main desire was to prevent that time from arriving. At the first sitting of the new legislature, two days after the *Champ de Mai*, Lucien Bonaparte was suggested for election as President of the Chamber; but the representatives ignored the official hint, and chose by an enormous majority Lanjuinais, one of the deputies for the Seine, a convinced Liberal. The constitutionalists were clearly determined that the old administrative regime should never be restored.

But domestic politics were not the worst problem in June, 1815. It was necessary to beat back the approaching armies of Europe, if the Constitution was to have even a chance of trial. Every man in France who looked at the military situation with unbiassed judgment felt himself constrained to doubt whether the breathing-space would be obtained. This was not the view of the soldiery; the rank and file started for the frontier in a state of fierce enthusiasm, such as had not been seen since the days of the Republic. It was the same with the lower ranks of the officers; the thousands who had been eating the bitter bread of half-pay during the reign of Louis XVIII had hastened back to their regiments with a firm determination that they would never again be reduced to such a life.

The memory of the slights and the poverty which they had endured made them fanatical adherents of their old master. No army that the Emperor had ever led fought with such truculent fury as that of 1815. But the spirit of the marshals and generals was very different; they knew enough of the strength of the Coalition to make them down-hearted as to the result of the coming campaign. They had thrown in their lot with Napoleon, but doubted their own wisdom, when they saw old comrades like Macdonald and Victor adhering to the Bourbons, and even Berthier refusing to return to France to join the master whose chief of the staff he had been for so many glorious years. Many took the field with a presentiment of disaster; a few who, like Ney, had fatally compromised themselves with the Bourbons, went forth like men possessed, with the vision of the hangman's rope before them in the event of defeat. Such a prospect might render them capable of acts of desperate courage but did not strengthen their judgment.

The weakest point in Napoleon's situation was that he found himself—what he had never been before, save in 1814—destitute of allies. When he returned from Elba, he had possessed one single supporter—

MARSHAL JOACHIM–NAPOLÉON MURAT

his brother-in-law of Naples. King Joachim felt sure that he would be evicted from his realm before the Congress of Vienna concluded its sessions and had resolved to link his fortunes with those of the Emperor. By good service in 1815 he might wipe out the memory of his treachery in the preceding year. His plan was to throw himself into the Emilia and Lombardy, hoping to rouse to arms the numerous partisans of the Imperial *régime*, who detested the restoration of Francis Joseph and Pius VII to their former dominions.

Murat took no counsel with his brother-in-law, but rushed forward with mad haste, and commenced the war while Napoleon was still hoping to lure Austria and Great Britain out of the league of the Continental Powers. The reorganisation of the French Army had hardly begun, when news reached Paris that Joachim had issued a proclamation calling the Italians to revolt and had invaded the Papal States at the head of 80,000 men. He occupied Rome, Florence, and Bologna, before the Austrians had collected an army to drive him back; and he was able to push on to the line of the Po. But on April 10 serious fighting began. The Austrians were far inferior in numbers, but Murat's troops were worthless.

Their old sovereign, King Ferdinand, once observed of the Neapolitan army, "You may dress it in blue, or in green, or in red; but, whichever you do, it will run." Checked at a series of combats in the Emilia, the invaders were pressed back to Tolentino, where Joachim was forced to deliver a pitched battle. The result was that he lost all his artillery and 4000 prisoners; the rest of his army dispersed (May 3). He could not rally even 10,000 men to defend Naples; and, when the Austrians pressed forward, he was forced to throw up the game and fly in disguise by sea (May 19).

A few days afterwards he arrived at Toulon, a penniless refugee. Napoleon refused to see him; he was enraged at the levity with which his brother-in-law had precipitated the war without asking his advice. He even believed (but wrongly) that, if Murat had restrained himself, Francis II might have remained neutral; under this impression he repeatedly declared that the Italian campaign had been one of the main causes of his ruin.

Since, therefore, there could be no subsidiary operations in northern Italy, Napoleon had to cast his eyes along the long eastern frontier of France, from Dunkirk to the Var, with a full knowledge that the enemy might break in at any point; there was no neutral border for a single mile, for even Switzerland had declared its adhesion to the Grand

TYPES OF THE BRITISH ARMY

Alliance. Nor could Spain be forgotten; Ferdinand VII was tardily collecting corps of observation behind the Bidassoa and the Muga. It was fortunate for the emperor that, except on one very short front of forty miles about Saarbrücken and Trier, France was surrounded by States of inferior rank—the kingdom of the Netherlands, Bavaria, Baden, Switzerland, and Sardinia. None of these could deliver an immediate attack with its own unaided resources; and the main hostile armies had to be brought from afar, from Hungary and Bohemia, from Brandenburg and Silesia, from the distant depths of Russia.

There were only two bodies of troops belonging to any of the Great Powers which lay in the immediate neighbourhood of the French frontier. In Belgium, at the moment of the emperor's return from Elba, there was a British force of some 10,000 men—the regiments which had served under Graham in Holland during the preceding year. In their company were two or three Hanoverian brigades. Out of this nucleus the British Government proposed to construct an army of 100,000 men. They ordered Wellington to Brussels, where he arrived on April 5, and began sending to him in twos and threes every corps on the home establishment that could be equipped for service.

Unfortunately, the larger part of the old Peninsular Army had been shipped to America; and, though the Peace of Ghent had been signed, these troops were still beyond the Atlantic. Very few battalions of the veterans of Spain could be put at Wellington's disposition. But, week by week, his British force was growing; by the middle of June it reached 30,000 men. In addition, a quantity of Hanoverian *Landwehr* had marched up to the Meuse and the Scheldt.

The rest of Wellington's miscellaneous host was composed of the contingents of Brunswick and Nassau, whose sovereigns, from jealousy of Prussia, had placed their little armies at the disposal of Great Britain, and of the levies of the Netherlands. The government of the new kingdom which had been created for the Prince of Orange had been surprised by the return of Napoleon at a moment when its army was still in the making.

Its whole regular force amounted on March 1 to only 10,000 men. Since then it had raised and equipped 20,000 more, mostly militia of the rawest sort. The Dutch-Belgian troops were the weakest element in Wellington's army; all the old soldiers were men who had served as conscripts under Napoleon; the rest were untrained recruits. There had always been a considerable French party in Belgium; and most of the Flemings and Walloons disliked their enforced union with Holland. The officers of the Netherland army were loyal; but too many of the rank and file, partly cowed by the reputation of their former master, partly attracted towards him by old memories, could not be trusted to give a good account of themselves. British, Germans, and Dutch included, Wellington had 105,000 men under him in June; but, of these, 20,000 were detached to form the garrisons of Antwerp, Ostend, and other Belgian fortresses.

The other army at hand was a Prussian force under General Kleist, quartered partly in the newly-formed Rhine Province, which the Congress of Vienna had given to Frederick William III, partly in eastern Belgium, about Namur and Luxemburg. It numbered only some 30,000 men in March; but the Berlin Government, acting with zeal and rapidity, had sent up three more army-corps from the east in April and May, and given the command to the indomitable Blücher. Early in June, Blücher had 117,000 men in line, four-sevenths of whom were line troops, the remainder *Landwehr* battalions. The weak part of this army consisted in the newly-raised regiments of Westphalia, Berg, and Rhineland men, who had formerly served either Napoleon or his brother Jerome as conscripts. But the preponderance of the old Prussian regiments in the whole force gave it a homogeneity which Wellington's host was far from possessing.

It was on the Prussian and Anglo-Dutch armies in Belgium that Napoleon concentrated his main attention; they were close at hand, while the Austrians had far to come, and the Russians had hardly yet crossed their own frontier. Reasoning correctly from the characters of the two generals opposed to him, he concluded that, if he waited much longer, they would attack him. His information from Belgian sympathisers, however, was to the effect that their mobilisation was not yet complete, and that both were awaiting reinforcements. Meanwhile their troops were scattered, the line of their advanced posts covering the whole frontier from the Scheldt to the Moselle. The Prussian cantonments extended from Liege to Charleroi, the Anglo-Dutch from Mons to Ghent. It would probably take three days for either army to mass on the common centre, the line Mons-Charleroi; while six would be required to concentrate them, if the British right or the Prussian left were the point selected for attack.

The emperor's whole plan of campaign was based on these facts. He resolved to collect every available man, and to throw himself upon the junction-point of the two hostile armies before they were expecting his approach. Secrecy was all-important, since with three days' notice the enemy would have time to draw together.

But, if only they failed to get wind of his approach, or to discover the exact line of his advance, he might hope to catch them in the midst of their process of concentration, and to deal with each separately. To meet them united would be almost certainly fatal, for they outnumbered his own available force almost in the proportion of two to one. It was a risky game; but in the emperor's present situation every move was hazardous, and this was the only one which promised great results. If the British and Prussians were crushed, he could hasten down to the Rhine to meet the Austrians and assail them before the Russians began to arrive. If he could but protract the game till September, his new levies would give him 400,000 more men; and with such a force anything might be possible. A crushing defeat administered to Wellington might cause the fall of the British Ministry; a second Ulm might break the spirit of Francis II and cause him to make peace. Prussia would be irreconcilable, but she might be destroyed. Looking forward, the emperor did not wholly despair; but he knew that he was staking his crown on the chance of gaining the three days that he required.

The total force which the emperor could employ against Belgium was about 125,000 men. It was 10,000 men weaker than he had intended, for, at the last moment, he had been forced to despatch against the Vendée, which had broken out in open insurrection on May 15, two divisions with a brigade of the Imperial Guard. The Vendeans were beaten; and their general, La Rochejaquelein, was killed at the combat of St Gilles, near Nantes, on June 4. But it was impossible to recall the missing divisions in time to take part in the invasion of Belgium.

The whole force which the emperor had collected under his own hand was composed of veterans of the regular army. For the defence of the eastern and southern frontiers he had told off comparatively small forces of the line, backed by masses of the National Guard. Only Rapp, who was sent to command the army of the Rhine, had a solid corps of 20,000 regulars and but few of the new levies. In the other divisions—those of the Alps under Suchet, of the eastern Pyrenees under Decaen, of the western Pyrenees under Clausel, of the Var under Brune, of the Jura under Lecourbe—the National Guards formed half, or more than half, of the total force under arms. All these six armies together numbered only 75,000 men. Of the rest of the emperor's available troops, about 130,000, mostly National Guards, had been thrown into the fortresses of the east and north.

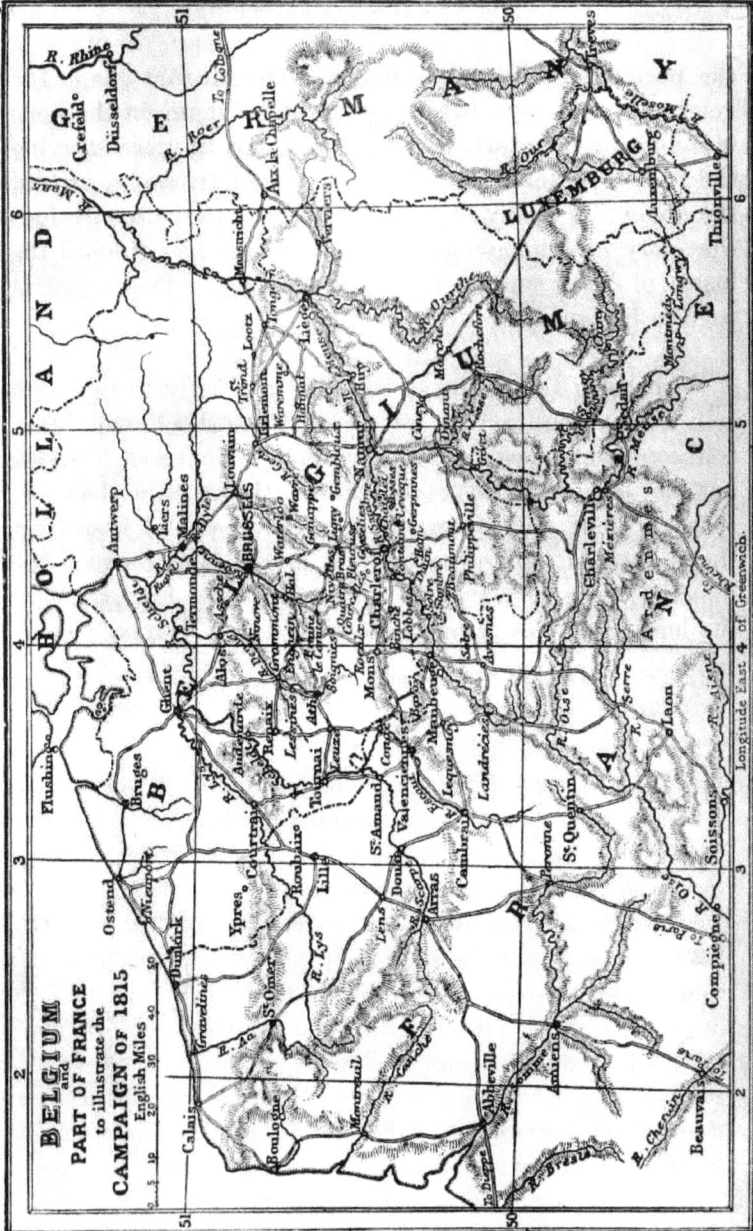

BELGIUM
and
PART OF FRANCE
to illustrate the
CAMPAIGN OF 1815
English Miles

Napoleon started for the front on June 12. His first and in some ways most important move was carried out with complete success. The five army corps which were to form the bulk of his army were drawn in from their scattered cantonments, extending from Valenciennes to Thionville, without alarming the enemy. On June 14 the whole force was concentrated on a front of not more than thirty-five miles, just where the French frontier (as it then was) projected most deeply into Belgium. Meanwhile nothing save the vaguest rumours had reached Wellington and Blücher. On June 13 the former wrote to his friend Graham:

> We have reports of Buonaparte joining the army and attacking us. But I judge from his speech to his Legislature that his departure is not likely to be immediate, and I think we are now too strong for him here.

CHAPTER 12

Ligny & Quatre Bras

When the duke was writing these words, the emperor's carriage was driving furiously forward from Laon to Avesnes; that night he slept within ten miles of the Belgian frontier. Blücher was of much the same opinion as Wellington; he was busily engaged in drawing out his plans for an advance into France, when the enemy burst across the frontier.

The emperor had thus secured the three days start over the Allies in the matter of concentration which was the necessary preliminary to a successful campaign in Belgium. He had his 125,000 men massed for the stroke, while their 210,000 were strung out on a front of a hundred miles. It remained to be seen how he would utilise this tremendous advantage. His five corps were commanded by d'Erlon and Reille—veterans of the army of Spain—Vandamme, Gérard, and Lobau. Of the marshals, only three were with the army. Soult acted as chief of the staff, a post which he had never before filled, and in which he showed himself, from lack of experience, markedly inferior to Berthier. Ney, who owing to his conduct in March had been kept in a sort of half-disgrace during the last three months, had been called up at the last moment and placed in command of the left wing—the corps of Reille and d'Erlon. Grouchy, whose reputation had been won as a leader of horse, took charge of the great cavalry reserve.

At dawn on the morning of June 15 the French Army passed the frontier and threw itself upon the outposts of the Allies. The blow was

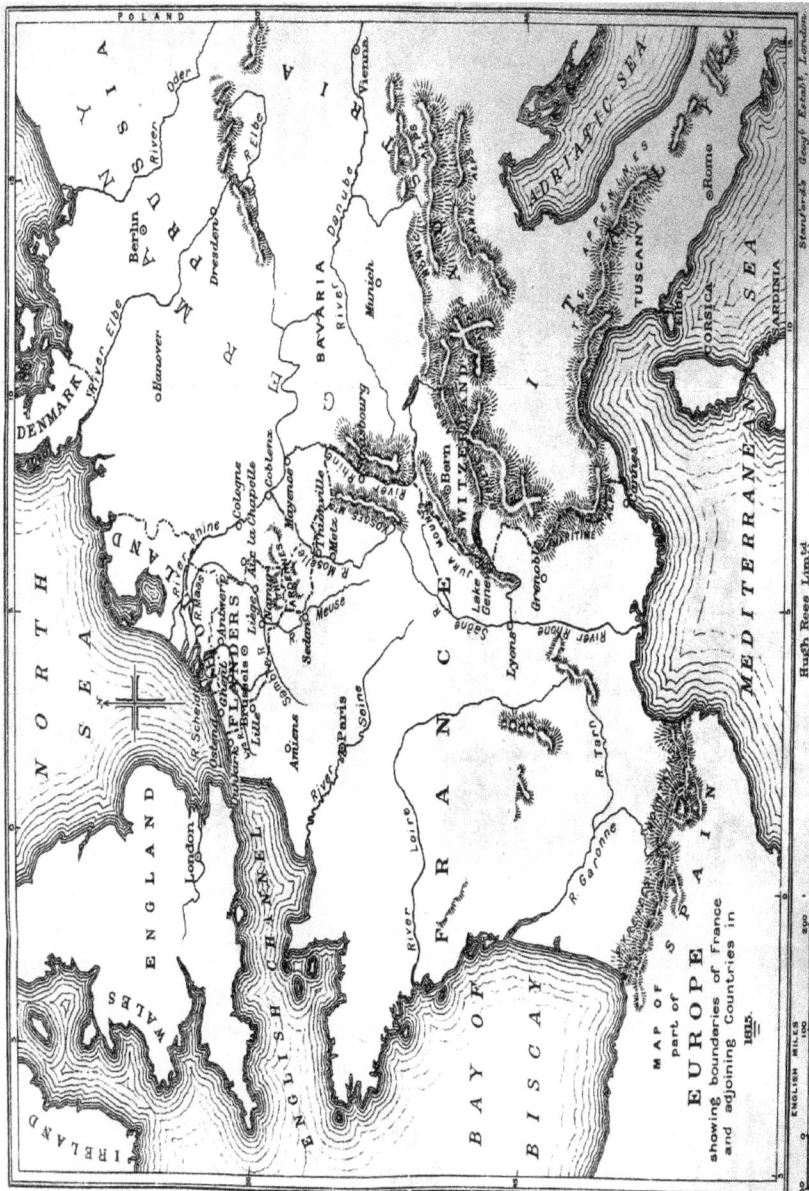

MAP OF
part of
EUROPE
showing boundaries of France
and adjoining Countries in
1815.

POLAND

NORTH SEA

DENMARK

River Elbe

River Oder

Berlin
Dresden
Hanover

Elbe

BAVARIA

Munich
River Danube
Vienna

ADRIATIC SEA

Rome

TUSCANY

CORSICA

SARDINIA

MEDITERRANEAN SEA

FRANCE

GERMANY

Cologne
Coblenz
Aix la Chapelle
River Rhine
River Meuse
Metz
Sedan
Meuse

FLANDERS
Brussels
Scheldt

Bern
SWITZERLAND
Lake Geneva
Grenoble
JURA MTS.

Paris
River Seine
Amiens
River Loire

SAONE
River Rhone
Lyons

BAY OF BISCAY

R. Garonne
R. Tarn

SPAIN

ENGLAND
London
WALES
IRELAND

ENGLISH CHANNEL

ENGLISH MILES

Stanford's Geog.l Estab.t London

Hugh Rees Lim.td

delivered on the extreme right of the Prussian Army, in and about Charleroi, and just failed to touch Wellington's extreme left at Mons. On the first day, only the corps of Ziethen was engaged on the side of the Allies; and this force, caught before it could concentrate, and assailed by superior numbers, was driven northward and eastward with considerable loss. By nightfall the emperor was in possession of Charleroi and the bridges of the Sambre; and Ziethen had fallen back behind Fleurus.

Blücher, on hearing of this first assault, had set his whole army on the march westward. At noon on June 16 Ziethen was joined by Pirch's corps from Namur, and Thielmann's from Dinant and Huy; Blücher had thus 90,000 men in hand. His fourth corps, that of Bülow, had not arrived. It had lain at Liége, forty miles from Charleroi, and was still a day's march from the main army. Blücher, however, had made up his mind to fight without waiting for Bülow, and drew up his host on the hill-sides behind Ligny and St Amand, looking down into the valley where Fleurus lies.

If the position of Blücher was not quite satisfactory at this moment, that of Wellington was much less so. The duke had received definite details of the enemy's movements many hours later than ought to have been the case. Ziethen had sent him news that his outposts were attacked early on the 15th, before anything decisive had happened. After this, engrossed in the details of fighting, the Prussian general forgot to keep the British headquarters informed of the developments of the French advance. It was only about 4 p.m. that Wellington received intelligence from several quarters which showed that the attack in the direction of Charleroi was being made by several army-corps and was evidently part of a general advance.

The duke immediately ordered all his divisions to concentrate at their headquarters and to be ready to march at a moment's notice. But he was still uncertain whether the movement on Charleroi was being carried out by the whole of the emperor's army, or whether a second column might not be advancing on the other high-road which leads to Brussels by way of Mons. His ignorance was due to the negligence of Dörnberg, the officer commanding the British cavalry-screen on the line Mons-Tournay, who failed to send any report as to matters in his front till night. The duke had been of opinion that the Mons road presented advantages for the enemy which the Charleroi road did not and refused to commit himself to a concentration on his extreme left till he was sure that his left-centre was safe. Hence it was only late in the evening that, reassured on this point, he directed his scattered divisions to concentrate on Nivelles, Braine-le-Comte, and Hal.

As they could not move till daybreak on the 16th, he was in the unfortunate position of having no troops on the Brussels-Charleroi road next morning save one Dutch and one Nassau brigade, at Quatre-Bras and Nivelles; while within supporting distance there were only the reserve from Brussels—some 26,000 British, Hanoverian, and Brunswick troops—and one or two brigades at Enghien and Braine-le-Comte. The duke clearly underrated the rapidity with which Napoleon would push forward when his crown was at stake. That night Wellington remained at Brussels and attended the Duchess of Richmond's famous ball. At daybreak he rode out to visit his outposts, and then to confer with Blücher.

Actual contact between the British and French outposts had been established late in the afternoon of the 15th, when the cavalry at the head of the emperor's left columns struck the pickets of the Nassau brigade under Prince Bernard of Saxe-Weimar at Frasnes, and drove them back to Quatre-Bras, where the prince showed fight. Ney, who was in command of this part of the French Army, reported the fact to the emperor, and encamped opposite Quatre-Bras, waiting for his infantry to come up. There were only 4000 men in front of him; and it would be many hours before the Brussels troops, which only started at daybreak on the 16th, could arrive to support Prince Bernard. But of this the marshal was necessarily ignorant; he could only report that he was in touch with the enemy, who seemed inclined to stand.

Thus, on the morning of the second day of the campaign, the position of the French Army was excellent. Blücher had not collected even three-fourths of his army at Ligny till noon; Wellington would not, till twelve hours were passed, be able to concentrate more than a third of his at Quatre-Bras. The emperor, however, seems to have overrated his advantage, great as it was. His orders for the 16th directed Ney to drive away whatever lay in front of him at Quatre-Bras, and then to fall upon the flank of the Prussian force at Ligny. This force Napoleon, in his earliest despatches, seems to have estimated at a single corps only. But, as the day were on, he discovered it to be much stronger than he had supposed and deferred his attack till his whole right wing had come up.

Ney, with less justification, behaved in a similar fashion in front of Quatre-Bras, and, before assailing Prince Bernard's brigade, waited till he had the whole of the infantry of Reille's corps under his hand.

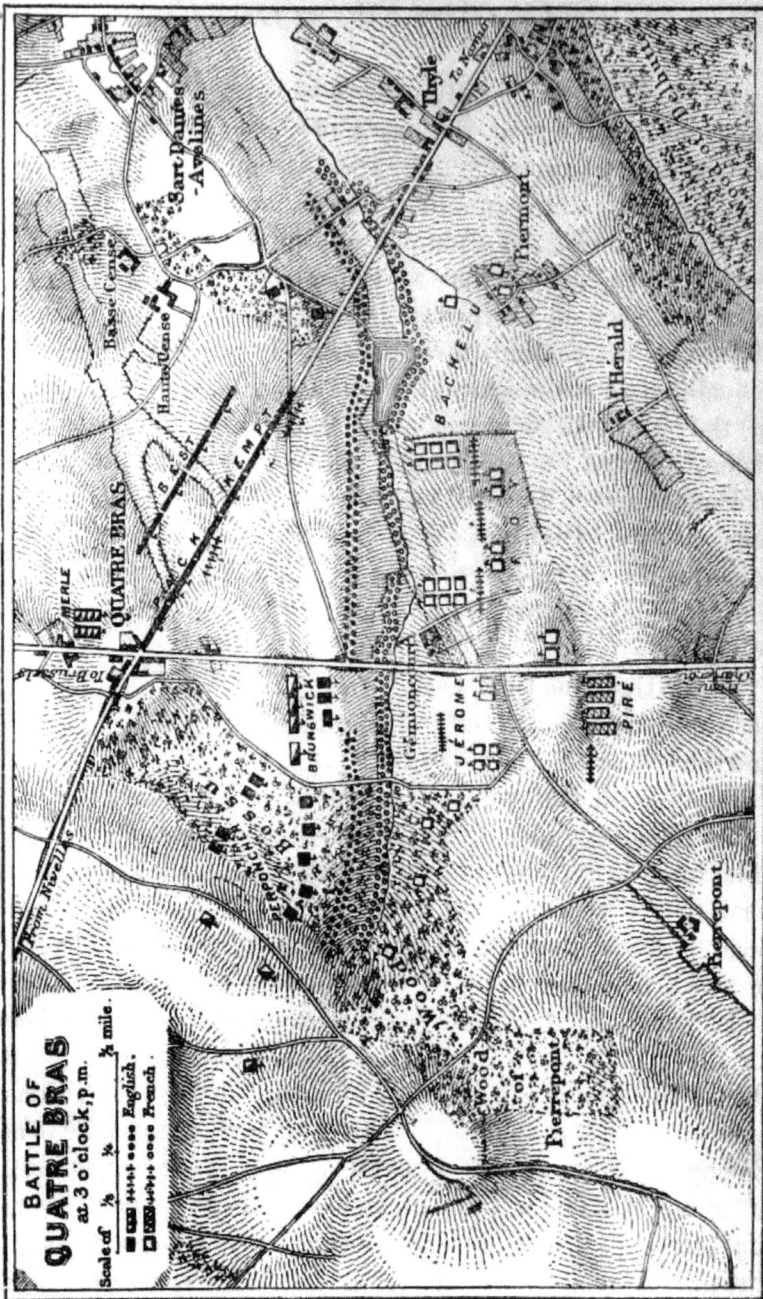

BATTLE OF
QUATRE BRAS
at 3 o'clock, p.m.

Scale of ⅛ ¼ ½ mile.

━━━ ┅┅┅ English.
━━━ ┅┅┅ French.

Sart-Dames
-Avelines

Doyle

To N.

Piermont

Bachelu

L'Herald

Basse Censée

Haute Censée

QUATRE BRAS

MERLE

To Brussels

Gémioncourt

JÉROME

PIRÉ

To Brussels

BRUNSWICK

From Nivelles

Bois

Pierrepont

Wood

col

Pierrepont

Thus, nothing happened on either field of battle till noon was well passed. Wellington, after visiting his force at Quatre-Bras, rode over to Ligny, interviewed Blücher, and told him that he would bring him aid if he was not himself attacked and detained by the French left. The promise was conditional, and could never be carried out, as Ney found full occupation for all the British divisions, as they successively reached Quatre-Bras during the afternoon. The duke then returned to his own advance-guard, just in time to meet Ney's attack, which was delivered a few minutes before his arrival.

Between 2 and 3 p.m. on June 16 the emperor, having massed in front of the Prussian position the Guard, the corps of Vandamme and Gerard, and all his reserve cavalry, thought himself strong enough to begin. As a matter of fact, he had 20,000 men less than Blücher on the field, and, even when Lobau's corps came up late in the afternoon, was still in a grave numerical inferiority. But, not fully aware of this, he commenced a vigorous attack upon the line of villages which covered the right and centre of the Prussian position; their left wing he merely "contained" with the numerous cavalry of Grouchy. This was the commencement of a long and obstinate struggle. The French repeatedly stormed Ligny and the three villages of St Amand; Blücher, perpetually feeding his fighting-line from his reserve, always won them back again.

But the Prussians suffered more heavily than their opponents, because their troops were exposed to the preponderating artillery fire of the French, whenever they descended the bare slopes above the villages in their counter-attacks. This was not the sort of battle that the emperor desired; he had been for some time expecting Ney to appear, in accordance with his orders, behind the Prussian right wing. But no French troops showed in this direction, the marshal being engaged in a bitter struggle with Wellington at Quatre-Bras and finding himself unable to spare a man for the turning movement.

The emperor, however, cared little for the subsidiary action far to his left; he sent orders directly to d'Erlon, the commander of the 1st corps, which formed Ney's reserve and was just approaching Quatre-Bras at the moment, bidding him draw off eastward and march towards Ligny, so as to fall upon the Prussian flank and rear. D'Erlon obeyed, but, by a slight misdirection in his march, headed for Fleurus rather than Ligny, and therefore came upon Napoleon's battlefield in such a way as to join the emperor's left, rather than to circumvent the Prussian right. Napoleon was for a moment puzzled by the ap-

BATTLE OF
QUATRE BRAS
at 8 o'clock, p.m.

Scale of ¼ ½ ¾ ½ mile.

English.
French.

BATTLE OF QUATRE BRAS

pearance of troops in this direction and slackened in his attacks on St Amand and Ligny. But, learning that the new-comers were his own missing corps, he recommenced the assault on Blücher's line. This final attack, however, obtained no support from d'Erlon, who at this juncture received pressing orders from Ney, bidding him return and save him from Wellington's overpowering numbers. Though he was now in a position to manoeuvre with splendid effect against the Prussian right, d'Erlon turned back and started for Quatre-Bras.

Thus, Napoleon had to fight out his battle with no aid from the west. He brought it, however, to a successful conclusion, by dashing the Imperial Guard against the Prussian centre just as night fell. Blücher had used up his reserves and was unable to withstand the tremendous impact of this mass of veteran troops. He himself charged at the head of his last remaining cavalry brigades, but was repulsed, thrown from his horse, and nearly taken prisoner. He was dragged off the field almost insensible from his fall; and his army at the same moment abandoned all its positions and rolled back to the villages two miles in the rear of its original position.

Blücher had lost more than 20,000 men, including many stragglers from the Berg and Westphalian *Landwehr*, who ran away and did not stop till they reached Aix-la-Chapelle. The emperor had also suffered heavily; his losses must have amounted to about 11,000 men, and he had taken few prisoners and only twenty-one guns. Thus, Napoleon had won a victory, but not a decisive one. The Prussians shook themselves together at dawn, and retired unmolested in the direction of Wavre, the point at which they could most easily put themselves in connexion with Wellington's army. This was quite contrary to the suppositions of the emperor, who imagined the Prussians to be far more disorganised than they were and thought it probable that they had retired due east, towards their own base at Liege, while really, they had marched north. This false hypothesis had results fatal to its framer on the next day but one.

Ligny, however, in spite of d'Erlon's mistake, was distinctly a victory; at Quatre-Bras neither party could claim so well-marked a success. Ney, as we have already mentioned, delivered his attack on Wellington's advance-guard at about 2 p.m., with the whole corps of Reille. The line of the Allies was at once crumpled up; but, just as it gave way there arrived on the field Picton's British division, the first of the Brussels reserves to reach the front, and, shortly after, the Duke of Brunswick and his corps. At the same moment Wellington himself

BATTLE
OF
LIGNY
16th June 1815

rode up. He had just time to deploy his fresh troops, when the French attack pressed up against them. After a fierce struggle, in which the Duke of Brunswick fell, it was beaten off.

Soon afterwards both sides received reinforcements, Kellermann's *cuirassiers* joining Ney, while the duke was strengthened by Alten's British division from Braine-le-Comte. Ney resumed the attack, dashing his cavalry fiercely against the allied centre. More than one British battalion was broken; and the *cuirassiers* penetrated as far as the houses of Quatre-Bras. But they were finally driven off, and the allied line reformed itself. Ney, who had now learnt that his master had called off the corps of d'Erlon, his sole reserve, was in a state of desperate fury. Napoleon, by stripping him of half his infantry force, had condemned him to defeat; in his rage, Ney sent to recall d'Erlon, despite the Imperial orders, and so ruined Napoleon's plan for making Ligny a decisive battle. But the missing corps was too late in its return to Quatre-Bras to save the day in that direction.

Long ere its arrival, Wellington assumed the offensive; he had just received Cooke's division, the British Guards, and with the aid of this reinforcement attacked the French along the whole line. His superiority in numbers was now very marked; he had 32,000 men in hand to Ney's 22,000, and could not be held back. The enemy, still fighting fiercely, had been forced to return to their original positions when darkness brought the battle to an end. The losses were equally distributed; each side had suffered about 4200 or 4300 casualties.

Looked at from the tactical point of view, Quatre-Bras was a severe check to Ney. But from the strategical point of view the action had served Napoleon's purpose fairly well, since the marshal had prevented Wellington from sending a single man to Blücher's aid. Ligny would have had very different results, if the duke had been able to crush the containing corps in front of him early in the day and had then marched for St Amand.

The reason why he failed to do so was the lateness of his concentration; he had to fight Ney with the Brussels reserves almost unaided. If his troops from Ghent, Oudenarde, and Ath had started twelve hours earlier, Ney must have been destroyed. During the night, the belated divisions poured in, till nearly the whole army was concentrated on the morning of the 17th. But it was now too late. The news of Ligny had arrived; and the duke saw that the emperor would infallibly join Ney before the day was out. He resolved to draw back at once from his advanced position, and to seek a junction with Blücher before he again gave battle. Early in the morning he sent word to the Prussian head-quarters that he would stand on the position of Mont St Jean, if he were promised the help of one of Blücher's army-corps.

Napoleon was slow to move during the morning of June 17. He was fatigued by the long running fight on the Thursday and by the battle on the Friday; but this fact does not wholly account for the strange lethargy that seems to have seized him on this day. He spent the morning in talking politics with his generals, in driving round the battlefield of the previous day, and in reviewing his victorious troops. Every moment was of importance to him, yet he squandered seven precious hours before he made a move.

Not till about noon did he issue the orders which were to govern the rest of the campaign. He directed Grouchy to take charge of the corps of Vandamme and Gérard and half the reserve cavalry—some 33,000 men, when the losses of Ligny were deducted—and to follow the Prussians in whatever direction they had retreated; He was to keep in touch with them at all costs, and to discover whether they were retiring towards their base, or showing any signs of moving towards Wellington. Napoleon himself intended to join Ney with the Imperial Guard, the rest of the reserve cavalry, and the corps of Lobau. Owing to the late hour at which the orders were given, neither of the columns got away till 2 or 3 p.m.

Meanwhile, owing to the emperor's tardy start, the whole Prussian army had slipped away unmolested; and the French cavalry had not even discovered the route which it had taken. Much time was lost in seeking for Blücher on the road to Namur. At nightfall, Grouchy knew that some of the Prussians must be moving on Wavre, which would bring them in the direction of the British but was still uncertain whether their main body was or was not retreating eastward in the direction of Liege. For this he cannot be seriously blamed; the responsibility lies partly with the emperor for losing time in the morning, partly with the two cavalry generals, Pajol and Excelmans, who had shown gross carelessness in letting the enemy slip away and failing to find him again.

Delayed by heavy rain, which fell all through the afternoon and evening, Grouchy's infantry did not reach Gembloux till nightfall. They had covered less than ten miles in the day; the Prussians had covered twenty, and were safely concentrated at Wavre, where they were joined by Bülow's intact corps, which had at last got up from Liege to the front.

In this part of the field Napoleon had practically lost twenty-four hours—one of the three precious days which he had gained by his rapid concentration and his vigorous advance. Things went almost as badly for him in its western portion. Wellington had begun to withdraw his army from Quatre-Bras at 10 a.m. on June 17. Owing to his late start from Ligny, Napoleon came on the ground only when the last of Wellington's infantry was far advanced on the route to Mont St Jean; a mere cavalry screen under Lord Uxbridge remained in his front. Recovering his energy when it was too late, the emperor drove in the British cavalry, and pursued it fiercely throughout the late afternoon. But he could neither catch it nor do it any serious harm; at the defile of Genappe, indeed, Uxbridge turned back and broke the leading brigade of the Imperial horsemen by a downhill charge of the Life Guards.

After this he was not so severely pressed; the same heavy thunderstorm which had delayed Grouchy did much to check the emperor's pursuit. It was nearly 7 p.m. on the 17th before the head of the French army reached the front of the position of Mont St Jean, where Wellington had been arranging his army as it came up. A reconnaissance in the rain showed the emperor that his enemy was standing ready to receive him; and he halted to allow the rest of his troops to arrive. So long was his column that much of the infantry did not reach the front till after midnight, and at least one division only on the following morning. The troops were much fatigued by their long tramp in the rain and had outmarched their commissariat; there was no proper distribution of rations either that night or the next day. They bivouacked in the mud of the fields, drenched through, fireless, and half-starved.

Wellington's position on that night was an anxious one, in spite of the fact that he had carried out his retreat without loss or disorder. All now depended on the Prussians; he had sent them, early in the morning, his offer to fight on the battle-ground he had chosen, if he were promised the aid of a single army-corps. If they replied that this was impossible, he would have to retire again, and to sacrifice Brussels, which lay some eleven miles to his rear. It was only after midnight that he received the all-important answer to his proposal. Blücher had been *hors de combat* on the 17th, owing to the contusions he had suffered at Ligny; and the details of the Prussian movements during that day had been regulated by Gneisenau, his chief of the staff. But at night the indomitable old man had recovered sufficiently to resume command; it was he who received the duke's offer, and he promptly accepted it.

Certain objections were made by Gneisenau and other generals, who thought that a flank march so near the enemy was full of dangers, and that it was wrong to throw up the safe line of retreat on Maestricht which the army now possessed. This was true enough; but the chance of catching Napoleon in flank and overwhelming him with superior numbers was too good to be lost. Blücher wrote that he would despatch Bülow's corps to join the English at daybreak and send after it that of Pirch. His other two corps should follow if not prevented. He knew Grouchy's exact position and thought it might be necessary to detach Thielmann and Ziethen to hold him back. Blücher had risen to the full height of the situation; and these orders, once given, decided the fate of the campaign. If they had been carried out with exactitude, they would have ended it with far less expenditure of blood than was actually incurred on June 18. The execution, however, was not equal to the conception; the plan worked, but it worked over-slowly and over-late.

Chapter 13
The Battle of Waterloo

Reassured as to the cooperation of the Prussians, Wellington drew up his army on the hill-side of Mont St Jean, across the two high-roads Nivelles-Brussels and Charleroi-Brussels, which there meet. The position does not at the first sight appear very strong; the slopes are gentle, and do not rise more than 120 or 150 feet above the level of the valley which divides them from the French lines. There was no cover in front, save at three isolated points. Before the British right lay the farm, orchard, and copse of Hougoumont, surrounded with hedges and walls; in front of the exact centre, on the Charleroi high-road, is the smaller farm of La Haye Sainte; far away on the extreme left lie two other farms, close together, Papelotte and La Haye.

All these were occupied: Hougoumont by a brigade of the British Guards; La Haye Sainte by a picked detachment of the German Legion; the other two by Bernard of Saxe-Weimar's Nassau brigade. The enemy would have to storm them, before he could make any solid lodgement in the British position. But the feature which Wellington regarded as most advantageous in his field of battle was that behind his fighting line the ground stretched away in a broad plateau falling slightly toward the north. Here he could array his reserves completely out of sight of the enemy and bring them to the front without expos-

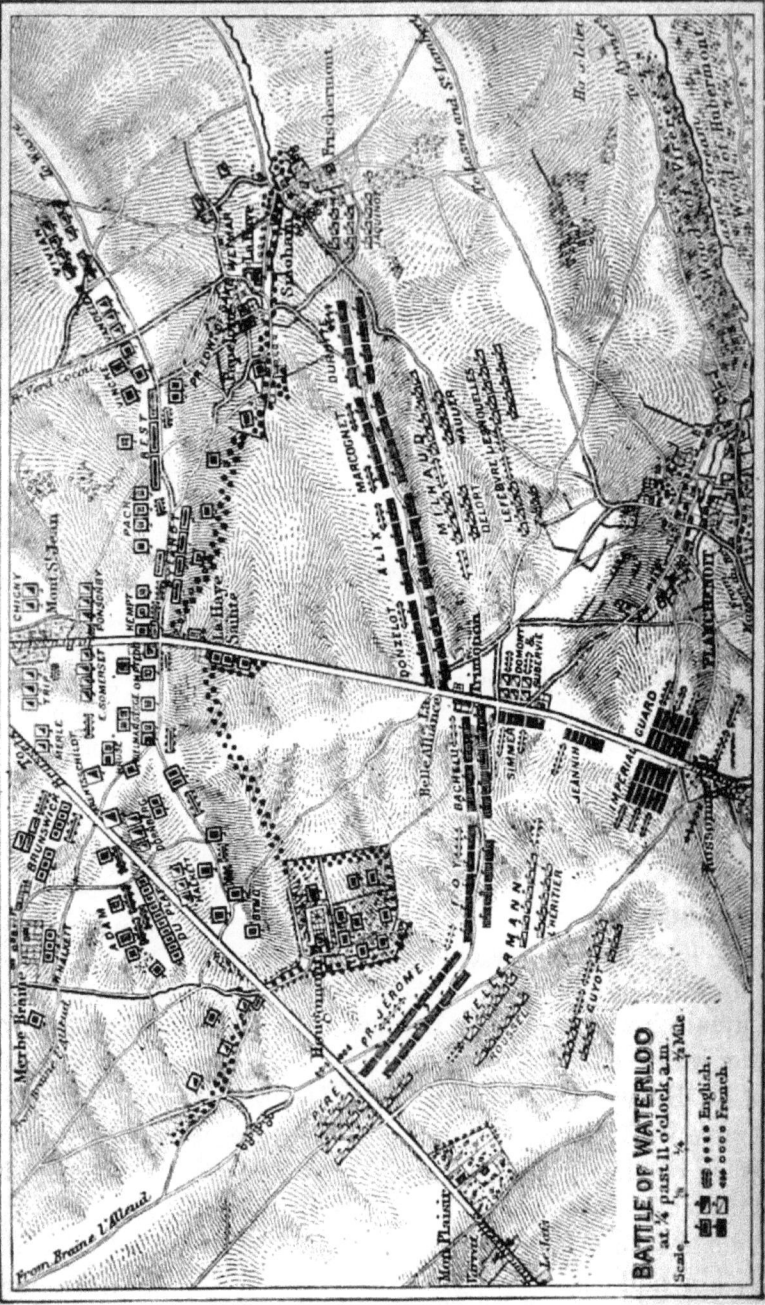

BATTLE OF WATERLOO
at ¼ past 11 o'clock, a.m.

Scale. ¼ ½ ¾ Mile.

∗∗∗∗ English.
∘∘∘∘ French.

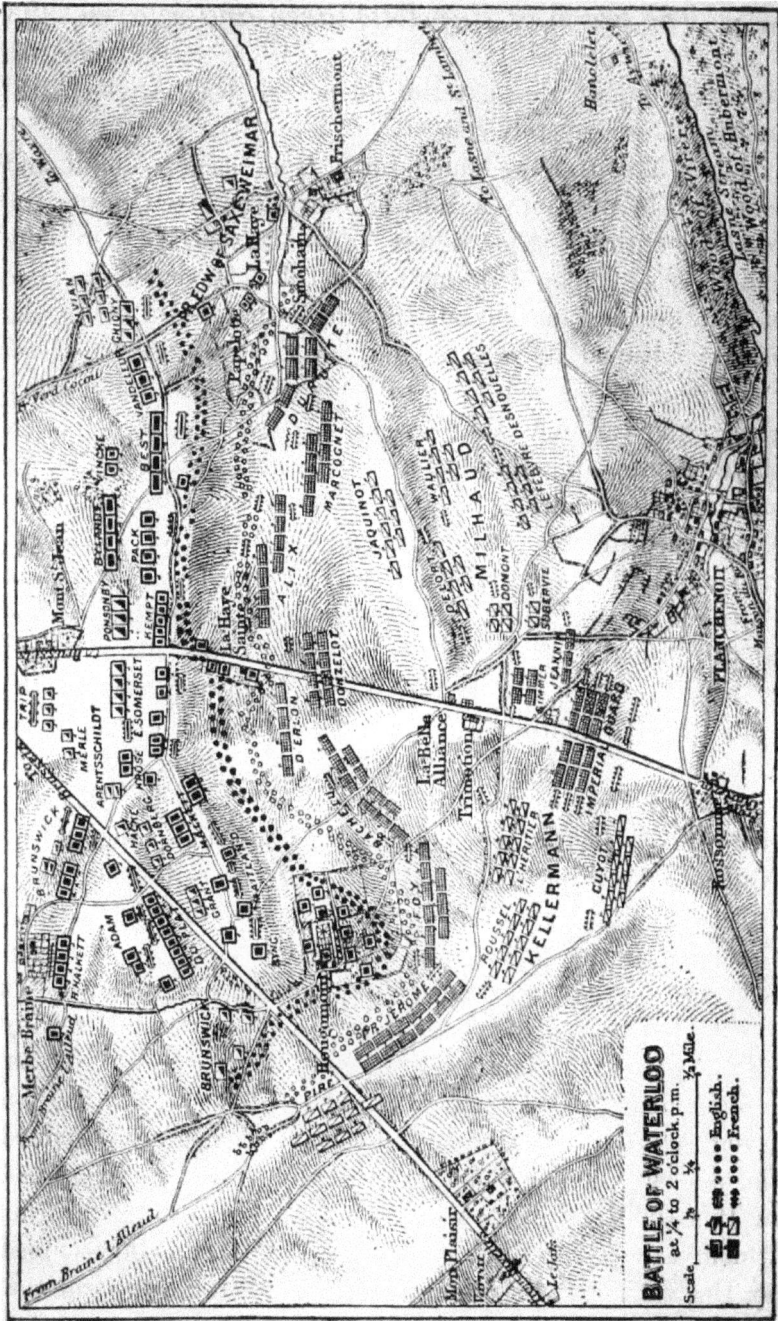

BATTLE OF WATERLOO
at ¼ to 2 o'clock p.m.

Scale ¼ ¼ ½ Mile.

●●●● English.
●●●● French.

From Braine l'Alleud

Mont Plaisir

Merbe Braine

BRUNSWICK

Braine

ADAM

H. HALKETT

MAITLAND

BYNG

COOKE

HALKETT

PACK

KRUSE

KIELMANSEGGE

ARENTSSCHILDT

MEALE

TRIP

E. SOMERSET

Mont S. Jean

KEMPT

PONSONBY

BEST

VINCKE

BYLANDT

CHILLY

PRINCE OF SAXE-WEIMAR

La Haye

Smohain

Frischermont

la Belle Alliance

Trimotion

DE LA COSTE

ALIX

MARCOGNET

JAQUINOT

DURUTTE

D'ERLON

DOMZELOT

BACHELU

FOY

JEROME

REILLE

KELLERMANN

IMPERIAL

CUYOT

GUARD

LEFEBVRE DESNOUELLES

SUBERVIE

DOMONT

MILHAUD

WALTER

DELORD

RUSSEL

PLANCHENOIT

Rossomme

From Genappe and S. Lambert

Bois de Paris

Lasne stream and S. Lambert Wood

Hanotelet

Mont S. Jean

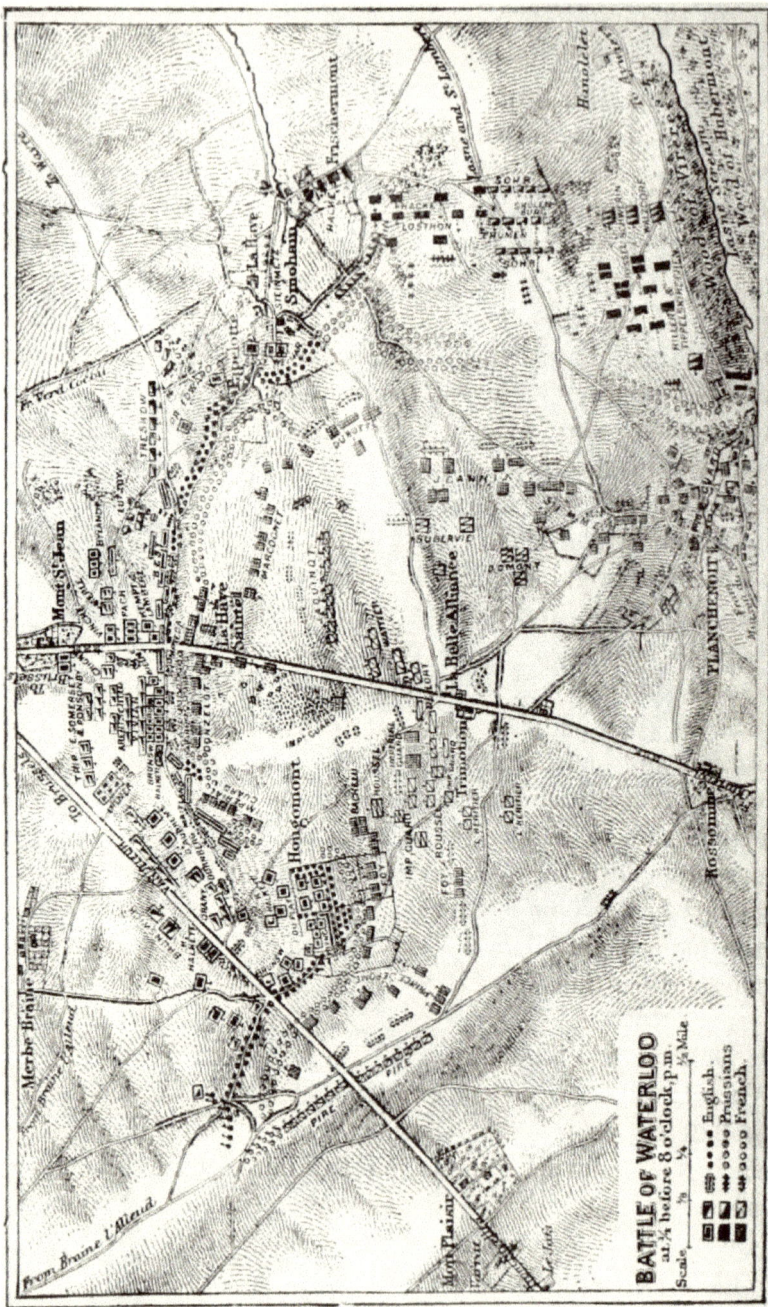

BATTLE OF WATERLOO
at ¾ before 8 o'clock, p.m.
Scale, ⅛   ¼   ½ Mile

English.
Prussians.
French.

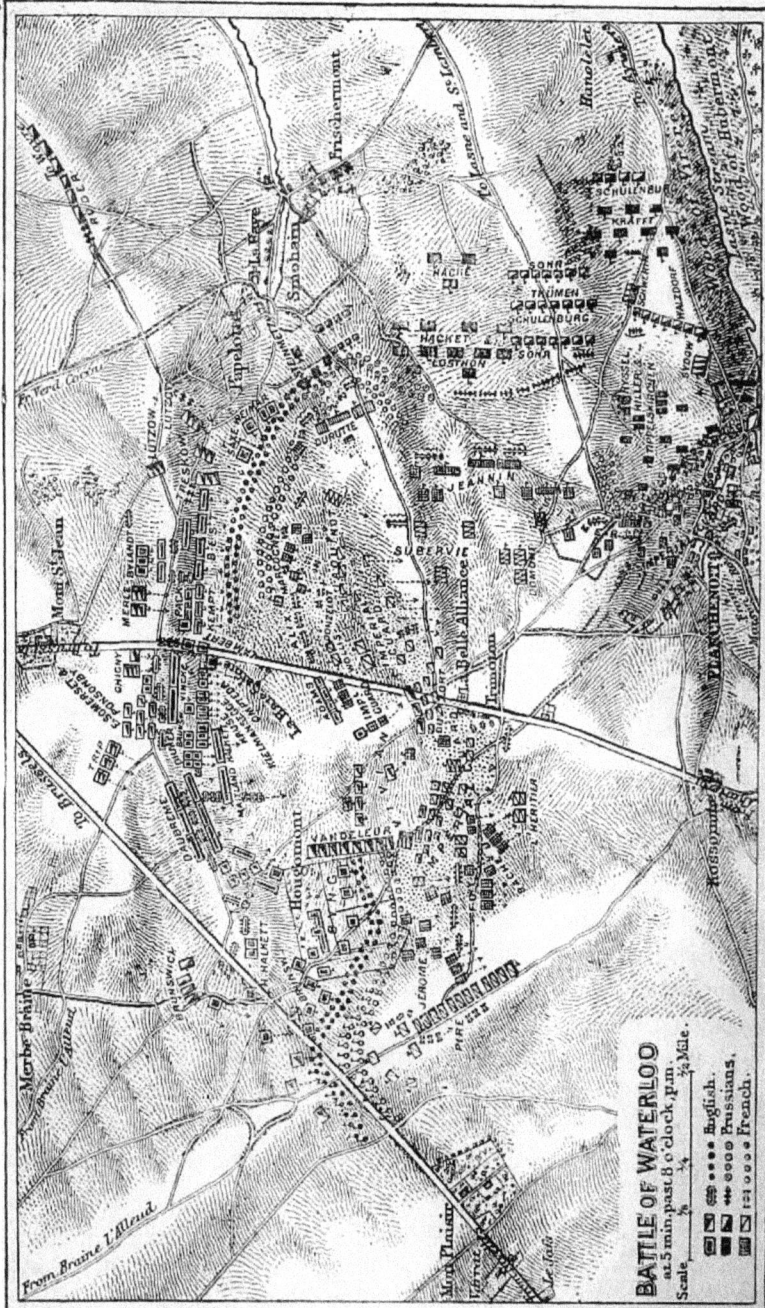

BATTLE OF WATERLOO
at 5 min. past 8 o'clock. p.m.
Scale. ¼ ⅓ ½ Mile.

English.
Prussians.
French.

ing them to view till the crest was reached. It was the exact converse of the Ligny position, where all the Prussian reserves had been exposed to Napoleon's eye, and many of them to his artillery, before they were brought into action.

Wellington had 67,000 men on the ground. Of these, 24,000 were British; 5800 belonged to the King's German Legion, of Peninsular fame; 11,000 were Hanoverians. There was the Brunswick corps, reduced to 5500 men by its losses at Quatre-Bras; two Nassau brigades (Kruse and Saxe-Weimar) over 6000 strong; and finally, 14,000 Dutch-Belgians. These last were the weak point in the line; horse and foot had behaved feebly at Quatre-Bras and did not redeem their reputation at Waterloo. It was a motley array at best, but, with Blücher due before noon, all seemed safe; the duke knew it would be more than a mere morning's work to wear down his stubborn British and German infantry.

It was probably in reliance on the early arrival of his ally that Wellington had left, far out on his right, a day's march from Mont St Jean, a force consisting of a strong Dutch-Belgian division, with one British and one Hanoverian brigade, under General Colville and Prince Frederick of Orange. They lay at Hal, on the Mons-Brussels road, nearly 14,000 strong, intended apparently to guard against a turning movement of the French. But it had long been ascertained that Napoleon had no detached corps to the west; it was a mistake not to call Colville in.

On the low ridge opposite Mont St Jean, Napoleon had arrayed some 74,000 veteran troops, on each side of the farm of La Belle Alliance and the high-road from Charleroi to Brussels. He showed no hurry to begin the battle on the morning of that eventful Sunday, June 18, 1815. Indeed, the rear of his infantry only reached the field after daybreak and required some hours of rest. Wellington lay quietly in his front, inviting attack: Blücher, so Napoleon supposed, was out of the game. He had news from Grouchy, dated from Gembloux at 10 p.m. on the 17th, to the effect that one Prussian corps had retired on Wavre, but that the rest of the troops defeated at Ligny were heading for Perwez, on the road to Liége, i.e. were falling back towards their base, and leaving Wellington to his fate.

The marshal added that he intended to follow the force that had moved on Wavre, in order to head it off from Brussels and separate it from the British Army. This information seemed to guarantee the emperor against any interference on the part of the Prussians. Grouchy, it is true, learnt more of the facts of the situation on the following morning, and wrote at 6 a.m. to inform his master that the bulk of Blücher's men had gone to Wavre, not to Perwez. But this despatch did not reach La Belle Alliance till after Napoleon had made his arrangements; and, even if it had arrived earlier, it contained no hint that the Prussians were moving on Mont St Jean.

Napoleon, therefore, gave his weary army a long rest after daybreak, and put off the hour of attack, so that the sodden ground might grow drier and permit of the free movement of his artillery across the fields. It was only about 11 a.m. that his forces were deployed for action. Their array was very simple, as simple as the emperor's own plan of battle, which contemplated nothing more nor less than the smashing in of the British centre by a tremendous frontal attack. His army was formed in three lines; in front were Reille's corps on the left, d'Erlon's on the right, each with cavalry on the outer wing. The second line was formed of Lobau's incomplete infantry corps (only 7000 men), with the reserve cavalry, no less than six divisions, deployed on its wings. Last of all came the Imperial Guard, 20,000 strong, the infantry in column on the high-road, the cavalry in line to right and left. It was a magnificent array, and every man was visible from the British position.

The emperor, on the other hand, could not make out much of Wellington's arrangements. There were visible to him only the four isolated farms on the slope, and above them a line of infantry and guns along the crest; the reserves were out of sight. The duke had formed a front line of twelve infantry brigades, six British, four Hanoverian, one Nassau, and one Dutch, with two British cavalry brigades on his extreme left, in the direction from which the Prussians were expected to appear. In second line, behind his centre, was the rest of his horse, British and Dutch. The infantry reserve was massed for the most part behind the right wing, because the Prussian aid was expected on the left. Blücher, according to the arrangements made on the preceding night, would form the true reserve of the duke's left wing.

Never, in any of his earlier fights, had Napoleon massed such numbers on so short a front; the whole French line was less than three miles long, including the cavalry on its extreme wings. In the tactical disposition the infantry was used in heavy columns of unprecedented solidity. They were to push their way through the British line by mere force of impact. This arrangement did not please those of the emperor's lieutenants who had seen the wars of Spain and remembered the poor exhibition that column-tactics had always made against the

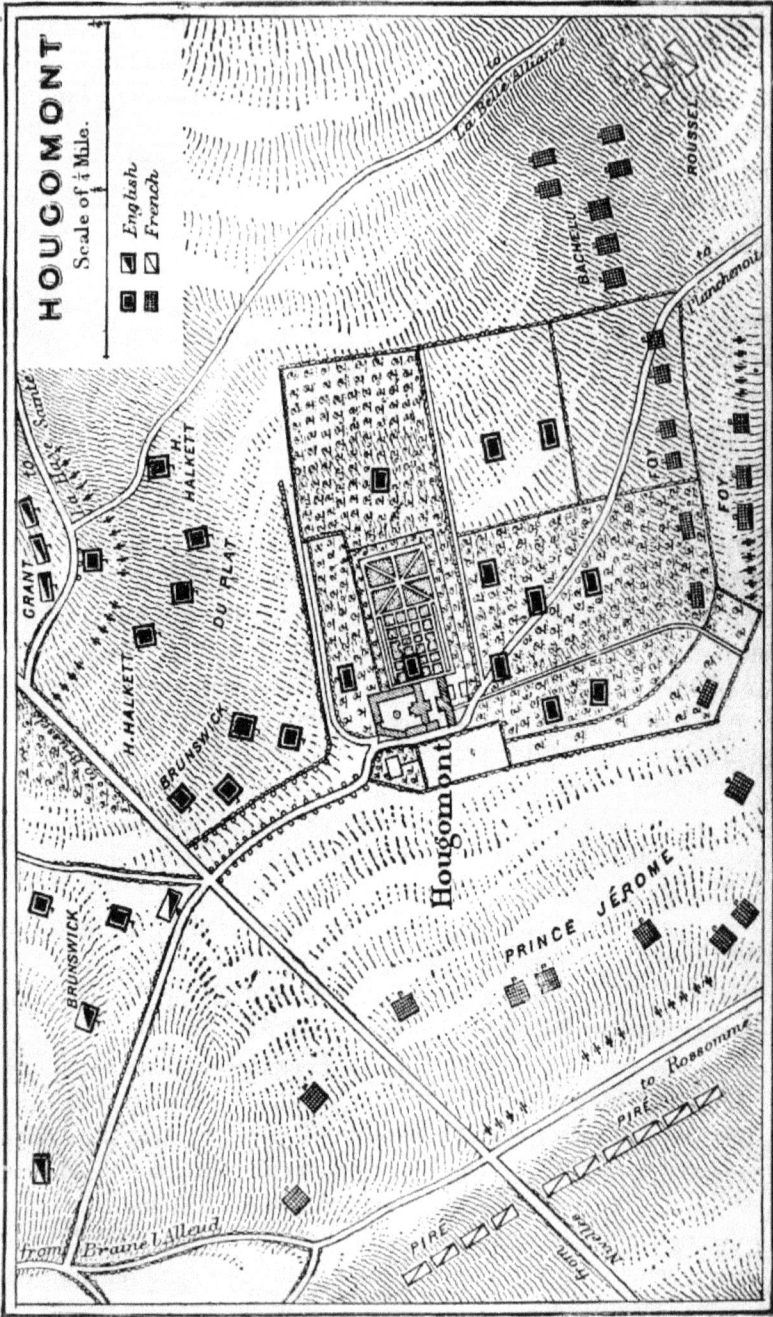

HOUGOMONT

Scale of ¼ Mile.

English
French

English two-deep formation. Soult urged caution; but Napoleon replied in an insulting outburst:

> You were beaten by Wellington, and so you think he is a great general. But I tell you that Wellington is a bad general, and the English are bad troops; they will merely be a breakfast for us!

A little later, Reille was asked his opinion of the British infantry; he replied that he thought that, in a good defensive position, they could repel any frontal attack. He hoped that his master would manoeuvre and try flank movements; front-to-front action would be costly and unsuccessful. The emperor paid no attention; he was determined to try the effect of assaults by massive columns upon the long red line that crowned the opposite hill-side.

About 11.30 a.m. the French Army was at last on the move. After some cannonading, a division of Reille's infantry pressed in upon the farm of Hougoumont. After some fighting, the copse and orchard were carried; but in the farm-buildings and the garden two battalions of the British Guards held their own and beat off regiment after regiment as it surged in upon them. This, however, was but a side-issue; the emperor's real attack was to be delivered on the other side of the highroad, half a mile further to the east. Here, under cover of the fire of a long row of batteries, eighty pieces in all, d'Erlon's corps was waiting the order to attack the British left-centre. It was formed in four great columns, each a species of *phalanx* containing eight battalions, ranged one behind another. This order of battle was extremely unwieldy; but, in many a fight, Continental troops had broken up in panic at the mere approach of such a moving multitude.

Just as Napoleon was about to order d'Erlon to attack, he received an unpleasant surprise. It was pointed out to him that masses of troops were coming into sight far to the north-east, on the heights of Chapelle St Lambert, some six miles away. A few hours earlier, the emperor would have been puzzled to guess what this force could be; but he had received, some little time back, Grouchy's despatch of the early morning, informing him that Blücher, far from retiring towards Liége, was massed at Wavre. The force in the distance must, then, be some fraction of the Prussian Army. Soon afterwards a prisoner was brought in, a hussar of Bülow's corps, who, when questioned, divulged the fact that his general was marching to join Wellington. The emperor reflected for a moment; then he gave d'Erlon orders to proceed with his attack. Bülow was still far away; Grouchy was probably in pursuit

BATTLE OF
WAVRE
18th & 19th June 1815.

S.A.JOHNSTON.F.R.G.S.

French   Prussians
Cavalry   Infantry   Artillery

SCALES

Military Steps 2½ Feet each

English Miles

First positions coloured light

of him; the battle might be won before the Prussians could intervene.

Accordingly, at about 1.30 p.m., the four vast columns forming the 1st corps crossed the little valley that separated them from the British position and began to climb the opposite hill. One brigade diverged to storm the farm of La Haye Sainte; the rest advanced straight against Wellington's left-centre. At the head of the slope they came under a hot musketry fire but continued to press forward. The first troops that they encountered were Bylandt's Dutch-Belgian brigade, which fled to the rear in disorder. A moment later they came upon Picton's two British brigades, reduced to little more than half their strength by the losses of Quatre-Bras, but steady as ever. A furious musketry engagement began; the French were five times more numerous, but, owing to their vicious formation, could bring no more muskets to bear than could their opponents.

While both sides were blazing into each other at close quarters, and the smoke lay thick around them, there was a sudden rush from the rear; and two brigades of British heavy cavalry—Somerset's Horse Guards and Life Guards, and Ponsonby's Union Brigade—charged into the thick of the French columns. D'Erlon's men were caught unprepared, while closely engaged with Picton's infantry. The unwieldy masses were riven to pieces, hurled down the slope, and chased back to their old position with the loss of two eagles, 3000 prisoners, and several thousands more of killed and wounded. Unfortunately, the British horse, drunk with the exhilaration of success, failed to check their career, and rode straight into the French lines, sabring the fugitives, till Napoleon flung upon them cavalry from right and left, and swept them home again with fearful loss. Of the 2500 who had charged, a full thousand were left behind dead or disabled. Ponsonby, the commander of the Union Brigade, was killed in cold blood after he had been made prisoner. Picton, too, had fallen in the very moment of victory.

Prudence would now have counselled Napoleon to break off the battle. Bülow had become visible in the nearer distance, advancing slowly towards the French right flank. Lobau's small 6th corps and two brigades of reserve cavalry had to be detached to the east to intercept him. This reduced by 10,000 men the number available for the attack on Wellington. Moreover, a new despatch was received from Grouchy, alarming because it showed that at 11 a.m. he was still far from Wavre and had no conception of Bülow's having marched to join Wellington. But Napoleon had no idea of ordering a retreat; he knew that he was

Farm of
LA HAYE SAINTE
*Defended by the 2*d* Light Battalion*
of the KING'S GERMAN LEGION
June 18th**1815.**

Belle Alliance

Orchard

Barricade

Pond

Yard

Barn

Open Gateway

Principal Entrance Small door Back Entrance

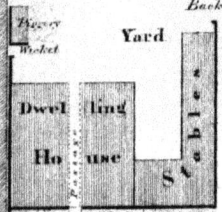

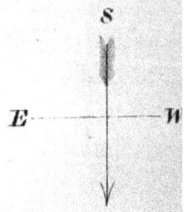

Piggery
Wicket

Yard

Dwelling
House

Stables

High Road from Waterloo to

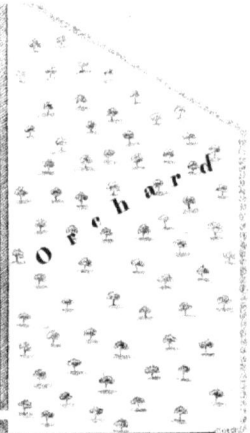

Garden

Ravine
held
by 95th Reg.t

S

E · · · · W

La Haye Sainte Farm

ruined if he failed to beat Wellington that afternoon. The British must be crushed at all costs before the Prussians came up in force.

Accordingly, at 3.30 p.m. the emperor directed Ney to take charge of his front line and resume the attack. The least injured regiments of d'Erlon's corps marched against La Haye Sainte; a fresh brigade of Reille's corps went forward to reinforce the baffled assailants of Hougoumont. Little or no progress was made at either point; and the marshal resolved to have recourse to a new expedient—a great cavalry charge against the front of the British line between the two farms. At about 4 p.m. Ney ordered Milhaud's two divisions of *cuirassiers* to charge; they moved up, supported by the light cavalry of the Imperial Guard, forming in all a mass of 5000 veteran horsemen.

At the sight of their approach, the fifteen British and Hanoverian battalions forming Wellington's right-centre fell into squares and prepared to withstand the shock. The tremendous episode which filled the next two hours was the part of the Battle of Waterloo which impressed itself most strongly on the memory of the survivors on the British side. Never, in all the Napoleonic wars, was there so prolonged a whirlwind of cavalry charges as those which filled the later hours of that afternoon. Milhaud's first onslaught was only the beginning; he breasted the slope, drove the allied gunners from their batteries, and then dashed at the squares. They did not flinch, and their fire blew the squadrons to pieces; then Wellington ordered his own cavalry reserves to advance and drove the enemy down the slope. But the attacks were renewed again and again; and, in the intervals, the French artillery played upon the British squares with deadly effect. It was their round-shot, and not the swords of the *cuirassiers*, which made such havoc among the battalions of Wellington's centre.

When Milhaud had failed to break a single British square, and his corps was hopelessly disorganised, Ney called up the rest of the reserve cavalry from the second line, Kellermann's two divisions of *cuirassiers*; they were followed by the heavy squadrons of the Guard. This splendid veteran cavalry, 5000 strong, fell upon the crippled squares; Milhaud's scattered brigades reformed themselves, and fell in as supports to the new attacking force. There followed an hour of confused *mêlée*; the horsemen rode through the line of squares and even to the very rear of the British position, charging every face of the dwindling blocks of British and German infantry, but always failing to break in. Yet the stress was so great that Wellington used up all his cavalry, save those of the extreme left wing, in the struggle, and gradually pushed

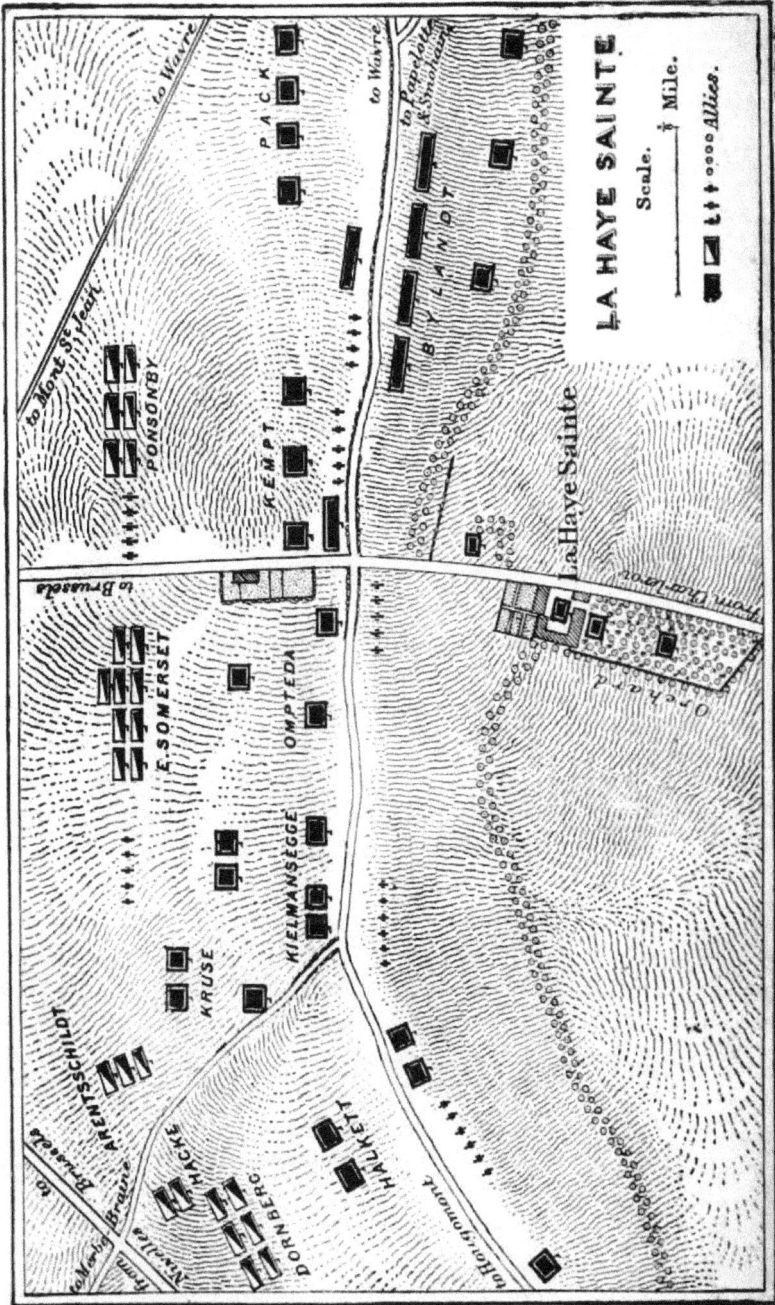

LA HAYE SAINTE.

Scale.

$\frac{1}{4}$ Mile.

Allies.

forward into the fighting line the whole of his infantry reserve, save one Dutch-Belgian division, which showed such unequivocal signs of demoralisation that the duke dared not risk it in the front.

The shrinkage in the ranks of the squares was fearful; they were dreadfully mauled by the French artillery during the intervals of the charges, and harassed by the fire of *tirailleurs*, who crept up close to them and could not be driven off, for to open out into line would have meant utter destruction at the hands of the cavalry. One battalion of the German Legion, ordered by the Prince of Orange to deploy, was absolutely exterminated by the *cuirassiers* before it could resume its formation.

What, meanwhile, were the Prussians doing? Wellington had expected to be succoured before noon and had only consented to fight on that understanding. Yet six o'clock had arrived, and no relief due to the Prussian operations was yet perceptible. It is impossible to explain the delay, as has often been done, by the bad state of the roads alone. The roads were much cut up, it is true; but Wavre is only thirteen miles from Mont St Jean, and it does not take from dawn (8.30 a.m. at that season of the year) till 4 p.m. to cover such a distance. The fact was that there had been bad staffwork and also a certain amount of hesitation at the Prussian headquarters. If Blücher had ordered his nearest corps, that of Thielmann, to march for the French flank at dawn, it would have been in contact with the enemy at 10 or 11 a.m.

What Napoleon would have done in this case it is idle to guess; he had not at that time committed himself to the battle with Wellington. But Bülow's corps, which had two miles further to march than the others, was chosen to lead the column, because it had not suffered at Ligny. It did not start till 6 a.m., was stopped in the streets of Wavre— which it ought not to have passed through—by an accidental fire, and then crossed the march of Pirch's corps. Both columns were blocked; and it was 1.30 p.m. before Bülow's leading division finally reached Chapelle St Lambert, where, as we have already seen, it at once attracted Napoleon's attention.

It was 4 p.m. before it got into actual contact with the French. This amazing delay, of nearly ten hours, was due not to Blücher, but to Gneisenau, his chief of the staff, who feared that Wellington might retreat, after committing the Prussian Army to the dangerous flank march. So late as 10.30 a.m., Gneisenau wrote to Muffling, the Prussian *attaché* at the British headquarters, adjuring him to find out if the Duke really intended to fight; and it was not, in fact, till the cannonade of Waterloo was making itself heard all over Brabant, that the Prussian advance was urged on with genuine energy. Then, at last, Blücher had reached the front; and he rode up and down the line of march, calling to his men that "they must not make him break his word," and encouraging the infantry to help in dragging the embogged cannon across the miry meadows along the Lasne.

It was only about 4 p.m., just as the great French cavalry charges were beginning, that Bülow's corps reached the wood of Paris, some two miles from Napoleon's right flank, and began to interchange shots with the French vedettes. The emperor, as we have seen, had told off Lobau to "contain" them, which he did in the most skilful fashion. Drawing out his troops at right angles to the main French line, he established himself in a good position, with the village of Planchenoit covering his right, and there fought fiercely for two hours against threefold numbers, for Bülow had over 30,000 men.

At last, despite all his efforts, Planchenoit was lost; but the emperor, who had now turned his attention for a space to this corner of the field, sent the four regiments of the Young Guard to retake it. These fresh troops, coming up with a sudden rush, completely cleared the village. It was now 6 o'clock; Bülow's last reserves had been used up; and it could not be said that he had turned the fate of the battle. The only positive difference that his presence had made was that it had compelled the emperor to divert against him, first and last, some 14,000 men of his reserves, who might otherwise have been used against Wellington. This was far from the support that the Duke had expected when he offered battle. Fortunately, however, at this moment, more Prussian troops drew near. The corps of Ziethen and Pirch, which had started later and moved even more slowly than Bülow, were at last at hand.

But, long before their arrival began to produce effect, Napoleon's last offensive moves had been made. Seeing that the cavalry attacks had achieved no definite success, and that the British line was still unbroken, Ney made a final attempt to force it with his infantry. While the wrecks of d'Erlon's corps made one more assault on La Haye Sainte, the infantry of the left-centre—the divisions of Foy and Bachelu, belonging to Reille's corps—pushed forward, to the east of Hougoumont, to assail the much-tried brigades which had just beaten off the cavalry. Though these divisions were fresh troops, engaging battalions wasted by three hours' desperate fighting, they were repulsed; once more the column withered away before the deadly discharge of the two-deep line.

"*C'était une grêle de morts*" ("It was a hail of the dead,") wrote Foy in his diary a few days later. But, a little further to the right, the French achieved at this moment the first real success that they had won against Wellington that day. D'Erlon's men carried La Haye Sainte at about 6.30 p.m. The buildings had been well-nigh pounded to pieces by the French guns; the gallant battalion of the German Legion which held them had exhausted all its cartridges; and the enemy at last burst in. This was the most dangerous moment of the battle for the allied army. A breach had been made in its front line; and the troops on each side of the gap were utterly exhausted and unable to fill it up.

Fortunately for Wellington, d'Erlon's and Reille's corps were also at the end of their strength; they were unable to push forward. Ney begged the Emperor to send more infantry; but the moment was not propitious for such a request. Napoleon had nothing left in reserve save the fifteen battalions of his Old and Middle Guard; and he grudged spending them. Moreover, he was watching a new and dangerous attack of the Prussians on Planchenoit which was just impending.

"You want more infantry!" he exclaimed, "*Où voulez-vous que j'en prenne? Voulez-vous que j'en fasse?*" ("Where do you want me to take it? Do you want me make it?") And for a critical forty minutes he refused to succour Ney. The only movement that he made was to send two of his precious battalions of the Old Guard to feed the defence of Planchenoit, where Bülow, now supported by Pirch's corps, had made a third irruption into the village. Like the previous assaults, it was defeated; the Old Guard swept the street and the churchyard free once more.

But, during this short moment of hesitation on the emperor's part, Wellington had found means to repair the damage in the neighbourhood of La Haye Sainte. Ziethen's corps had at length arrived and had come into touch with his extreme left. He drew from that quarter his last two brigades of British cavalry, those of Vivian and Vandeleur, and ranged them in the rear of his depleted centre. The much-tried brigades between La Haye Sainte and Hougoumont were drawn in together and strengthened by other regiments called up from the right. A solid front was once more displayed to the enemy.

It was at this moment that the emperor made up his mind to deliver his last blow, and to throw the Guard into the thick of the battle. The alternative of retreat was still open to him; and there were good military reasons for accepting it. But the political reasons against tak-

212

ing this line were too cogent to be resisted. As one of his own generals wrote a few days later,:

> The emperor might have refrained from making his last attack, and could have gone off in good order, without leaving a gun behind. But then he must have repassed the Sambre, after having lost 30,000 of the men with whom he had crossed it two days before. How could he have hoped to take up the campaign against the Russians, the Austrians, and the rest of the Allies, after having been forced to retire with loss from before the English Army alone? In spite of the fearful result I cannot blame Napoleon.

Though a retreat might save the army for a few days, it could only mean ultimate disaster. The emperor, then, was right to attack; his mistake was that he did not send the Guard to the front *en masse*, the moment that La Haye Sainte fell.

It was past seven when Ney led out from the French position the last column of assault. It was composed of six battalions of the Middle Guard, arrayed in hollow squares—a curious formation for attack, dictated probably by the fear that Wellington might have cavalry waiting to receive them. Two battalions of the Old Guard followed some distance behind, to act as supports. The remaining five were still held back in reserve near or behind La Belle Alliance. The attack was delivered not directly up the high-road towards La Haye Sainte, but half a mile further west and near to Hougoumont.

By chance or design the battalions took a formation *en échelon*, with the right in advance and the left somewhat refused. The leading square, that furthest to the east, came up the slope opposite Halkett's British brigade; the others were making for the ground held by Maitland's brigade of the Guards. The moment that they began to ascend the heights, all came under a heavy fire of artillery, for Wellington's gunners, though often driven from their pieces by the cavalry charges, were still holding their positions. The smoke was dense; and the different units seem to have lost sight of each other and to have fought each its own battle.

The shock was short and decisive. The right-hand *échelon* first reached the crest, engaged in a close and murderous musketry fight with Halkett's brigade, and then recoiled. A little later the central force, apparently three battalions, came up against Maitland's Guards and the British battery beside them.

When they were seen looming through the smoke, Wellington, who was present himself at this point, bade the Guards rise to their feet—they had been lying down to escape the fire of the French artillery—and give one volley, after which they were to advance firing. Now, as so often in Peninsular battles, the first point-blank discharge of a well-formed British line was irresistible. The heads of the French squares went down in one weltering mass; then, when their enemy marched on them, still pouring in deliberate volleys, the survivors broke and fled downhill. The advance of Maitland's brigade was only checked by the appearance of the last French *échelon*, two battalions strong, somewhat on their flank.

But, while the Guards were reforming to meet this new attack, another force came on the scene. Colonel Colborne of the 52nd, whose corps belonged to Adam's brigade, the unit next to the right of Maitland, had wheeled his battalion out of the main line, so as to place it at right angles to the advancing French and parallel to their flank. His fire tore away the whole left flank of these two battalions, which broke in helpless disorder and rolled down the slope after their beaten comrades. Their retreat carried with it the two battalions of the Old Guard which were crossing the valley in their support, as well as the half-formed and depleted masses of Reille's corps which were lingering under the lee of Hougoumont.

The cry, "*la Garde recule*," was already running along the whole French line, when Wellington let loose upon the wavering masses below him his last British reserves, the two cavalry brigades of Vivian and Vandeleur. They crashed down the hill-side east of Hougoumont, across the *débris* of the fight, and fell upon the retreating Imperial Guard and the exhausted and disordered remnants of Kellermann's and Milhaud's cavalry. All gave way, almost without resistance; and the French centre was transformed in a minute into a panic-stricken crowd. Wellington had bidden his whole front line to advance in support of the cavalry, but it found no enemy to fight; after ascending to the crest of the French position it halted and left the pursuit to the Prussians. There was no strength to march left in the remnants of the shattered battalions which had borne the burden and heat of the day.

At the moment when Napoleon's last attack was repulsed by Maitland and Colborne, Ziethen's Prussian corps had broken in between d'Erlon's and Lobau's troops at the north-eastern point of the French front. The right angle formed by the enemy's line gave way inwards, and the Prussian cavalry arrived near La Belle Alliance, driving their immediate opponents before them, at the same moment that the brigades of Vivian and Vandeleur reached the same point from the other side.

The last resistance made to the Allies was offered by three squares of the Old Guard near the high-road; they held out for some time, in order to protect the retreat of the Emperor, who had lingered with them while there was any hope of rallying his centre. Charged without success by both British and Prussian cavalry, these veterans at last retired, and mingled with the flying masses in their rear. The Young Guard in Planchenoit held out almost as long; had they given way earlier, the Prussians would have reached the high-road south of the French position and cut off the whole army. But this was prevented by the admirable obstinacy of Lobau's men, who held their own till night fell, and the main battle had long been lost.

The Emperor's army, now no more than a helpless horde of fugitives, was chased all night by the Prussian cavalry, and never allowed a moment to rally. After being driven out of seven successive bivouacs, which it had attempted to form, it fled over the Sambre next morning, and crossed the frontier in isolated bands. In the last great battle, it had lost all its artillery, more than 250 guns, and about 30,000 men in killed and wounded alone. The prisoners were comparatively few, probably not more than 6000 or 7000; but, in many units of the Imperial army, the actual casualties exceeded 50 *per cent*, of the men present. Wellington's army had lost over 13,000 men, of whom 7000 were British. The Prussians reported a loss of over 6000.

CHAPTER 14

The End of Empire

It may be said that till within the last few years there were no definite data available for the calculation of the losses of the French Army during the Waterloo campaign. Siborne, the most careful of English writers on the subject, contented himself with stating that they were 'immense, but difficult to estimate,' and did not commit himself to figures. More modern narrators of the campaign from this side of the Channel have either copied his example or reproduced French estimates, which are themselves usually echoes from Gourgaud's 36,940, or the 36,500 of the *Victoires et Conquêtes*. Henry Houssaye, whose volumes on 1814-15 have completely superseded the earlier French accounts, because of his infinitely greater care in consulting original documents, gives much higher figures. He allows for 35,000 men lost at Waterloo alone, 12,800 at Ligny and Quatre-Bras, some 2,000 for

Grouchy's casualties at Wavre and Namur, and a few hundred for the skirmishes with the Prussians on June 15, in all a total of 51,000 men. (*1815, Waterloo* by Houssaye published by Leonaur.) This estimate is undoubtedly far nearer to the truth than any which had hitherto appeared, but I think that it is now possible to arrive at a result which approaches even closer to exactitude.

The new evidence which enables us to attack the problem from a secure basis is contained in M. Martinien's *Tableaux par Corps des Officiers tués et blessés pendant les Guerres de l'Empire 1805-1815.* This magnificent work of 824 pages consists of regimental lists of all officers killed and wounded in the Napoleonic campaigns, extracted item by item from the records of the regiments at the Archives of the Ministry of War at Paris. It is no mere table of figures but gives the name and rank of each person cited, and even notes the death of all officers who, though returned as merely wounded, ultimately succumbed to their injuries within a couple of months of the engagement in which they had been disabled. The whole being drawn up by regiments, not by battles, the inquirer must go through the titles of all units engaged in a campaign, if he wishes to obtain the total of losses in it, and then add up the results for himself.

This I have done for all the regiments which took part in the Waterloo campaign, in the hope that by the aid of the figures thus obtained we may arrive at some general facts concerning the French losses in 1815. The results are embodied in the annexed tables. It will be seen that they differ very appreciably from the totals given by M. Houssaye; *e.g.*, he asserts that 720 French officers were killed or wounded on 18 June and cites M. Martinien as his authority. But the *Tableaux*, published a year later than his book, show that the real total was not 720, but 1,405. Similarly, his estimate for the casualties of Ligny and Quatre-Bras is 346, but Martinien's list of names gives no less than 707 killed and wounded officers.

But it is not only the losses of the whole army considered in general that M. Martinien's tables display to us. We can also deduce from them how the stress of each battle bore upon the larger units of Napoleon's host, the corps, divisions, and brigades. To show the proportion in which each suffered, it is only necessary to prefix to its losses the total number of officers present at the opening of the campaign. These figures I have procured from another admirable work, which has appeared within the last few years, Couderc de Saint-Chamant's *Dernières Armées de Napoléon* (1902). Not till this book came to hand was it possible to arrive at the exact number of officers who took the field with each unit. But by printing in full the last morning-states of the Waterloo army, those of 10-15 June, recovered from the miscellaneous documents of the *Section Historique*, Captain Couderc has enabled us to see what precisely is the meaning of M. Martinien's lists of losses.

For example, if we had only the latter before us, we could merely know that at Waterloo the 1st Léger and the 21st of the Line each lost twenty-three officers. But when we note in Captain Couderc's columns that the former regiment had 61 officers in the field, while the latter had but 42 officers, we realise that the one lost only 37 *per cent*, of its commissioned ranks, the other more than 50 *per cent*. These percentages of loss in the various units of the army have turned out to be so interesting that I have devoted several paragraphs of comment to them.

The method in which the figures thus collected can be utilised is that which has been applied in many similar cases by military statisticians—the multiplying of the number of casualties among the officers by twenty, as a rough but fairly accurate way of arriving at the number of casualties among the rank and file. This proportion is not that of the actual officers and men present at the opening of the campaign, which seems to have stood at 23 to 1, but allows for the undoubted fact that 'the epaulette attracts the bullets;' *i.e.* that in all the Napoleonic wars, no less than in the wars of today, the officer took more than his fair proportional risk, because his duty sent him to the front.

That this figure of 20 to 1 errs rather on the side of understatement than of overstatement seems to result from an examination of the French losses in the Peninsular war. In ordinary line versus column engagements, such as the imperial troops were wont to wage with the British in Spain, the average number of casualties of men per officer was decidedly over twenty. The figures of Albuera, Salamanca, and Vittoria were never properly returned by the French commanders, but those of the other main battles of the Peninsular war stand as follows:

Talavera . 266	officers killed or wounded :	7,002 men ::	1 officer : 26	men
Busaco . 243	,,	,,	4,241	,,	1 officer : 17·4 men
Barrosa . 113	,,	,,	2,451	,,	1 officer : 21·6 men
The Pyre-nees . 377	,,	,,	10,448	,,	1 officer : 27·7 men
Nivelle . 174	,,	,,	4,096	,,	1 officer : 23 men
Bayonne & St. Pierre. 268	,,	,,	5,095	,,	1 officer : 21·3 men

At Busaco, if Masséna's return is accurate, the proportion of officers to men disabled is abnormally great; at Talavera and the Pyrenees it is abnormally light. Taking the whole series of battles together, we find that the proportion is one officer killed or wounded to 23.2 men. But we must remember that the Waterloo army was heavily officered; the regiments had their full *cadres* in the commissioned ranks, even when (as in many cases) they were not up to regulation strength in men. In several cavalry regiments the officers stood to the men in a proportion so high as 1 to 12, and in the infantry 1 to 24 was the average.

In the Peninsula, on the other hand, it is a repeated complaint of the French commanders, especially of Soult in 1813-14, that the regiments were short of officers. Statistics bear out this allegation: in Masséna's army in 1810 the infantry showed one officer to 26 men; in Soult's army in 1813 there was but one officer to 28 men. We should allow, therefore, that in the Waterloo campaign fewer men per officer were likely to fall, simply because there were fewer men per officer in line. If we find that the Peninsular battles show an average of 23 men hit to one officer, when 26 or 28 men per officer were present, we may grant that a loss of 20 men per officer should be the probable figure for 1815, when only 23 men per officer were in line.

The headings of the columns in the annexed tables for the most part explain themselves. But it is perhaps necessary to point out that the casualties in the column headed 'Small Fights' include (1) the losses of 15 June suffered by the Guard Cavalry, the Reserve Cavalry (Excelmans and Pajol) and Vandamme's infantry, while driving in Ziethen's corps towards Fleurus; (2) the casualties of 17 June which Subervie's Lancers suffered at the combat of Genappe, when they were engaged with the 7th Hussars and the Household Cavalry of Wellington's rearguard; (3) the casualties of Maurin's cavalry, and of Gérard's and Vandamme's infantry during Grouchy's retreat on 20 June; (4) those of Teste's division of the 6th Corps, while defending the walls of Namur against the pursuing Prussians on 21 June, on the second day of this same retreat. The third item is far the heaviest, and accounts for just over half of the total of 109 officers killed and wounded in the 'small fights.'

I have included the losses of Ligny and Quatre-Bras in the same column, as they were fought on the same day by different fractions of the French Army, and there can be no confusion between them. Those of Quatre-Bras belong to the 2nd Corps (minus Girard's division), L'Héritier's *cuirassiers*, and the light cavalry of the Guard: they amount to 33 officers killed and 158 wounded. The far heavier losses of Ligny (76 officers killed and 440 wounded) are distributed between the 3rd and 4th corps, Girard's division of the 2nd Corps, the Reserve Cavalry corps of Pajol, Excelmans, and Milhaud, and the infantry and heavy cavalry of the Guard. Of the casualties of the staff in these two battles I have identified and distributed those of the generals by name, but in regard to the 26 *aides-de-camp, adjoints de l'état-major* &c, the only possible course (since M. Martinien gives them simply as 'losses on 16 June') was to credit them to Ligny and Quatre-Bras in the proportion of the other losses of the day—*viz.* 19 to the first named, and 7 to the second engagement.

Division	Regiment	Officers Present	Ligny and Quatre-Bras		Waterloo		Wavre		Small Fights		Total		General Total
			k.	w.	k.	w.	k.	w.	k.	w.	k.	w.	
1st Corps D'Erlon													
Infantry Allix.	54th Line	41	—	—	6	14	—	—	—	—	6	14	20
	55th „	45	—	—	5	14	—	—	—	—	5	14	19
	28th „	42	—	—	6	11	—	—	—	—	6	11	17
	105th „	42	—	—	11	22	—	—	—	—	11	22	33
Donzelot .	13th Léger	61	—	—	7	20	—	—	—	2	7	22	29
	17th Line	42	—	—	5	16	—	—	—	1	5	17	22
	19th „	43	—	—	9	13	—	—	—	—	9	13	22
	51st „	42	—	1	8	11	—	—	—	—	8	12	20
Marcognet .	21st Line	42	—	—	7	16	—	—	—	—	7	16	23
	46th „	43	—	—	3	21	—	—	—	—	3	21	24
	25th „	40	—	—	1	30	—	—	—	—	1	30	31
	45th „	43	—	—	3	28	—	—	—	—	3	28	31
Durutte .	8th Line	40	—	—	1	19	—	—	—	—	1	19	20
	29th „	40	—	—	2	8	—	—	—	—	2	8	10
	85th „	40	—	—	5	17	—	—	—	—	5	17	22
	95th „	40	—	—	1	18	—	—	—	—	1	18	19
Cavalry Jacquinot.	7th Hussars	28	—	—	—	9	—	—	—	—	—	9	9
	3rd Chasseurs	29	—	—	1	10	—	—	—	—	1	10	11
	3rd Lancers	27	—	—	2	6	—	—	—	—	2	6	8
	4th „	22	—	—	3	6	—	—	—	—	3	6	9
		792	—	1	86	309	—	—	—	3	86	313	399
2nd Corps Reille													
Infantry Bachelu .	3rd Line	42	—	5	5	20	—	—	—	—	5	25	30
	61st „	41	3	11	4	13	—	—	—	—	7	23	30
	72nd „	40	2	3	1	8	—	—	—	—	3	11	14
	108th „	61	3	14	5	15	—	—	—	—	8	29	37
Prince Jerome	1st Léger	64	—	3	5	18	—	—	—	—	5	21	26
	2nd „	95	—	12	5	10	—	—	1	—	6	20	26
	1st Line	69	6	21	5	13	—	—	—	—	11	34	45
	2nd „	65	1	5	6	20	—	—	—	—	7	25	32
Girard [1]	11th Léger	42	—	20	—	—	—	—	—	—	—	20	20
	82nd Line	27	1	21	—	—	—	—	—	—	1	21	22
	12th Léger	51	—	23	—	—	—	—	—	—	—	23	23
	4th Line	44	1	24	—	—	—	—	—	—	1	24	25
Foy . .	92nd Line	40	4	2	1	12	—	—	—	—	5	14	19
	93rd „	41	1	1	6	11	—	—	—	—	7	12	19
	4th Léger	59	6	23	2	6	—	—	—	—	8	29	37
	100th Line	51	1	14	1	8	—	—	—	—	2	22	24
Cavalry Piré . .	1st Chasseurs	40	—	2	—	14	—	—	—	—	—	16	16
	6th „	34	—	1	2	11	—	—	—	—	2	12	14
	5th Lancers	25	1	9	—	3	—	—	—	—	1	12	13
	6th „	34	3	8	—	9	—	—	—	—	3	17	20
		965	33	222	48	191	—	—	1	—	82	413	495

Division	Regiment	Officers Present	Ligny and Quatre-Bras		Waterloo		Wavre		Small Fights		Total		General Total
3rd Corps **Vandamme**													
Infantry	15th Léger	62	3	11	—	—	1	14	—	1	4	26	30
Lefol	23rd Line	62	1	12	—	—	4	1	—	—	5	13	18
	37th „	59	1	10	—	—	—	1	—	—	1	11	12
	64th „	40	2	11	—	—	1	8	—	—	3	19	22
Habert	34th Line	55	3	14	—	—	2	2	—	1	5	17	22
	88th „	57	12	16	—	—	—	2	1	—	13	18	31
	22nd „	55	—	17	—	—	1	6	1	2	2	25	27
	70th „	45	1	10	—	—	2	2	—	—	3	12	15
	2nd Swiss	21	—	—	—	—	—	9	—	—	—	9	9
Berthezène	12th Line	41	—	13	—	—	—	—	1	4	1	17	18
	56th „	42	1	7	—	—	—	3	—	1	1	11	12
	33rd „	39	—	—	—	—	—	—	2	13	2	13	15
	86th „	44	—	7	—	—	—	—	2	8	2	15	17
Cavalry Domon[2]	4th Chasseurs	31	—	—	—	9	—	—	1	2	1	11	12
	9th „	25	—	2	—	10	—	—	—	—	—	12	12
	12th „	29	1	2	1	10	—	—	—	—	2	12	14
		707	25	132	1	29	11	48	8	34	45	241	286
4th Corps **Gérard**													
Infantry	30th Line	41	8	13	—	—	—	—	1	2	9	15	24
Pécheux	96th „	41	3	5	—	—	—	—	2	2	5	7	12
	63rd „	44	2	8	—	—	—	—	—	—	2	8	10
	75th „	42	—	—	—	—	—	—	1	4	1	4	5
Vichery	59th Line	41	2	11	—	—	3	5	—	—	5	16	21
	76th „	41	1	12	—	—	2	9	—	—	3	21	24
	69th „	40	5	5	—	—	—	—	—	—	5	5	10
	48th „	42	2	13	—	—	—	—	—	—	2	13	15
Hulot	9th Léger	45	4	10	—	—	—	—	—	—	4	10	14
	111th Line	45	2	10	—	—	—	1	—	—	2	11	13
	44th „	44	1	9	—	—	—	—	—	—	1	9	10
	50th „	36	3	10	—	—	—	2	—	—	3	12	15
Cavalry Maurin	6th Hussars	25	—	—	—	—	1	—	—	1	1	1	2
	8th Chasseurs	25	—	—	—	—	—	6	—	—	—	6	6
	6th Dragoons	20	2	7	—	—	—	—	—	—	2	7	9
	16th „	24	—	4	—	—	—	—	—	—	—	4	4
		596	35	117	—	—	6	23	4	9	45	149	194

[1] This division was detached from its corps, and fought at Ligny, not Quatre Bras.
[2] This division was detached from its corps, and fought at Waterloo, though the 3rd Corps was present at Wavre.

Division	Regiment	Officers Present	Ligny and Quatre-Bras		Waterloo		Wavre		Small Fights		Total		General Total
			k.	w.	k.	w.	k.	w.	k.	w.	k.	w.	
6th Corps **Lobau**													
Infantry	5th Line	42	—	—	4	18	—	—	—	—	4	18	22
Zimmer	11th „	61	—	—	2	16	—	—	—	—	2	16	18
	27th „	39	—	—	1	16	—	—	—	—	1	16	17
	84th „	45	—	—	5	11	—	—	—	—	5	11	16
	5th Léger	42	—	—	4	9	—	—	—	—	4	9	13
	10th Line	40	—	—	2	21	—	—	—	—	2	21	23
Jeannin	47th „	Never joined	—	—	—	—	—	—	—	—	—	—	—
	107th „	44	—	—	4	11	—	—	—	—	4	11	15
	8th Léger	42	—	—	—	—	2	4	—	1	2	5	7
Teste[3]	40th Line	Never joined	—	—	—	—	—	—	—	—	—	—	—
	65th „	22	—	—	—	—	—	—	1	7	1	7	8
	75th „	42	—	—	—	—	—	—	1	4	1	4	5
		419	—	—	22	102	2	4	2	12	26	118	144

Division	Regiment	Officers Present	Ligny and Quatre-Bras		Waterloo		Wavre		Small Fights		Total		General Total
CAVALRY RESERVE													
1st Corps Pajol													
P. Soult . {	1st Hussars	—	—	—	—	—	—	—	—	7	—	7	7
	4th „	97	—	9	—	—	—	—	—	—	—	9	9
	5th „		—	5	—	—	—	—	—	1	—	6	6
	1st Lancers		—	1	1	13	—	—	—	1	1	15	16
Subervie [b] . {	2nd „	122	—	—	—	3	—	—	—	14	—	17	17
	11th Chasseurs		—	—	2	10	—	—	—	—	2	10	12
		219	—	15	3	26	—	—	—	23	3	64	67
2nd Corps Excelmans													
Strolz . {	5th Dragoons		—	7	—	—	1	2	—	—	1	9	10
	13th „	146	—	—	—	—	—	4	—	—	—	4	4
	15th „		—	—	—	—	—	—	—	3	—	3	3
	20th „		—	—	—	—	—	—	1	6	1	6	7
Chastel . {	4th Dragoons		—	12	—	—	—	—	—	—	—	12	12
	12th „	141	1	8	—	—	—	—	—	—	1	8	9
	14th „		2	3	—	—	—	—	—	—	2	3	5
	17th „		1	7	—	—	—	—	—	—	1	7	8
		187	4	37	—	—	1	6	1	9	6	52	58
3rd Corps Kellermann													
L'Herétier . {	2nd Dragoons		—	—	6	12	—	—	—	—	6	12	18
	7th „	138	—	—	1	15	—	—	—	—	1	15	16
	8th Cuirassiers		—	13	—	4	—	—	—	—	—	17	17
	11th „		1	3	2	15	—	—	—	—	3	18	21
Roussel . {	1st Carabineers		—	—	8	13	—	—	—	—	8	13	21
	2nd „		—	—	3	10	—	—	—	—	3	10	13
	2nd Cuirassiers	122	—	—	2	14	—	—	—	—	2	14	16
	3rd „		—	—	2	11	—	—	—	—	2	11	13
		260	1	16	24	94	—	—	—	—	25	106	135
4th Corps Milhaud													
Wathier . {	1st Cuirassiers		—	—	4	13	—	—	—	—	4	13	17
	4th „	117	—	—	4	10	—	—	—	—	4	10	14
	7th „		—	—	3	11	—	—	—	—	3	11	14
	12th „		—	—	4	12	—	—	—	—	4	12	16
	5th Cuirassiers	39	1	—	2	12	—	—	—	—	3	12	15
Delort . {	6th „	22	—	2	—	16	—	—	—	—	—	18	18
	9th „	34	—	2	2	11	—	—	—	—	2	13	15
	10th „	32	1	4	2	11	—	—	—	—	3	15	18
		244	2	8	21	96	—	—	—	—	23	104	127

[a] This division was detached, and fought at Wavre, though the corps was at Waterloo.
[b] This division was detached and served at Waterloo, though Pajol was at Wavre.

Division	Regiment	Officers Present	Ligny and Quatre-Bras		Waterloo		Wavre		Small Fights		Total		General Total
			k.	w.	k.	w.	k.	w.	k.	w.	k.	w.	
Artillery													
Horse .	13 batteries of 1st, 2nd, and 4th Regiments	44	—	—	2	1	—	—	—	—	2	1	3
Field .	26 batteries of 2nd, 5th, 6th, and 8th Regiments	90	2	1	4	7	—	—	—	2	6	10	16
		134	2	1	6	8	—	—	—	2	8	11	19

Division	Regiment	Officers Present	Ligny and Quatre-Bras		Waterloo		Wavre		Small Fights		Total		General Total
Train	28 companies of 1st, 2nd, 3rd, 5th, 6th, 7th, 8th battalions	57	1	1	1	3	—	—	—	—	2	4	6
Engineers	'Etat-major particulier'	?	—	1	—	8	—	—	—	—	—	9	9
	Sappers and Miners	46	—	—	3	9	—	2	—	—	3	11	14
		46	—	1	3	17	—	2	—	—	3	20	23
IMPERIAL GUARD													
Infantry													
Old Guard													
Friant	1st Grenadiers	86	—	—	1	11	—	—	—	—	1	11	12
	2nd „		—	1	1	15	—	—	—	—	1	15	16
Morand	1st Chasseurs	89	—	—	1	6	—	—	—	—	1	6	7
	2nd „		—	—	—	11	—	—	—	—	—	11	11
Middle Guard													
Roguet	3rd Grenadiers	65	—	2	3	13	—	—	—	—	3	15	18
	4th „		—	2	4	13	—	—	—	—	4	15	19
Michel	3rd Chasseurs	80	—	—	8	17	—	—	—	—	8	17	25
	4th „.		—	—	4	11	—	—	—	—	4	11	15
Young Guard													
Duhesme	1st Tirailleurs	80	—	—	—	6	—	—	—	—	—	6	6
	3rd „		1	—	1	8	—	—	—	—	1	8	9
Barrois	1st Voltigeurs	82	—	—	2	8	—	—	—	—	2	8	10
	3rd „		—	—	2	7	—	—	—	—	2	7	9
Heavy Cavalry													
Guyot	Grenadiers à cheval	117	—	—	2	17	—	—	—	1	2	18	20
	Dragoons		1	—	3	16	—	—	—	—	4	16	20
	Gendarmes	4	1	—	—	1	—	—	—	—	1	1	2
Light Cavalry													
Lefebvre-Desnouettes	Lancers	139	—	2	1	9	—	—	—	—	1	11	12
	Chasseurs		—	—	6	14	—	—	—	—	6	14	20
Artillery	9 field batteries / 4 horse „	54	—	—	2	9	—	—	—	—	2	9	11
Train		?	—	—	—	1	—	—	—	—	—	—	1
		806	3	7	41	193	—	—	—	1	44	201	245

STAFF AND NON-REGIMENTAL OFFICERS

Rank	Officers Present	Ligny and Quatre-Bras		Waterloo		Wavre		Small Fights		Total		General Total
		k.	w.	k.	w.	k.	w.	k.	w.	k.	w.	
Généraux de division [5]	?	1	4	3	18	—	1	1	1	5	19	24
Généraux de brigade [6]	—	1	11	4	16	1	1	—	—	6	27	33
Adjudants-commandants	—		2	1	8	—	—	—	—	1	11	12
Adjoints d'état-major	—	1	11		9	—	—	—	—	1	20	21
Ingénieurs-géographes	—				1	—	—	—	—		1	1
Aides-de-camp	—		11	3	21	1	—	—	1	4	33	37
Commissaires des guerres	—		1		—	—	—	—	—		1	1
Total	?	3	40	11	68	2	2	1	2	17	112	129
Grand total of whole campaign	?	109	598[7]	267	1,138	22	79	17	95	415	1,910	2,325

[5] These were:—Killed at Ligny, Girard, of the 2nd Corps; wounded at Ligny, Habert, of 3rd Corps, and Domon and Maurin, of the cavalry. Wounded at Quatre-Bras, Kellermann. Killed at Waterloo, Desvaux, Michel, and Duhesme, of the Imperial Guard; wounded at Waterloo, Bailly de Monthion, Barrois, Colbert, Friant, Guyot, of the Guard, Durutte, of the 1st Corps, Bachelu and Foy, of the 2nd Corps, Zimmer, of the 6th Corps, Delort, L'Héritier, Roussel, of the cavalry reserve, Haxet 'Grand Prévot de l'armée.' Wounded at Wavre, Gérard, commanding 4th Corps, Teste of 6th Corps. Small Fights: killed, Letort, of Imperial Guard, on 15 June, near Charleroi; wounded, Vandamme, commanding 3rd Corps, in front of Namur, 20 June.

[6] These were :—Killed at Ligny, Le Capitaine, of 4th Corps; wounded at Ligny, Billard and Dufour, of 3rd Corps, Berruyer, of 4th Corps, Devilliers and Piat, of Girard's division of 2nd Corps, Farine, of reserve cavalry; wounded at Quatre-Bras, Gauthier, of 2nd Corps. Killed at Waterloo, Aulard, of 1st Corps, Baudoin and Janin, of 2nd Corps, Donop, of reserve cavalry. Wounded at Waterloo: Gobrecht, Noguez, and Bourgeois, of 1st Corps, Campy and Vathiez, of 2nd Corps, Farine, Guiton, Dubois, Picquet, Travers, Blancard, of reserve cavalry. Cambronne, Harlet, Henrion, Lallemand, of the Guard, Durrieu, of the staff. Killed at Wavre, Penne, of 6th Corps.

[7] Of this Quatre-Bras 33 killed, 157 wounded = 190; Ligny 76 killed, 443 wounded = 519.

The first observation called forth by a study of these tables is that the French losses at Ligny must have been considerably understated by all the historians. We note that at Quatre-Bras 191 officers fell; on an estimate of 20 men hit to each officer, this should give a total casualty list of 3,800 men: as a matter of fact, the number was somewhat greater, for Ney and Reille report 4,300 disabled, (these figures seem perfectly genuine and certain; see Houssaye and the notes of Gourgaud, who gives the figure at 4,140, Foy, and others), a proportion of 22 not of 20 to 1. But at Ligny we find that 516 officers were killed or wounded, while in deference, apparently, to Napoleon's statement that he had lost only some 6,000 or 7,000 men, the historians, down to M. Houssaye himself, state the French casualties at figures varying up to, but never exceeding, 8,500 men.

This proportion, which would give only 16 men hit per officer, seems entirely improbable. There was nothing in the character of the fighting at Ligny which would make it likely that the officers should suffer in such an abnormal proportion: neither the long cannonade, nor the street firing in Ligny and the two St. Amands, ought to have proved so peculiarly deadly to the commissioned ranks. I am driven to conclude that it would be safer to estimate the total French loss at 10,000 men; even this would be lower than the proportion of 20 to 1 which we have agreed to accept as normal. Descending to details, we find that by far the heaviest casualties at Ligny fell upon Girard's division of the 2nd Corps, the unit detached from Reille which fought so desperately in the Hameau de St.-Amand. It lost 90 officers out of 164 present, more than 54 *per cent*. This fact corroborates all the narratives which speak of it as practically *hors de combat* at nightfall, and accounts for Napoleon having left it behind him on the field of Ligny, to recuperate itself, when he marched off upon the following day.

Of the other troops present at Ligny Vandamme's corps lost 157 officers out of 707 present, a portion of about one in five, or more exactly 22.2 *per cent*. Gerard's corps suffered 152 casualties among 596 officers present, or about 25.5 *per cent*. The Reserve Cavalry, who were mainly occupied in observing the Prussian left wing, and of whom only one or two divisions were seriously engaged, seem to have lost only 66 officers out of some 700 present, about 8 *per cent*. The Imperial Guard suffered even less: the infantry had 5 officers wounded and one killed, the heavy cavalry two killed. It is clear, therefore, that Gourgaud's estimate of 100 of all ranks killed and wounded for the whole Guard is not far wrong, though 160 would be nearer the mark. M.

Houssaye's hypothetical estimate of 300 must be hopelessly erroneous; it would give 37 men hit per officer.

The figures also render incredible his statement that the 4th Chasseurs of the Guard were so cut up at Ligny that they were reduced from two battalions to one at Waterloo: they had not in the Battle of Ligny one single officer killed or wounded, and probably not a score of men. It is clear, therefore, that they had still two battalions on the day of Waterloo, and that Ney's final charge on 18 June was conducted by six not (as M. Houssaye asserts) by five battalions of the Guard.

★★★★★★

M. Houssaye quotes General Petit's narrative as his authority for the statement that the 4th Chasseurs were thus cut up at Ligny and were a battalion short at Waterloo. But there is no such allegation in this narrative, printed *in extenso* in the English Historical Review for 1903.

★★★★★★

The figures for Quatre-Bras have nothing very noticeable in them. Reille's corps had 801 officers present (Girard's division being detached at Ligny) and lost 165, one in five, or 20.4 *per cent.* The unit that suffered most was Foy's division, which had 52 casualties among 191 officers, *i.e.* 27 *per cent.* Kellermann's *cuirassiers*, who gave the English squares so much trouble, must be considered to have got off very lightly with 17 officers hurt out of some 50 present in the one brigade that was engaged. Of these 17, only one, by a curious chance, seems to have been killed outright. Piré's Lancers, who broke the British 69th and nearly rode over the 42nd also, had four officers killed and 17 wounded out of 59—exactly the same proportion of losses as that suffered by the *cuirassiers*.

Passing on to 17 June we find that the only serious fighting on that day was the combat of Genappe, where Subervie's Lancers, the head of Napoleon's pursuing column, drove in the British 7th Hussars, but were themselves ridden down by the Life Guards. They are recorded to have lost 15 officers out of 73 present, a sufficient proof that the sharpness of the check has not been exaggerated in British accounts of the skirmish. Of Wellington's two regiments engaged, the 7th lost 4, the 1st Life Guards 1 officer—so that it seems probable that the total French casualties were as three to one compared with the British.

We now come to the awful slaughter of Waterloo. M. Martinien's figures show 267 officers killed and 1,138 wounded as the casualty list of the great battle. This total of 1,405 would seem to give a probable loss of 28,100 for the French Army, putting un wounded prisoners aside. Of the latter, as we gather from Wellington's and Blücher's despatches, there were about 7,500 or 8,000, of whom a very small proportion were officers; for at Waterloo, as in other battles, the rank and file surrendered freely when cut off, while the officers either resisted and were shot down, or made desperate efforts to get away and succeeded. In the rout and pursuit after nightfall, during which the majority of the prisoners were taken, this last was more especially the case.

Nearly the whole of the remainder of the unwounded captives were taken during the charge of the Union Brigade, when the British cavalry got in among the infantry of Allix, Donzelot, and Marcognet and captured whole companies *en masse*.

★★★★★★

Several narrators speak of one of the main features of the battlefield next morning as being whole rows of muskets neatly laid down in line opposite Picton's position, where organised bodies of French had surrendered simultaneously, on being cut off by the Union Brigade.

★★★★★★

Two thousand men laid down their arms in ten minutes at this point, but I am compelled by M. Martinien's figures to believe that, while the rank and file yielded, the officers resisted and were cut down. For in the 45th and 105th regiments, which bore the brunt of the charge and both lost their eagles, I find that 64 officers out of 85 present were killed or wounded, though the number of unwounded rank and file taken was very large indeed. But while it is certain that in this part of the field the officers as compared with the men suffered much heavier casualties than their normal one-to-twenty percentage, I imagine that the general average of losses must have been corrected in the pursuit after dark, where the rank and file surrendered, but the officers, having greater initiative and a stronger dislike for capture, got off and escaped.

I should conclude, therefore, that we must place the total loss of the French Army at Waterloo at something like 37,000 men out of the 72,000 present, or about 50 *per cent*. This would allow for the 1,405 officers whom we know to have been killed or wounded, for 28,100 rank and file killed or wounded, and for 7,500 unwounded prisoners, of whom I should guess that not more than 100 were officers. When we turn to look at the details of the losses of the various units of Napoleon's army, the first fact that strikes us is the very moderate casualty list of those divisions which were opposed to the Prussians, as compared with that of those which fought the British. The force with which Lobau so long held back Blücher consisted of the two infantry divisions of Zimmer and Jeannin, the Young Guard under Duhesme and Barrois, and Domon and Subervie's Cavalry, with the addition late in the day of three battalions of the Old Guard (one each of the 2nd Grenadiers and the 1st and 2nd Chasseurs). The casualty list of these units stands as follows:

Zimmer's division	. 187	officers present,	73	killed or wounded,	or 39	p.c.
Jeannin's division	. 126	,,	,,	41	,,	,,	or 32·5 ,,
Young Guard	. 161[7]	,,	,,	34	,,	,,	or 21 ,,
Domon's cavalry	. 80[7]	,,	,,	30	,,	,,	or 37·5 ,,
Subervie's cavalry	. 106[7]	,,	,,	29	,,	,,	or 27·3 ,,

The losses of the three battalions of the Old Guard cannot be separated from those which the other battalions of their regiments suffered in the main battle. But taking the rest of Lobau's force together, we find that it lost 207 officers out of 649 present, or a percentage of 31.8. This would be considered sufficiently heavy in any ordinary battle, but at Waterloo it contrasts very strongly with the awful casualty list of the divisions which were engaged with the British Army, where no less than 44 *per cent*, of the officers present were disabled. After making all due allowance for the fact that Lobau's men were acting on the defensive, and partly protected by the buildings of Planchenoit, it still remains astounding that they should have held their own for five hours against an adversary who had at first a threefold and afterwards a sevenfold advantage in numbers. One can only conclude that the Prussian fire was far less deadly than the English—one of the many consequences of column as opposed to line formation. It was not without reason that Soult observed to Napoleon that morning, '*Sire, l'infanterie anglaise en duel, a' est le diable.*'

Taking together all the fractions of the Imperial Army which were opposed to the English alone, we get the following results:—

1st Corps .	. 788	officers present,	395	killed or wounded,	or 50·6	p.c.
2nd Corps .	. 635[8]	,,	,,	240	,,	,,	or 37·7 ,,
Middle Guard	. 141[9]	,,	,,	73	,,	,,	or 51·8 ,,
Reserve Cavalry :						
Kellermann	. 243[8]	officers present,	118	killed or wounded,	or 48·5	p.c.
Milhaud	. 234[8]	,,	,,	117	,,	,,	or 50·0 ,,
Guard Cavalry	. 255[8]	,,	,,	69 .	,,	,,	or 27 ,,
Total .	. 2,296	,,	,,	1,012	,,	,,	or 44 ,,

[7] Deduction being made of the losses of these units at the battle of Ligny and the combat of Genappe.

[8] After deducting previous losses at Quatre-Bras and Ligny.

[9] After deducting previous losses at Ligny.

I have had to leave the infantry of the Old Guard out of the calculation, as five of its battalions were engaged with the British and three with the Prussians, while M. Martinien's tables only give the losses by regiments not by battalions, so that they cannot be properly distributed between the two halves of the battle. It will be noted that the Old Guard's casualty list was only 46 officers out of 174 present, *i.e.* 26.4 *per cent.*, a smaller proportional loss than that of any other unit of the French army, save the infantry of the Young Guard. The literary tradition which will have it that the famous squares of the Old Guard perished *en masse*, while covering the retreat of the emperor, is obviously erroneous. These veterans suffered far less than the line and the cavalry.

On the other hand, we note that the 1st Corps, which, after enduring the charge of the Union Brigade, maintained for the rest of the day a bitter strife with the infantry of the British left wing, lost a full half of its officers killed and wounded. If we allow for the unwounded prisoners made by the British cavalry in addition to the casualties, it is evident that much more than half of this unfortunate corps was destroyed. The *cuirassiers* of Milhaud and Kellermann, who delivered the great charges on Wellington's squares during the afternoon hours, also suffered a loss of about 50 *per cent.* So did the six battalions of the Middle Guard, with which the emperor delivered his last thrust at nightfall against Wellington's right centre.

It is somewhat surprising to find that the Guard cavalry, who joined in the same charges as the *cuirassiers*, show the much smaller casualty list of only some 27 *per cent.* This is partly, but not wholly, accounted for by the fact that the emperor retained four of the light Guard squadrons about his person till the end of the day. They were only engaged for a few minutes with Vivian's Hussars after nightfall and can have suffered little. But, even allowing for this, the numbers lost seem small: is it possible that there is some small omission of names in M. Martinien's rolls of the lancers and *chasseurs?* Those of the horse-grenadiers and dragoons show a far higher proportional loss, yet we know that the light cavalry was as deeply engaged as the heavy.

The greatest individual losses in cavalry regiments at Waterloo are those of the 6th Cuirassiers, 16 officers disabled out of 20 present; the 11th Cuirassiers and 1st Carbineers lost almost as heavily in proportion. In the infantry the greatest sufferers were the 105th line, 33 casualties out of 42 present, the 45th and 25th, with 31 casualties each out of 40 and 43 respectively present—all in the 1st Corps—and then the 61st of the line of the 2nd Corps, with 17 casualties out of 27 present.

The heaviest losses of the Guard infantry were in Roguet's brigade, which supplied half the column that delivered the last great attack on Wellington's right-centre: in it 37 officers fell out of 61 present. But a score of regiments in the 1st and 2nd Corps show heavier proportional losses than this.

It only remains to speak of Grouchy's casualties at Wavre and Namur. Those at Wavre were very moderate, as might be expected from the rather slack way in which the marshal pushed the inferior Prussian force in front of him. Four of his seven infantry divisions seem hardly to have been engaged: Berthezène, Pécheux, Teste, and Hulot have only 12 officers wounded between them. The other three divisions show 16 officers killed and 51 wounded out of 472 present, a mere 14 *per cent*. The cavalry was lightly engaged and shows only 15 officers hit. The marshal's total loss must have been well under 2,000 men. The combat in front of Namur on 20 June, indeed, must have been almost as serious a business, though so little is made of it in most histories. Probably the total of Grouchy's losses from 18 to 21 June may have amounted to 3,200 men, as he would seem to have lost about 162 officers in that period.

Our general estimate, therefore, of the French losses in the whole campaign is somewhat as follows:

Quatre-Bras .	. 4,800	killed and wounded.
Ligny . .	. 10,000	„ „
Waterloo .	. 29,500	„ „
„ .	. 7,500	prisoners unwounded
Wavre . .	. 1,800	killed and wounded.
Small fights .	. 2,100	„ „
Total .	. 55,200	

These figures as it will be seen, exceed those of M. Houssaye by some 4,000 casualties—partly owing to what I am inclined to consider his under-estimate of the loss of Ligny, partly because of the high figure which must apparently be allowed for the small fights, more especially the combat of 20 June. As the emperor took the field with 126,000 men, he lost some 43 *per cent*. of his army in the week between 15 June and 22 June.

★★★★★★

In dealing with the French losses in the Waterloo campaign I was compelled to give the figures for the strength of the Imperial Guard from the last return then accessible to me, that of 1 June, as given by Couderc de Saint-Chamans in his *Dernière Armée de Napoléon*. Since then I have discovered that a later return exists, one signed Dériot, and dated 16 June, the very morning of the battles of Ligny and Quatre Bras. Thus, it is now possible to give as precise an estimate of the force of the Guard when it took the field, as has been already given for the other units of the French Army. I owe this return to my friend Commandant Balagny, who was good enough to search for it in the archives of the French war office. The number of officers is somewhat lower, except in the artillery, than the earlier figures; for the return of 1 June, drawn up before the Guard quitted Paris, includes a good many officers (though very few of the rank and file) who were ultimately left behind and thrown on to the strength of the half-formed 5th and 6th regiments of *Voltigeurs* and *Tirailleurs*, or of the *depôts* of the Guard. The figures stand as follows:—

—	Officers Present, 1 June	Officers Present, 16 June
Infantry.—Old Guard:		
1st Grenadiers 2nd ,,	86	78
3rd ,, 4th ,,	65	61
1st Chasseurs 2nd ,,	89	68
3rd ,, 4th ,,	80	64
Young Guard:		
1st Tirailleurs 3rd ,,	80	54
1st Voltigeurs 3rd ,,	82	63
Heavy Cavalry:		
Grenadiers à cheval Dragoons	117	95
Gendarmes .	4	4
Light Cavalry:		
Lancers Chasseurs	139	106
Artillery	54	97
Total	806	690

It will thus be seen that the percentages of loss which I gave in my previous article all need to be revised—the proportion of casualties to officers present being in all cases, save the artillery, perceptibly higher than those which I first stated, owing to the fact that a smaller number of officers were present than I had supposed.

It will be unnecessary to state again in full the percentages of loss at Ligny and Quatre Bras, where the Imperial Guard only lost, in all, three officers killed and eight wounded out of over 650 present; but those of Waterloo are worth giving, in order to show how the fighting bore on the various units.

—	Officers Present [1]	Officers Killed	Officers Wounded	Total	
Infantry :					
1st Grenadiers ⎱ 2nd ,, ⎰ · ·	77	{ 1 { 1	11 15	12 ⎱ 16 ⎰	28
3rd ,, ⎱ 4th ,, ⎰ · ·	57	{ 3 { 4	13 13	16 ⎱ 17 ⎰	33
1st Chasseurs ⎱ 2nd ,, ⎰ · ·	68	{ 1 { —	6 11	7 ⎱ 11 ⎰	18
3rd ,, ⎱ 4th ,, ⎰ · ·	64	{ 8 { 4	17 11	25 ⎱ 15 ⎰	40
1st Tirailleurs ⎱ 3rd ,, ⎰ · ·	53	{ — { 1	6 8	6 ⎱ 9 ⎰	15
1st Voltigeurs ⎱ 3rd ,, ⎰ · ·	63	{ 2 { 2	8 7	10 ⎱ 9 ⎰	19
Heavy cavalry · · ·	94	5	34	39	
Light cavalry · · ·	104	7	23	30	
Artillery · · · ·	97	2	11	13	
Total · ·	678	41	194	235	

1. Deducting previous losses at Ligny etc. in each unit.

Of these, as was shown in my article of October 1904, the 3rd and 4th Grenadiers and Chasseurs and all the cavalry were opposed entirely to the English. Their percentage of loss works out at

—	Present [2]	Casualties	Per cent.
3rd Grenadiers ⎱ 4th ,, ⎰ · · ·	57	33	57·8
3rd Chasseurs ⎱ 4th ,, ⎰ · · ·	64	40	62·5
Heavy cavalry · · ·	94	39	40·6
Light cavalry · · ·	104	30	28·8

2. After deducting Ligny casualties

or in all a loss of 44.2 *per cent*, of the officers in the field. Of the Young Guard, all of whom were opposed to the Prussians, the much more moderate casualty list stands thus:—

—	Present [2]	Casualties	Per cent.
1st Tirailleurs ⎱ 3rd ,, ⎰ · · ·	53	15	28·3
1st Voltigeurs ⎱ 3rd ,, ⎰ · · ·	63	19	30·1

2. After deducting Ligny casualties

or an average of about 29.3, showing clearly enough how far less was the stress of battle at Planchenoit than on the slopes east of Hougoumont. The 1st and 2nd Grenadiers and 1st and 2nd Chasseurs having been divided and used partly against the English and partly against the Prussians, it is impossible to distribute with accuracy their losses, which ran to 46 casualties out of 145 present, or 31.7 *per cent.*

The return of 16 June, giving the exact strength of the Guard when it took the field, has never before been published, so that it may not be out of place to give it here. It will be noted that it makes out the Guard to have been some 1,300 stronger than is shown by Siborne and the other standard authorities.

	Present		Sick or Depôt		Total	
	Officers	Men	Officers	Men	Officers	Men
Infantry :						
1st Grenadiers	41	1,239				
2nd ,,	36	1,055	10	294	148	4,211
3rd ,,	34	1,130				
4th ,,	27	493				
1st Chasseurs.	36	1,271				
2nd ,,	32	1,131	14	308	146	4,779
3rd ,,	34	1,028				
4th ,,	30	1,041				
1st Tirailleurs	26	1,083				
3rd ,,	28	960	15	284	132	4,450
1st Voltigeurs .	31	1,188				
3rd ,,	32	935				
Total Infantry .	387	12,554	39	886	426	13,440
Cavalry :						
Lancers .	47	833	20	433	67	1,266
Chasseurs à cheval .	59	1,138	10	97	69	1,235
Dragoons	51	765	10	116	61	881
Grenadiers à cheval	44	752	19	191	63	943
Gendarmes	4	102	9	148	13	250
Total Cavalry .	205	3,590	68	985	273	4,575
Artillery .	97	3,071	21	452	118	3,523
Sapeurs .	3	109	1	39	4	148
Marins .	3	104	—	42	3	146
Equipages	8	390	10	192	18	582
Ouvriers .	17	261	4	60	21	321
Grand total .	720	20,079	143	2,656	863	22,735

This set of figures disposes of M. Houssaye's statement that only five battalions of the Guard were engaged in Ney's final attack on the British light centre at Waterloo. He says that the 4th Chasseurs was a small regiment originally and suffered so severely at Ligny that it was consolidated into a single battalion on 18 June. These assertions are contradicted (1) by the fact that it certainly had 1,041 bayonets—two full battalions—on the morning of Ligny, as shown by this return, and (2) by the tables of M. Martinien, which demonstrate that the regiment lost not one single officer killed or wounded at Ligny. It cannot possibly, therefore, have had more than 20 or 30 casualties in the rank and file—probably less. At Waterloo, therefore, it must have been still over 1,000 strong, and formed two full battalions. Ney's attack, therefore, was delivered by six, not five battalions, supported, as we believe, by two more of the 2nd Chasseurs somewhat to the rear of the echelon formed by the others.

★★★★★★

It has often been endeavoured to fix the responsibility for the loss of Waterloo upon Grouchy; Napoleon himself, and countless later writers on the French side, have alleged that he had it in his power to intervene effectively in the battle and failed to do so. The answer to this accusation is that the marshal, like Napoleon himself, had not foreseen Blücher's bold flank march to join Wellington, and acted in strict accordance with his master's orders. In the first despatch that he received on the 18th, written from the field of Mont St Jean at 10 a.m., the emperor told him to march on Wavre, pushing before him the Prussians in his front, and at the same time to keep up his communications with the main army and send frequent reports.

This was exactly what Grouchy, long before he received the despatch, had determined to do. His troops were already on the march for Wavre, when the opening guns of Waterloo were heard. Some of his officers urged him to march toward the cannonade: but he refused, saying that his duty was to look after the Prussians. As soon as his advanced cavalry reported the enemy in strength beyond the River Dyle—it was Thielmann's corps, left behind to detain him—he made preparations to attack them. When the emperor's despatch reached him, he congratulated himself on having foreseen and carried out his master's orders. The critical hours of Waterloo passed while Grouchy was forcing the fords and bridges of the Dyle, slowly driving back Thielmann, who fought desperately to gain time for his commander-in-chief to reach Wellington.

Not till 5 p.m. did the marshal receive Napoleon's last despatch, telling him that Bülow had been sighted on the heights of Chapelle St Lambert, and ordering him to turn westward and crush this Prussian corps, which he would catch "*en flagrant délit!*" It was far too late for Grouchy to do anything of the kind; at that hour Bülow was attacking Planchenoit; and, even if the marshal had at 5 o'clock despatched towards the field of Mont St Jean such of his troops as were not already engaged at Wavre, they would not have reached it till long after the fate of the battle had been decided. By 8 p.m. the main struggle was over; and there was much more than a three hours' march (as the Prussians proved) between the Dyle and Planchenoit. Had Grouchy detached troops in that direction, they would have found the emperor already routed.

Grouchy fought his way across the Dyle on the 18th but received no news of the great battle that night. He therefore renewed his assault on Thielmann next morning, beat him by sheer force of numbers, and was about to pursue him northward, when he at last heard of the results of Waterloo. Promptly perceiving the danger that Blücher might cut him off, Grouchy ordered an instant retreat. He executed it in very skilful style, reached Namur just in time to avoid being intercepted, defended that town by a rear-guard action till his main body had got clean away, and escaped to France up the valley of the Meuse. He returned with his 33,000 men intact, thinking that he had deserved well of his country, but found that he was to be made the Emperor's scapegoat and to have the loss of Waterloo imputed to his stupidity or treason. It was a hard fate; his only crime was that, like Napoleon, he had failed to foresee Blücher's great flank march.

Napoleon, after ordering the wrecks of his army to rally at Laon, set out for Paris at once, and arrived there in a state of great mental and bodily prostration on June 21. The news of his disaster had reached the capital on the preceding night and was not generally known till a few hours before his arrival. He did not at first grasp the completeness of his own ruin, and spoke to his Ministers of his intention to continue the war, raise a *levée en masse*, and defend Paris. He had to be reminded that he was no longer the autocrat that he had been when he returned from Moscow or from Leipzig; and that he would have to reckon not only with the enemy in the field, but with the Chambers at home. The Houses had allowed him to appeal to the arbitrament of the sword; but, after his disaster, it was unlikely that they would continue the struggle against united Europe, merely in order to keep him on the throne.

The Allies had proclaimed that they were attacking not France but the emperor; peace, then, might be secured by his abdication. Napoleon had no intention of throwing up the game; and, for a moment, he contemplated dissolving the Chambers and declaring himself absolute. Deceived apparently by treacherous assurances from Fouché, to the effect that the spirit of the deputies was not so hostile as he supposed, he took no decisive measure on the morning of his arrival.

In a few hours it was too late for him to act. The Chambers no sooner met than, at the suggestion of La Fayette, they declared themselves in permanent session, and voted that anyone who attempted to dissolve them would be guilty of high treason.

To defend themselves, they called out the National Guards, on whose loyalty they could rely. This move struck the emperor's counsellors with terror. Lucien Bonaparte alone dared to advise his brother to collect the few regular troops which were in Paris, appeal to the *faubourgs*, and disperse the Chambers. But Napoleon's spirit was broken. He declared that he "would never lead a Jacquerie"; the idea of conducting a civil war at the head of the rabble was hateful to him. That night he made up his mind to abdicate; and when, on June 22, the Chambers sent him word that his choice lay between resignation and deposition, he bowed before the storm, and signed a declaration by which he abdicated in favour of his son. On June 25 he retired to Malmaison.

The Chambers believed that it was now in their power to decree a new Constitution for France, though they were much divided as to its form. They appointed a Provisional Government, of which Fouché and Carnot were the leading members. But already it had been practically settled that the Bourbons should be restored. Immediately after Waterloo, Wellington wrote to Louis XVIII at Ghent, advising him to cross the frontier in the wake of the allied armies.

The old king saw the wisdom of this counsel, and, on entering French soil at Cateau Cambrésis (June 25), published a proclamation in which he announced that he came to resume his rights, that he should adhere to the Constitution of 1814, repair the horrors of war, reward his faithful subjects, and punish the guilty in accordance with the forms of law. Next day he made a triumphal entry into Cambrai, which, after a feeble resistance, had been stormed by the British on the 24th. Within the next few days, all the towns north of the Somme which were not held down by regular troops hoisted the white flag; and a "royal army" of 5000 or 6000 irregulars assembled at Arras. The movement spread to Normandy, where the Imperialists were forced to shut themselves up in the larger towns; and the whole country rose to hem them in.

When Louis XVIII had been recognised as legitimate king by the greater part of northern France, it was too late for the Chambers to debate on what form of government they would inaugurate, too late also for the Allies to take into consideration any other plan for dealing

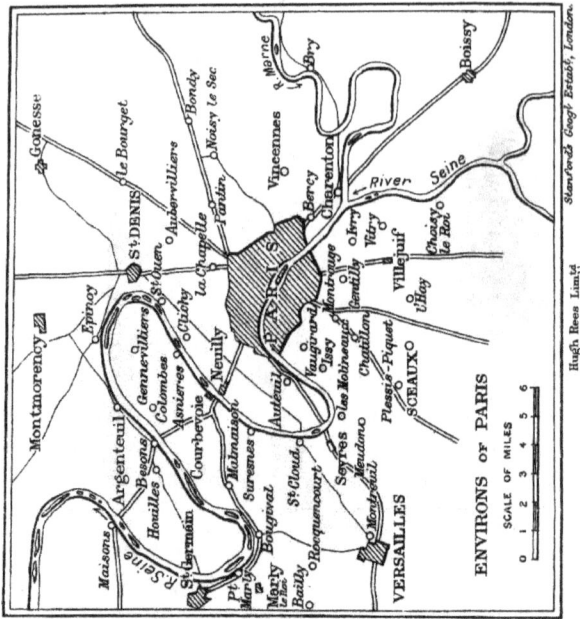

ENVIRONS OF PARIS

SCALE OF MILES

0 1 2 3 4 5 6

Hugh Rees Lim.td

Stanford's Geog.l Estab.t, London.

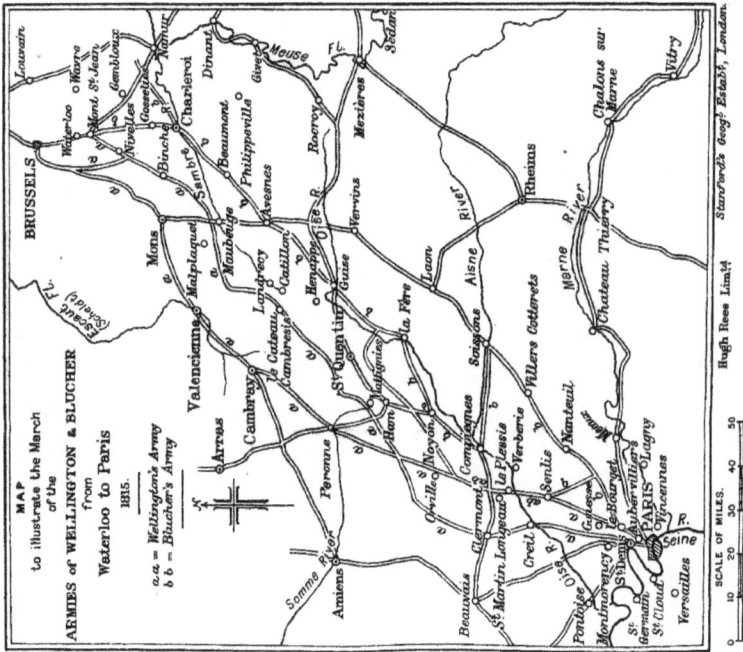

MAP
to illustrate the March
of the
ARMIES of WELLINGTON & BLUCHER
from
Waterloo to Paris.
1815.

a.a = Wellington's Army
b b = Blucher's Army

SCALE OF MILES.

0   10   20   30   40   50

Hugh Rees Lim.td

Stanford's Geog.l Estab.t, London.

with France than that of restoring the *status quo* of 1814. Several of the Powers were not too well pleased. Prussia, in particular, had intended to extort many things before allowing the king to be restored; and her ministers were indignant with Wellington for having permitted or rather encouraged Louis to take possession of his kingdom again.

Meanwhile the British and Prussian armies were advancing against Paris with all speed. Their leaders had agreed that the enemy must not be allowed time to rally. On their approach, the wrecks of Napoleon's army at Laon, and Grouchy's corps also, retired into Paris. On June 29 the heads of the Prussian columns appeared on the heights to the north of the capital; Wellington's army was about a day further off, but within good supporting distance. The Provisional Government sent messenger after messenger to the Allies, requesting them to grant an armistice and stay their advance, now that Napoleon had abdicated. Blücher and Wellington wisely refused; there was no knowing what might happen if the enemy were allowed to rally, and to bring up reserves from the south.

Napoleon, from his retreat at Malmaison, was already offering to take command of the army in Paris; and, though this was the last thing that Fouché and his colleagues desired, they were well aware that many regiments would have gone over to their old master if he had invited them to follow him against the Allies. The four days, June 25-29, which Napoleon spent at Malmaison were full of possibilities of danger. The Provisional Government, however, at last succeeded in inducing him to depart; had he stayed a day longer, they would have had either to arrest him or to suffer him to fall into the hands of the Prussians.

Blücher had sent off a flying column with orders to seize him, dead or alive, and had expressed his intention of shooting him offhand, as an outlaw, if he were captured. The Prussian cavalry reached Malmaison only a few hours after Napoleon had driven off on the road to the south. His last idea had been to quit Europe and betake himself to the United States; the Provisional Government had eagerly fallen in with the idea and promised him the use of two frigates then lying at Rochefort. On June 29, therefore, Napoleon disappeared; and several days passed before the Allies ascertained his whereabouts. It was only discovered on July 10, when he sent a message to Captain Maitland, commanding the blockading squadron off Rochefort, in which he asked whether he would be allowed to put to sea and sail for America.

Meanwhile, after Napoleon's departure from Malmaison, the Provisional Government was left face to face with Wellington and Blücher; and no suspension of hostilities had yet been arranged. Indeed, there was sharp fighting in front of Paris on July 1. The allied generals, after reconnoitring the strong line of fortifications along the northern front of the city, had determined to cross the Seine, with the object of presenting themselves before its undefended southern side. The brigade of cavalry which formed Blücher's advance-guard was routed near Versailles by a superior force of French horse; but this did not prevent the prince from taking up his position on the heights which command Paris on the south. At the same time Wellington occupied positions observing the northern front of the city.

The Provisional Government had now to make its choice whether it would fight or capitulate. There were some 70,000 men of the regular troops within the city, besides the National Guards. Blücher's and Wellington's armies united did not much exceed 120,000 sabres and bayonets. But the British and Prussians were only the van of the advancing hosts; it was known in Paris that the Austrians had crossed the eastern frontier on June 23, had beaten Rapp and his small army of the Rhine on June 28, and had shut him up in Strassburg.

Their columns were already advancing across Lorraine unopposed. At the same time, the Austro-Sardinian army of Italy had crossed the Alps and attacked Suchet, who, on hearing the news of Waterloo, asked for and obtained an armistice (June 28). If there had been any great national cause to defend, if any appeal to loyalty could have been made, it might have been worthwhile to fight. But no one knew whether the Chambers and the Provisional Government intended to acknowledge Napoleon II, to proclaim a Republic, to recall Louis XVIII, or to choose some new ruler—for example, the Duke of Orleans. The only persons who knew their own mind were Fouché and a few others, who had determined that the best thing for France and for themselves was to make a prompt submission to Louis XVIII.

Further resistance would be useless; it would only irritate the Allies, and lead to the dismemberment of the realm. It was by arguments of this kind that Fouché won over Davout, who combined the functions of Minister of War and commander of the army in Paris, to face the unpalatable prospect of concluding a capitulation and admitting the King. The two acts must be done simultaneously; for, if the city surrendered before the king was recognised, it would be treated as a conquered place. Blücher was for some time inclined to press matters to extremity, and to offer the Provisional Government nothing save the alternatives of unconditional surrender and a storm; but he was induced by Welling-

ALLIES ENTER PARIS

ton to accept a capitulation. The French Army was to retire beyond the Loire; the allied troops were to enter the city, but to respect all private and public property, except military stores and the works of art which Napoleon had plundered from Italy, Germany, and Spain. The allied generals undertook to make no attempt to arrest or punish any French subject for having borne arms under Napoleon (July 3).

Fouché and Davout had considerable difficulty in inducing the army and the Chambers to accept these terms. But all the military authorities agreed that Paris was indefensible on the southern side, and that the army was too disorganised to make a successful resistance. In face of such statements it was necessary to yield; and on July 5-6 the French troops marched for the Loire. On July 7 the Allies made a triumphal entry; and on the 8th Louis XVIII returned to the Tuileries. Fouché and Davout had already settled with him the terms on which he was to be received. As soon as the army had left Paris, the Provisional Government recognised Louis as king, and the Chambers dissolved themselves. New Houses, duly summoned by royal writ, were to meet within two months. They actually commenced their session before August was out and showed themselves "more royalist than the king."

For Napoleon there would be no honourable exile in Europe, but to the lonely island of St. Helena, in the South Atlantic, where he had to eat out his heart for six years in enforced idleness, and finally died of cancer in 1821.

CHAPTER 15

After the War

There was nothing to be feared from France, where the weak rule of the restored Bourbons gave their neighbours no trouble for some years. So, Europe was able to settle its accounts at the Congress of Vienna without further disturbance. Great Britain was paid handsomely, but by no means lavishly, for the part that she had taken in the long struggle against the Corsican usurper. In Europe she received two strongholds to make firm her hold on the Mediterranean—the invaluable strategical point of Malta, and the Ionian Islands further to the east. She also kept the small island of Heligoland, in the North Sea, which had served as a great smuggling depot during the Great War.

In America Britain retained the Dutch colony of Demerara on the Southern Continent—the tropical region now known as British Guiana; in the West Indies Britain took from the French St. Lucia and Tobago. In the Indian Ocean the valuable Isle of Mauritius (Isle de

France) was ceded by France, and Holland gave up her settlement of the Cape of Good Hope, which served as an admirable halfway house to Btitish Indian possessions and was the nucleus of its South African empire. The English Government might have asked and obtained still more; but it was thought that by securing complete domination in the commercial and manufacturing world during the war, Britain had gained so much that she need not be over-exacting. Valuable colonies by the dozen were handed back to France and Holland, with an almost extravagant liberality.

The settlement of Continental Europe concerned Britain comparatively little, save in one point. Holland and Belgium were formed into a new "Kingdom of the Netherlands," which was expected to prove a firm ally of Britain and a barrier against the northern extension of France. For the rest, Austria took Venice and Lombardy; Prussia received broad grants on the Rhine and in Saxony. The iniquitous partition of Poland that had disgraced the previous century was repeated—Austria kept Galicia, Prussia took back Posen and Danzig, while Russia absorbed the greater part of Napoleon's "Grand Duchy of Warsaw." The petty despots of Central and Southern Italy—the Pope, the King of Naples, and the rest—secured an undeserved return to their long-lost realms. France was confined within her old boundaries of the year 1792.

The England which emerged from the great war of 1793-1815 was a very different country from the England of the days before the French Revolution. In all her history there had never been a period of twenty-two years into which so many changes have been compressed. Not merely in matters political and economic, but in all social matters—in literature, in national feeling, in everyday thought and life—there was a profound alteration visible. For the most part the change had been for the better: the great war had exercised a most wholesome and sobering effect on the national character. Few men had watched the atrocities of the French Revolution or lived through the long period of suspense in 1802-1805, when foreign invasion was daily expected, without taking a profound impression from those times of storm and stress.

In the eighteenth century we often hear complaints of the want of patriotism and public spirit in Great Britain: no such reproach could be made to the generation which had fought through the great French war. The slackness and cynicism of the eighteenth century had been completely lived down. Political morality had been enormously improved: in the latter years of the war Whig and Tory had learnt to work together for the common national good despite of mere party interests. In 1806-7 a Tory majority had accepted a Whig ministry because it seemed for the moment desirable: in the following years the better Whigs refrained from captious opposition to the later Tory cabinets—though of course they did not cease to criticise their measures. There were none of the selfish and immoral combinations of cliques and groups which used to disgrace the eighteenth century. Parliamentary corruption of the bad old sort—the buying of members by hard cash or gifts of sinecures—had practically disappeared. Statesmen suspected of a want of private integrity could no longer come to the front.

The improved standard of political morals only reflected the general rise in the social morality of the nation. There was a growing feeling against drunkenness, foul language, gambling, and open profligacy, which had been looked upon with such a tolerant eye thirty years before. Nothing shows it better than the deep unpopularity of the Regent, George, Prince of Wales, who carried far into the nineteenth century the evil manners of the eighteenth. The contempt and dislike felt for him by the majority of the nation would never have been felt to such an extent by the older generation.

The revival of religious earnestness, which had begun with Wesley and the Methodists, was enormously developed by the influence of the war. The blasphemous antics of the French Revolutionists had shocked thousands of Englishmen into a more serious view of life, and twenty years of national peril had put flippancy at a discount. Prominent men who made no secret of their earnest religious convictions were no longer liable to be sneered at as enthusiasts or condemned as fanatics. All through the period the Low Church or Evangelical party was working hard and gaining an increasing hold on the nation. The religious indifferentism of the eighteenth century was disappearing.

Nothing shows the general improvement of the nation better than the higher tone of its literature. To the men of 1820 the coarse taste of the men of 1750 had become intolerable. Many will remember Sir Walter Scott's story of his friend who read over in old age the books which had seemed amusing fifty years back and found that they only raised a feeling of shame and disgust. It was a fact of a very typical sort that Scott himself was by far the most popular poet of his own day; men preferred his healthy, vigorous, patriotic strains to the work of his younger contemporaries, Byron and Shelley: though both were greater poets than the author of *Marmion* and the *Last Minstrel*, the one was too morbid and satanic, and the other too hysterical and anarchic for the taste of the time.

Turning to matters of a more tangible kind, we find as great a difference in the England of 1792 and of 1815. The population and resources of the country had grown in those twenty-two years in a measure for which previous history could afford no parallel. The distribution of the newly-gotten wealth was far less satisfactory, and numerous social problems had grown up which were bound to force themselves upon public attention the moment that the stress of war was removed. In population, the United Kingdom had increased from 14,000,000 to 19,000,000 souls, in spite of the considerable waste of life in the foreign war and in the Irish troubles of 1797-8.

But the rise in trade and commerce had been far more startling. British exports had more than doubled: in 1792 they had stood at £27,000,000; in 1815 the figures were £58,000,000. The imports had gone up between the same years from £19,000,000 to £32,000,000. Still more astounding was the rise in the national finances. The ordinary peace revenue had produced £19,000,000 in 1792: the same heads of taxation, as opposed to the extra war-revenue, brought in £45,000,000 in 1815. It was this marvellous expansion of the nation's resources alone which had enabled it to last out the Napoleonic struggle. If, as generally happens during war, the national resources had decayed rather than multiplied under the stress of heavy taxation and constant alarms, Britain should have been exhausted long before Bonaparte had run through his full career.

We have spoken already of the main factor of British prosperity, the monopoly of the carrying trade of the world, which had been won by naval victories, and which the enemy's insane "Continental System" had done much to confirm. The other great element in the growth of the wealth of Britain had been the immense development of internal manufactures. Even before 1792 the development of machinery in factories had already begun, and the country was rapidly asserting a superiority over its neighbours. The war completed British ascendency. While every other land in Europe was repeatedly overrun by hostile armies. Great Britain alone was free to work out her new discoveries without interruption. Many of her industries were notably fostered by the lavish expenditure on the army and navy: the demand for iron and steel, cloth and cotton, for military purposes had been enormous. Factories had been working for continental paymasters

243

also: even Napoleon himself, it is said, had been compelled to secretly procure from Yorkshire looms the cloth for the coats of the army which took the field in 1813, so entirely had continental manufactures failed him.

There was a general and very natural expectation in 1815-16 (as in 1919!) that the termination of the great war would bring about a period of even greater expansion and commercial supremacy for Great Britain. "Peace and Prosperity" have always been linked in men's minds. But after the First World War it is not strange that the five years which followed Waterloo were among the most troublous and unhappy periods in British domestic history. So widespread and long-continued was the distress and unrest, that men of gloomy and pessimistic frame of mind feared that the country was on the edge of a social revolution. The causes of the misery of the years 1816-21 are, however, not difficult to understand. They affected both the agricultural and the manufacturing interests.

The war had naturally caused an enormous rise in the prices of all agricultural produce. Britain had been cut off from the corn-markets of Europe, and after 1812 from those of America also. Moreover, the unwise system of "protection," which the Tory party consistently carried out, tended to keep corn artificially dear by the heavy import duties imposed on the supply from foreign countries. This monopoly of the English grower of cereal products had led to an altogether unnatural inflation of prices: thrice between 1810 and 1814 the annual average value of the quarter of wheat had risen over 100s.

In those days the conception of government food control had not been thought out. While the town dwellers suffered from the exorbitant cost of the loaf, the land-owners and farmers had gained: the rents of the one, the profits of the other, had increased to an immoderate degree. The poorer agricultural classes had not shared to any great extent in this prosperity, owing to the iniquitous system of the Poor Law. But from 1814 onward the inflated war prices ceased, and during the next three years the cost of wheat varied from 60s. to 80s. the quarter, instead of from 90s. to 120s. This was a terrible blow to the farmers and landlords, who had calculated their rents and their expenditure on the higher average, as if the war was to last for ever. The whole agricultural interest was very hard hit, and many individuals were ruined.

But the worst of the stress fell on the unfortunate labourers, though they had not shared in the profits of the time of inflated prices that had just ended. When the farmers were turning off their hands and cutting down wages, the poorer classes in the country were not compensated by the fact that the loaf had become appreciably cheaper. There followed acute distress, which ended in riots and rick-burning over large districts of the southern and midland shires. There were wild rumours of secret associations, of plots for a general rising like that of the French peasants in 1789, with plunder and massacre to follow. Most of this talk was groundless, but there was a certain amount of fire beneath the smoke, and in many parts the labourers were ready for mischief.

While rural England was in this unhappy state, the great towns were also in evil case. In 1815-18 the manufacturing classes were suffering from their own set of troubles almost as much as the agricultural classes. The cessation of the war had put an end to the unnatural expansion of the industries which had profited by British naval and military expenditure: the price of iron, for example, fell from £20 to £8 a ton when the government ceased to be a buyer. In many trades, too, over-speculation on the part of the great employers of labour led to distress. There had been a widespread notion that the countries of the continent would be able to absorb almost any amount of English goods the moment that the Continental System was removed. Factories at once threw upon the world such a vastly-increased output that the foreign market was glutted: indeed, the final struggle of 1812-14 had so drained the resources of France, Russia, Spain, and Germany, that they had little or no money to buy luxuries or even necessaries.

The exported goods had to be sent back or sold at an actual loss. Hence came bankruptcies and wholesale dismissal of operatives at home. The labour market was at the same time affected by the disbanding of many scores of thousands of soldiers and sailors. As many as 250,000 men were released from service in 1816-17-18 and had to find themselves new trades at short notice. Another source of trouble was the dying out of the old trades which had subsisted on hand-labour and were being superseded by machinery. The last generation of the workmen in these industries suffered bitter privations before they could or would transfer themselves to other occupations. It was they who distinguished themselves by the so-called *Luddite* outrages, in which gangs went by night to destroy the machinery in the new factories which were underselling their labour.

The government which had to face all these difficulties, social and economic, was unfortunately not in the least competent to deal with them. George III. had fallen into his last fit of melancholy madness in

1810, and his son George, Prince of Wales, was a sorry substitute for him. The father had often been obstinate and wrong-headed, but at least he was always honest, courageous, and a model of all the domestic virtues: no one could help respecting the good old king, whatever he might think of his wisdom. But the Regent was frankly disreputable: he tried the loyalty of England to the monarchical system as no other ruler has done since James II. A debauchee and gambler, a disobedient son, a cruel husband, a heartless father, an ungrateful and treacherous friend, he was a sore burden to the ministries which had to act in his name and palliate his misdoings. There was a widespread hope that his ruined constitution would not carry him through many more years, and that the succession might pass to his young daughter, the Princess Charlotte. But she died in childbirth in 1816, a year after her marriage to Leopold of Saxe-Coburg, and her father was destined to prolong his worthless life for fourteen years longer.

The cabinet which held office under the Regent was the Tory administration of Lord Liverpool. Its chief was an honest man and a good financier, but narrow-minded, prejudiced, and blindly opposed to all measures of political reform. His home secretary was Addington (now Lord Sidmouth), the unsuccessful premier of 1801-4, a man even more bigoted than his chief. Foreign affairs were in the hands of Lord Castlereagh, another high Tory, who had done good service as a diplomatist during the Napoleonic war, but was a reactionary, and suspected of being too great a friend of the despotic monarchs of the continent.

Lord Liverpool's ministry acted according to the best of its lights in dealing with the crisis of 1816-20. They cut down expenses as far as they were able, reduced the army and navy to the lowest limit consistent with safety, and did good service by restoring the currency, and replacing by a new coinage of gold sovereigns the depreciated banknotes which had carried England through the war.

★★★★★★

In the worst years of the war the bank-note for £5 would only buy about £3 18s. in gold. There had been practically no coinage of guineas since 1797, nor of silver since 1787. The new issue of gold was made in sovereigns, not in guineas, a great convenience in all payments.

★★★★★★

But thrift and honest finance were not sufficient to deal with the national troubles: measures of political and economic reform were urgently needed, and these the Liverpool cabinet was determined not to grant. They looked upon the strikes and riots that vexed the land, not as manifestations of poverty and starvation—which was in the main their real character—but as symptoms of a dangerous revolutionary conspiracy against the monarchy. The few noisy demagogues who were endeavouring to make capital out of the national discontent, they treated as if they were embryo Robespierres and Marats. Against the demonstrations and meetings of the distressed they employed armed force with a wholly unnecessary harshness. In the one or two cases where the rioters acted with violence, as at the Spa Fields Riot in London (1816), the Derby rising (June, 1817), and the Bonnymuir rising in Scotland (June, 1820), they made a very feeble show when resolutely faced: but the Government none the less had some dozens of them executed for treason.

A much less formidable indictment and a far milder punishment would have sufficed for such half-hearted revolutionaries. The greatest of the mistakes of the ruling powers was the unhappy business at Manchester on August 16, 1819. An orderly demonstration by an unarmed multitude was dispersed by a cavalry charge, in which some five or six people were trodden to death, and sixty or seventy injured or wounded.

The cabinet had just so much excuse that there were a few hotheaded demagogues who really meant mischief. The best known was a certain Arthur Thistlewood, a bankrupt adventurer who had a small following in London. He was a wild incendiary of the type of the French Jacobins, whose language and violence he carefully imitated. To avenge the "Manchester Massacre," he plotted the wholesale murder of the ministers. Learning that the whole cabinet were about to dine together on February 23, 1820, he persuaded a score of frantic desperadoes to join him in an attempt to break into the house where they were to meet, for the purpose of slaying them all. He was betrayed by an accomplice, and his band was surrounded by constables and soldiers at their trysting-place in Cato Street, and arrested after a bloody scuffle. Thistlewood and several of his accomplices were very properly hung. Abhorrence for their atrocious plot had a good deal of effect in restraining further agitation.

Just before the "Cato Street Conspiracy" had been frustrated, the old king George III. died, and the regent ascended the throne under the name of George IV. It was assuredly not from any merit of his that the national troubles began soon after to die down. The fact was that they were mainly the result of famine and despair, and that about 1820

The Massacre of Peterloo

there was a marked recovery in trade in the manufacturing districts, while in the countryside the farmers and labourers had succeeded in adapting themselves in some degree to the new scale of prices for agricultural produce. Riots and outrages gradually subsided, but there remained a strong political dislike for the Tory cabinet and its harsh and repressive measures.

The middle classes had begun to go over to the side of the Whigs, who now, for the first time since the outbreak of the great French war, began to find that they had a solid and powerful backing in the nation. Men had willingly consented to put aside all demands for constitutional change as long as the struggle with Napoleon lasted. It was now high time that the projects for political reform, which Pitt had sketched out thirty years before, should be taken in hand. As Pitt's heirs in the Tory party showed small signs of carrying them out, all those who were anxious to see them brought forward joined the other camp.

The chief of these burning questions was the Emancipation of the Catholics from political disabilities—a topic which had not been seriously raised since 1807—and the reform of the House of Commons, which was growing more unrepresentative of the nation every day. On certain other points—such as Free Trade, the removal of the protective duties placed on foreign corn and other commodities, the abolition of slavery in the British colonies, the reform of the Poor Laws—there was division in the Tory camp: the older generation were for leaving everything where it was: the younger were more ready to move on. In face of a vigorous and growing opposition, it is astonishing how long the Liverpool cabinet succeeded in staving off all manner of reforms: the delay was only rendered possible by the fact that the House of Commons so grossly misrepresented the nation. As long as the system of "rotten boroughs" went on, a government supported by the majority of borough-mongers could defy public opinion in a manner that has long ceased to be possible.

It is a notable fact, as illustrating the politics of that day, that the first checks to the policy of this rigid Tory Government came not on any great question of reform, but on a personal matter concerning the king. Caroline. George IV. had been separated for many years from his unfortunate wife, Caroline of Brunswick. Deserted by her husband, she had fallen into an unwise and undignified manner of life, wandering round the continent with a train of disreputable foreign attendants. She was a vain, silly, and vulgar woman, in whom no one could have felt any interest if she had not been so ill-treated by the man who should have been her protector. When George III. died, she announced her intention of returning to England in order to be crowned along with her husband. The king looked upon her approach with dismay and tried to frighten her away with threats of cutting off her income.

But she came back in spite of him, whereupon George took the invidious step of persuading Lord Liverpool to allow a bill for her divorce to be brought before Parliament. His own conduct had been so disgraceful that he should not have dared to attack his wife. With deep feelings of secret shame, the ministers lent themselves to this miserable scheme. A long parliamentary inquiry followed, which led to no conclusive proofs of the queen having been guilty of more than silly vanity and indecorum. The Whig leaders and the mob of London took up her cause, and meetings and demonstrations followed in quick succession. Disgusted at their position, the ministers in November, 1820, suddenly dropped their bill and let the queen go free. She started a violent agitation against her husband and would have caused much trouble if she had not died suddenly in the next year.

In modern days a ministry would resign after such a blow to its credit as the cabinet of 1820 had sustained in the matter of the queen's trial. Lord Liverpool and his colleagues, however, clung to office, but for the future had lost the complete command over Parliament which they had hitherto possessed. In 1821 the character of the ministry began to change: Addington (Lord Sidmouth), who had been mainly responsible for the mismanagement of home affairs, resigned; Lord Castlereagh in the next year committed suicide in a moment of insanity caused by overwork; several other of the old Tories disappeared from office. To replace them Lord Liverpool introduced younger men, who were not so entirely reactionary in their views, and were ready to follow the teaching of William Pitt in his earlier days, by linking the name of the Tory party with the idea of domestic reform. The chief of these were Canning, Huskisson, and Sir Robert Peel. The first-named statesman succeeded Castlereagh as foreign secretary, and promptly carried out a radical change in European policy.

Huskisson, who was a convinced free-trader, began to do his best to get rid of the protective duties that were cramping English commerce and manufactures. His great principle was to reduce the import duties on all raw materials—such as wool or silk—which were afterwards worked up in English factories. When once these commodities came in unburdened by taxes, their increased cheapness enabled manufacturers to produce their fabrics at a rate which defied foreign competition. Huskisson would have got rid of the corn-duties also, but Tory prejudice foiled him.

Peel, though not yet so far advanced in his views as his two colleagues, did admirable work as home secretary in the direction of administrative reform, and the mitigation of the unreasonable harshness of the criminal law. By a barbarous survival of mediaeval practice, there were still many scores of offences for which the death-penalty was prescribed: among them were such comparatively insignificant crimes as sheep-stealing, shop-lifting, and coining. Peel was the first minister of the Crown who began to cut down this dreadful list. He still left the gallows as the doom of those guilty of forgery, murderous assaults, and many other acts which are now sufficiently punished by penal servitude but struck out a good many items from the appalling total. The rest were all removed within fifteen years, and murder and treason were for a long time the only offences for which capital punishment is retained.

Canning's work at the Foreign Office demands a longer explanation. Ever since 1815 the continent had been under the control of the autocratic monarchs who had put down Napoleon. They lived in dread of a recrudescence of the revolutionary ideas which had been started by the Jacobins of France, and governed their subjects with a very tight hand, utterly refusing to listen to any petitions for the introduction of representative government or constitutional reforms. This was all the more hard because of the liberal promises which they had made to their peoples, when they were rousing them in 1812-13 to join in the general crusade against Bonaparte and the Continental System. The nations felt that they had been scurvily treated by their rulers, and from Poland to Portugal the whole continent was full of ferment and unrest.

There were plots, conspiracies, and agitations in every quarter, some aiming at the overturning of autocratic government and the obtaining of a free constitution, others more national in character, and directed against the ruthless cutting up of ancient states and peoples which had taken place at the Congress of Vienna in 1814-15. In Germany and Spain, the former idea prevailed, in Italy and Poland the latter. The Emperor of Russia conceived the idea of joining all the monarchs of Europe in a league against reform and liberal ideas, and framed the celebrated "Holy Alliance" in conjunction with Francis of

Austria and Frederick William of Prussia. The restored Bourbons of France, Spain, and Naples were wholly in agreement with them.

This reactionary confederacy had dominated Europe from 1815 to 1822. Castlereagh, while controlling the foreign policy of England, had refused to join the "Holy Alliance"; but, on the other hand, he had done nothing to hinder its work or to mark English disapproval of its narrow and despotic principles. Continental Liberals had always hoped for moral if not for tangible aid from free and constitutional England and had failed to get it. Britain had looked on while the troops of Austria invaded Italy and put down the new Constitution which had been unwillingly granted by King Ferdinand of Naples (1821), and while the armies of Louis XVIII. were being directed against the Spanish Liberals.

When Canning replaced Castlereagh at the Foreign Office (1822), this period of passive acquiescence came to an end, and English influence was used against the alliance of the despots. It was too late to save Spain, policy. which was overrun by the French in the spring of 1823, but Portugal was preserved from the same fate by the energetic threats which were made against French intervention there. The independence of the Spanish colonies in America, which had long been in revolt against the misgovernment of the mother-country, was recognised. In the east of Europe, where the Greeks had rebelled against the Sultan after four centuries of miserable oppression, Canning used all his influence in their aid. Money and volunteers from England were permitted to make their way to the Ægean.

Among the English "Phil-Hellenes" the most notable were the daring seaman Lord Cochrane, and the poet Byron, who roused himself from a life of idleness and luxury in Italy to give his aid to an ancient people in distress. He died of fever not long after his arrival in Greece; but his stirring poems and his excellent example did much to strengthen the wave of feeling in Western Europe which ultimately secured the freedom of Hellas. Canning, meanwhile, did all that he could short of declaring war to bring pressure on Sultan Mahmood, and to compel him to recognise the independence of his revolted subjects. He was prevented from going further by the uncertain attitude of the other powers, and especially of France and Russia, who could not make up their minds whether to regard Mahmood as a legitimate monarch endeavouring to suppress Liberals, and therefore a friend, or as a Mahometan persecutor, outside the pale of a "Holy Alliance" of Christian kings.

CHAPTER 16

Wellington as a Politician

In February 1827 Lord Liverpool was stricken down with paralysis, and the king, after some hesitation, offered Canning the vacant post of prime minister. He accepted it, and promptly got rid of the remnant of the old Tories who had still clung to office under his predecessor. Their places were filled with the more enlightened members of the party. It was hoped that a period of progress and prosperity, as marked as that of Pitt's famous rule in 1784-92, was about to commence, for the new premier had great schemes on foot both at home and abroad. But Canning had hardly time to settle down into office when he was carried off by an attack of dysentery (August 8, 1827). His death, only five months after he had reached the position in which he had the power to carry out his policy, was a most unfortunate event both for England and for the Tory party. His ministry continued in office for a few months under the nominal premiership of Lord Goderich, and then broke up for want of a master mind to keep them together.

The king, whose sympathies were all with reaction and the older Tories, invited the Duke of Wellington to take Canning's place. A more unfortunate appointment could not have been made; the great general proved to be a very poor politician. Personally, he had no sympathy with his predecessor's views; he believed in keeping things where they were in domestic politics. Free-trade, Catholic emancipation, and parliamentary reform were as distasteful to him as they had been to Addington or Castlereagh. In foreign policy his rooted principle was a dislike of continental Liberals; he had seen a great deal of the Spanish reformers in 1809-13 and had imbibed a great contempt for them and all their compeers in other lands.

The duke was thoroughly honest and upright in all his principles and prejudices, and he came on the scene with a splendid reputation for loyalty and patriotism. But he had never learnt the art of managing Parliament, of facing a determined opposition, or keeping together a party which consisted of two sections of divergent views. He very soon turned out of his ministry Huskisson, and the rest of Canning's followers, replacing them by Tories of the old reactionary breed. His first important action in foreign policy was to abandon his predecessor's support of the Greek insurgents, though England had been fully committed to their cause.

In the summer of 1827, while Canning still lived, an English fleet had been sent to the Levant with directions to bring pressure to bear on the Turkish Army in the Peloponnesus, and force its commandant, Ibrahim Pasha, to agree to an armistice with the Greeks. Admiral Codrington interpreted his orders in a stringent sense, forbade the *Pasha* to move, and when he continued the usual policy of massacre sailed into Navarino Bay and blew to pieces the large Turko-Egyptian fleet which was lying there (October 13, 1827). He was given unstinted applause by the English nation, but not by the prime minister, who disavowed his action, styled the Battle of Navarino "a most untoward event," and refused to take any further action against the Porte. Russia stepped in when Wellington withdrew; the new *Czar*, Nicholas I., sent an army across the Balkans, forced the *Sultan* to recognise the independence of Greece, and paid himself by confiscating a large slice of Turkish territory (August, 1828).

Throughout the three years during which he held office (1828-30), the "Iron Duke" did little to justify his reputation for firmness and steadfast purpose. There can be no doubt that his own inclination would have been to avoid all manner of constitutional change and keep things exactly as they stood. But he showed an unexpected faculty for yielding when he was attacked and worried by the opposition. When his plans were defeated in the House of Commons he did not resign, as most ministers with a parliamentary training would have done, but retained office, and often ended by allowing measures of which he disapproved to become law. As has been well remarked by one of his critics:

> He treated politics as if they were military campaigns, and when beaten out of his position did not throw up the game, but gave way, and only retired on to another similar position in the rear.

This line of conduct had, to the outside observer, every appearance of weakness, and looked like an undignified clinging to office. The duke, however, was honestly convinced that he was necessary to the State, and only retained the premiership because he thought that his resignation would open the way to revolution and civil strife.

His first retreat was carried out after a dispute on a religious question. The "Test Act" and "Corporation Act," which obliged members of corporations and office-holders under the Crown to make a profession of conformity to the Church of England, had long been a dead letter. Dissenters of all sorts had been allowed to evade their provisions. Yet when it was proposed to abolish these relics of seventeenth-century bigotry, the duke made a great show of resistance. The Whigs, however, succeeded in passing a resolution against them in the Commons; thereupon Wellington suddenly yielded, gave the measure the support of the ministry, and allowed the Acts to be repealed (1828).

His next show of weakness was even more startling. For some years the question of Catholic Emancipation, the old bugbear of George III., had been much obtruded on public notice, mainly by an agitation in Ireland, headed by the ablest Irishman whom the century has produced. The grievance of the Irish Catholics was a perfectly legitimate one; they had assented to the Union in 1800, because Pitt had promised that they should be given in the United Kingdom the same rights as their Protestant fellow-subjects. Pitt had failed to redeem his pledge, owing to no fault of his own, but to the old king's obstinacy. Now that George III. was dead, there was no reason why the promise given in 1800 should not be fulfilled: no one could believe that George IV. had any conscientious objection to it—unlike his father, he had no conscience at all. Nevertheless, the Tory party, with the exception of Canning and his friends, had refused to take up Pitt's engagement to the Catholics. Wellington, himself an Anglo-Irish Protestant by birth, had been as unbending as Liverpool or Addington.

In 1823 O'Connell had founded a league called the "Catholic Association," to bring pressure on the English Government.

It was a powerful, well-organised body, which and the worked by proclamations and monster demonstrations in the usual Irish style; it even collected a kind of impost called the "Catholic Rent," which was paid with a good deal more regularity than the king's taxes. Nominally suppressed by law in 1825, it was still in full vigour in 1828. O'Connell was a man of splendid eloquence and ready wit, with considerable organizing power. He was as completely the master of the Association as Parnell in later days was of the "Land League"; but he set his face against outrages and worked wholly by moral suasion. With all Ireland at his back, and the support of the Whig party in England, he was a most formidable power. To show his strength he had himself elected as Member of Parliament for County Clare, though he could not of course take his seat so long as the old laws against Catholics were still in force.

Confronted with this great agitation, continually harassed by the Whigs, and opposed by the Canningite wing of his own party, Wellington for some time refused to listen to any proposal for Catholic Emancipation. But suddenly, in the spring of 1829, his resistance collapsed; to the surprise and disgust of his own bigoted followers, he announced that he had become convinced that further resistance would only lead to civil war in Ireland, and that, rather than force matters to extremity, the ministry would bring in a bill placing the Catholics in the same position in matters political as members of the Established Church. Every post in the State was thrown open to them save those of King, Regent, Lord Chancellor, or Viceroy of Ireland. This measure was passed by the aid of the Whigs and the Canningites. A great proportion of the Duke's old Tory friends in both houses voted against it; for the future they distrusted Wellington and could not be relied on to vote solidly at his order.

Nothing could have been more calculated to encourage the duke's adversaries than this display of weakness on his part. In Ireland O'Connell at once started another agitation, this time in favour of the dissolution of the Union of 1800—"Repeal" as it was popularly styled in 1830, Home-Rule as we should call it now. For nearly a score of years this movement was to convulse the sister island; meanwhile O'Connell himself appeared at Westminster with a following of fifty Irish Catholic members ready to make trouble for English ministries, Tory or Whig, in every possible way.

That Wellington retained office for more than a year after he had conceded Catholic Emancipation, was only due to the fact that in respect for his personal character and the great things he had done for England in 1808-15, his adversaries refrained from pressing him to extremity. All his measures in 1829-30 were weak and ill-judged; he even abandoned Portuguese allies, whom Canning had saved in 1826, and allowed Dom Miguel, a usurper of most reactionary views, to be established as king in their country. But the overthrow of the ministry was deferred till November, 1830, before which date there was a general change in English politics caused by outside events.

On June 26, 1830, George IV. had died in his sixty-eighth year, unregretted by any single class of his subjects. It was a great boon to the nation that his successor was a prince of a very different stamp.

William, Duke of Clarence, the king's next surviving brother, who now ascended the throne under the name of William IV., was a simple, good-hearted, genial old man, who had served with credit in the navy, and had long occupied the honorary post of Lord High Admiral. His intelligence was limited, but his intentions were good, and no one could dislike or despise him. The only thing against him was an eccentricity which sometimes led him into absurd speeches and actions, and made men fear that he was tainted with the insanity of his father,

George III. Fortunately, their dread turned out to be unfounded; he kept his head and made an admirable constitutional king. It was of enormous benefit to the nation as well as the monarchy that he was not a party man like his brother and got on with the Whigs as well as with the Tories. He had married late in life (1818) and had two daughters, but both of them died in infancy, so that the succession to the throne now passed to his ten-year-old niece Alexandrina Victoria, the only child of Edward Duke of Kent, the fourth son of George III., who upon ascending the throne would have a golden age for the British Empire named in her honour.

During the very week in which William IV. ascended the throne the political horizon of Europe grew overcast. The domination of the "Holy Alliance" was suddenly threatened by popular risings in every region of the continent, the natural result of fifteen years of despotic rule, during which every national and constitutional aspiration had been crushed by brute force. The trouble began in Paris, where the narrowminded and reactionary Charles X. was expelled by a revolt in which the army joined the mob. France did not become a red republic, as many had feared, but merely changed its dynasty; for Louis Philippe, Duke of Orleans, a very astute intriguer, succeeded in putting himself at the head of the movement and was saluted as constitutional "King of the French"—the old title, "King of France," was dropped as savouring of feudalism. From Paris the wave of revolution spread right and left; there followed a vigorous rebellion in Poland against the despotism of Czar Nicholas I., a rising of the Belgians against their enforced union with Holland, insurrections in Spain and Portugal, and troubles of a less desperate sort in Germany and Italy.

In the midst of these foreign complications the Wellington ministry at last came to an end. The death of the late king was followed by a general election, in which more than fifty seats in the Commons were lost by the old Tory party. The fact was that the duke's weak policy had disgusted his own supporters, and even the knot of borough-mongers who were its firmest adherents had not exerted themselves very ardently in his cause. In the English counties, where popular feeling was able to express itself better than in the boroughs, more than sixty out of the eighty-two members returned were Whigs. When the new parliament met in November the ministers were defeated by a majority of twenty-nine on the first contentious topic that came up. Wellington resigned. The final giant of the 'Great Contest' had at last left the arena.

WELLINGTON IN OLD AGE

www.ingramcontent.com/pod-product-compliance
Lightning Source LLC
Chambersburg PA
CBHW032040080426
42733CB00006B/140